DAVID HAYDOCK

CHANNEL TUNNEL

25 YEARS OF EXPERIENCE

Published by Platform 5 Publishing Ltd, 52 Broadfield Road, Sheffield, S8 0XJ. England.

Printed in England by The Amadeus Press, Cleckheaton, West Yorkshire

ISBN: 978 1 909431 77 5

WELCOME!

Over the next 134 pages, "Channel Tunnel: 25 Years of Experience" describes how the services using the Tunnel were conceived and how they have developed over the past 25 years. This book is not intended to examine the history of the Channel Tunnel before the structure was built – this has been done well by several other authors in the past. Our aim is to record how operations have evolved through experience gained and in the light of a series of immense challenges. The Channel Tunnel is a massive achievement but, as we show here, operations have not always gone according to plan and the story certainly has more twists and turns to come!

Front Cover (main image): Eurostar e320 set 4008/7 stands at Temple Mills depot on 2 March 2015.

Back Cover: Eurotunnel locomotive 9033 brings up the rear of a car shuttle train entering the Channel Tunnel in France on 23 June 2010. *Keith Fender (2)*

Above: A Freight Shuttle approaches the French Tunnel portal in this magnificent aerial view. *Courtesy Eurotunnel*

CONTENTS

THE TUNNEL AND ITS ASSOCIATED INFRASTRUCTURE

In order to examine operation of the Tunnel it is important to understand that the "Channel Tunnel" is not a single bore but three – two running tunnels (RT1, the south running tunnel and RT2 the north running tunnel) and a "service tunnel" between them which is linked by "cross passages" to the running tunnels and can be used for maintenance and emergency purposes. The two running tunnels, which are 7.6 metres in diameter, are also linked by "piston relief ducts" which help adjust pressure between the two bores.

The continuous welded rails are laid in concrete slab track and there is a "platform" on the service tunnel side which can be used for evacuation if necessary (see diagrams). On the other side is another, lower, "platform" but there are also pipes and cables attached to the wall of the Tunnel. The overhead power cables

(25 kV AC 50 Hz) are attached to the roof of the running tunnels; these are particularly high up in comparison to the roof of trains built to the UK loading gauge, due to the very high loading gauge needed for Shuttle vehicles.

There is no conventional colour light signalling – all trains using the Tunnel need to be equipped with the TVM 430 cab signalling system, the same system as installed on French high speed lines (TVM means *Transmission Voie Machine*, which means "track to train transmission" – the system is based on fixed track circuit blocks). The only visible (to train drivers) signs of this in the Tunnel are blue/yellow signs marking the blocks every 500 metres. The signalling in the cab is not by conventional red (for stop), green (for go) or amber (for caution) but a display of the speed to which a driver may increase,

or to which speed must be reduced. If the driver accelerates above this speed or does not brake quickly enough, the brakes are applied automatically. In fact, in normal circumstances, most drivers set a "cruise control" in the Tunnel to maintain a constant speed. If capacity is at a premium all trains will be instructed to set the cruise control at 140 km/h. This is the standard speed for all Eurotunnel Shuttle trains, which are the most frequent. Eurostars may operate at 160 km/h through the Tunnel when there is no Shuttle train just in front. Through freight services all operate at less than 140 km/h (usually at 100 km/h) and are only allowed through the Tunnel when they will not slow down other services.

Intervals

In order to facilitate maintenance and operation in a degraded situation (train failure, accident), the Tunnel is divided into six "Intervals". At about one-third and two-thirds of the way through the Tunnel about 16 km from the Tunnel portals, there are "cross-overs" – vast caverns in which there are points allowing trains to cross between one running tunnel and another. Fortunately the Intervals are rarely evoked, except for maintenance and when there are major incidents in the Tunnel. In this book we give some details of the disastrous day when five Eurostars gave up the ghost in the Tunnel, and of the two major fires on Freight Shuttles. In cases like this, more than one Interval may be blocked.

In the case of the two fires, repair work meant one Interval was out of use for months. In such a case the Eurotunnel control centre is obliged to "flight" trains. This means that several trains pass through, one after the other, in one direction, then a "flight" of trains pass through in the opposite direction.

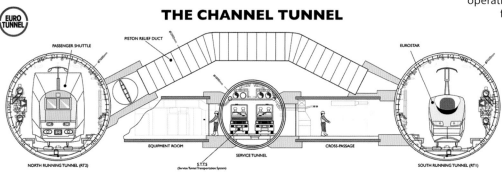

THE CHANNEL TUNNEL

EURO TUNNEL

PASSENGER SHUTTLE | PISTON RELIEF DUCT | EUROSTAR

NORTH RUNNING TUNNEL (RT2) | EQUIPMENT ROOM | S.T.T.S (Service Tunnel Transportation System) | SERVICE TUNNEL | CROSS-PASSAGE | SOUTH RUNNING TUNNEL (RT1)

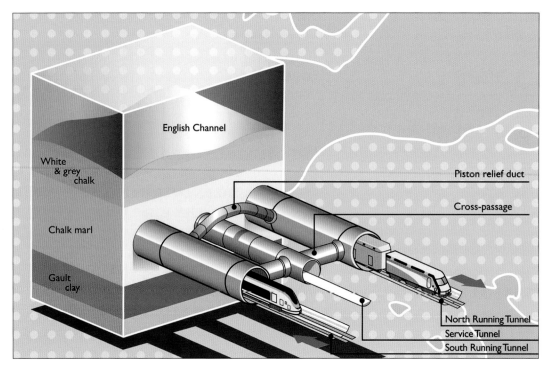

English Channel

White & grey chalk

Chalk marl

Gault clay

Piston relief duct

Cross-passage

North Running Tunnel
Service Tunnel
South Running Tunnel

Left: Cross-sections of the Channel Tunnel bores. *Courtesy Eurotunnel*

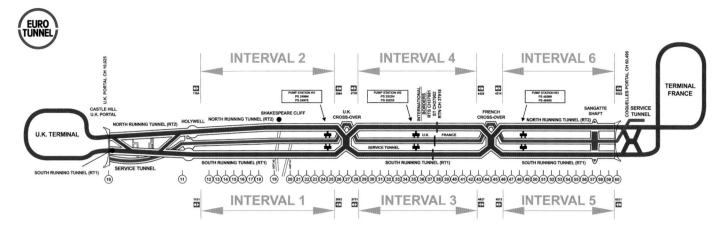

INTERVAL 2   INTERVAL 4   INTERVAL 6

CASTLE HILL U.K. PORTAL CH 10,025

PUMP STATION W1 PS 2496N PS 2497S

PUMP STATION W2 PS 3522N PS 3523S

INTERNATIONAL CROSSOVERS RTS CH37881 ST CH37902 RTN CH 37918

PUMP STATION W3 PS 4258N PS 4848S

COQUELLES PORTAL CH 60,495

TERMINAL FRANCE

CASTLE HILL U.K. PORTAL

HOLYWELL   NORTH RUNNING TUNNEL (RT2)   SHAKESPEARE CLIFF

U.K. CROSS-OVER

FRENCH CROSS-OVER

SANGATTE SHAFT

NORTH RUNNING TUNNEL (RT2)   NORTH RUNNING TUNNEL (RT2)

SERVICE TUNNEL

U.K. TERMINAL

U.K.   FRANCE

SERVICE TUNNEL

SOUTH RUNNING TUNNEL (RT1)   SERVICE TUNNEL   SOUTH RUNNING TUNNEL (RT1)   SOUTH RUNNING TUNNEL (RT1)   SOUTH RUNNING TUNNEL (RT1)

10 11 12 13 14 15 16 17 18 19 20 21 22 23 24 25 26 27 28 29 30 31 32 33 34 35 36 37 38 39 40 41 42 43 44 45 46 47 48 49 50 51 52 53 54 55 56 57 58 59 60

INTERVAL 1   INTERVAL 3   INTERVAL 5

Above: A simplified diagram of the Channel Tunnel network used by the Shuttle service showing the running tunnels, service tunnel and crossovers plus the "Intervals".

Right: A simplified diagram of how the Tunnel was bored, mainly through chalk marl (blue). *Courtesy Eurotunnel (2)*

Below: On 23 April 1994 Eurotunnel locomotive 9013 brings up the rear of a Freight Shuttle taking the curve into the Cheriton terminal and passing under the line to London. This was just over a month before the start of revenue services carrying lorries. *Chris Wilson*

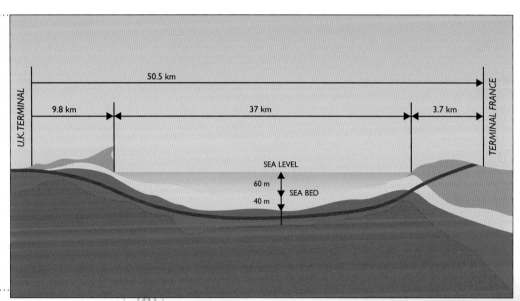

U.K. TERMINAL

50.5 km

9.8 km   37 km   3.7 km

TERMINAL FRANCE

SEA LEVEL

60 m   SEA BED

40 m

EUROTUNNEL'S TERMINALS

At each end of the Tunnel are two massive terminals to allow the transfer of cars, coaches and lorries on and off the Shuttle trains. Each one consists of ten platforms where trains can stop; these are accessed by road vehicles from overbridges and ramps at each end – vehicles drive onto the train at the rear and drive off at the front. The terminals were built with eight platforms each but two more were added in October 2002. The platforms are theoretically divided equally between passenger and freight activities but the middle platforms can be easily "re-purposed" if conditions warrant.

At the exit end of the terminal vehicles are able to drive straight onto adjacent motorways – there are no customs checks at the exits thanks to agreements between the UK and French governments. The vehicle

entrances to the Tunnel in each country consist of long approach roads (separate for lorries in France) to avoid queuing traffic backing up onto the motorways, then an array of gates where drivers "check in" their vehicles. These have been gradually automated and, for example, cameras now read car number plates, and the computer compares them with booking details, then asks the driver to confirm departure time, then automatically issues a card with a letter which can be hung inside the windscreen on the rear-view mirror. The letter identifies which Shuttle service the car should travel on.

At Cheriton, cars then move forward to the terminal to await being called for departure. After taking advantage of shops and food and drink outlets, the driver and

Above: The Cheriton terminal and associated infrastructure seen on 20 August 2018 from Castle Hill above the Channel Tunnel portal, with a Passenger Shuttle train leaving one of the ten tracks in the loading/unloading terminal. The train is about to join the France-bound track from High Speed 1. Immediately to the left is the London-bound track to HS1, while tracks branching to the left will join the Eurotunnel depot, which is clearly visible, with the tracks to left skirt the depot then curve around to the right, joining the terminal after passing under HS1.
Julien Gersing

passengers rejoin their cars and drive to the customs and security gates where staff check ID documents and carry out security checks. These are continuously evolving but currently include sampling and analysing dust from a car dashboard to full searches of a car if police or customs staff have suspicions. In Coquelles the customs and security checks take place before occupants can drive to shops and catering outlets.

When called forward – from about half an hour to 15 minutes before departure – cars are driven to holding areas before being called on to drive onto the Shuttles. Operation of the Shuttles is dealt with in greater detail later in this book.

The procedures for lorries are much more complicated given the greater danger of fire and the possibility of migrants sneaking on board, in particular. A series of checks take place before vehicles can be driven on board. Again more details can be found later in this book.

Lorry traffic through the Tunnel has grown to such an extent that relatively minor disruption to Freight Shuttle services (or ferry services, meaning that lorries move over to the Shuttle), including bad weather delaying ferries in Dover or industrial action, can lead to massive tailbacks on motorways, particularly in Kent. This has led Kent Police and the Port of Dover to devise a contingency plan known as "Operation Stack" under which lorries may be "stacked" in the area leading to the Channel Tunnel, usually by queuing on the hard shoulder and/or left-hand lane of the M20 motorway from London.

Cheriton terminal

The terminal at Cheriton is considerably smaller that the one at Coquelles (Calais) due to the need to squeeze it into a very cramped site between the town of Folkestone and the hills to the north. Access lines to the terminal actually start to branch off from the high speed line to London (HS1) within Castle Hill Portal at Cheriton Junction

(see diagram below). HS1 continues almost directly west at a slight gradient while two tracks for the terminal branch off to the south and curve away from HS1 before turning north to pass under HS1. By the time HS1 passes over the terminal access tracks, sidings split off into Dollands Moor yard, where Tunnel freight trains change locomotives, and not far beyond this, at Sandling, HS1 starts to run alongside the Dover–Ashford line, all the way to Ashford.

The land between HS1 and this curve is taken up by a Eurotunnel depot and Shuttle stabling sidings. The depot is much smaller than the one in Coquelles and maintains the diesel locomotives used in the Tunnel – the ten Krupp-MaK Bo-Bos and the 12 small Schöma maintenance vehicles.

After curving through 180° and passing under HS1 the pair of access tracks to the terminal fan out into ten tracks alongside platforms plus an additional emergency track. The platforms are almost a kilometre long as they have to accommodate Shuttle trains over 800 metres long. At the Tunnel end, the 11 tracks rapidly combine into three tracks which join HS1 just outside or inside the Tunnel portal.

Coquelles terminal

The Coquelles terminal site is several times larger than at Cheriton – the terminal and depot were built on flat, marshy land where drainage was the only major construction problem. The arrangement both on the approaches to, and within the terminal area is much more complicated in France than in the UK. The Tunnel portal is about 4 km from the coast and the tracks emerge in a south-easterly direction. The Tunnel–Lille high speed line (LGV Nord Europe) climbs away from the Tunnel and within 3 km serves Calais Fréthun station which has two through tracks and two loops serving platforms. The LGV then carries on towards Lille, gradually turning east.

Just short of Calais Fréthun, two tracks turn north-east, leading to Fréthun freight

Below: Track diagram of the Eurotunnel terminal at Cheriton. *Courtesy TRACKmaps*

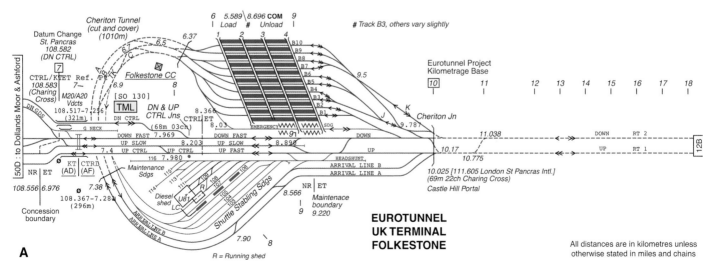

Above: The 840 metre long F46 building dominates this aerial view of installations at Coquelles. In the top left-hand corner is the Shuttle terminal. Shuttle trains arrive from the tunnel on the running line on the bottom right of the photo, just to the left of the fence, to the right of which are five SNCF tracks in Fréthun yard. To the left of F46 is the locomotive maintenance depot in front of which are two Krupp-MaK diesels, two Shuttle locomotives, a Class 92 electric and, unusually, a Euro Cargo Rail Class 77 diesel. *Courtesy Eurotunnel*

Below: Two former British Rail Class 20 diesel locos head out of the southern running tunnel with a tracklaying train during construction in 1991. *David Haydock*

yard, which has nine tracks for changing locomotives on through freight trains and stabling trains. This yard now has one track with a scanner for freights heading for the UK (see chapter on freight trains). At the north end tracks from Fréthun yard join the Boulogne–Calais main line and at Les Fontinettes a chord branches east to join the Calais–Hazebrouck–Lille route. The Calais–Boulogne line skirts the east of Fréthun yard, then turns south-east, serving the low-level island platform at Calais Fréthun station. The Boulogne line then passes under the LGV just after the station and a chord joins the low-level station to the LGV here.

The two tracks towards the Eurotunnel terminal run just north of the above SNCF tracks for about 2 km then divide to add a third track and go through a 180° curve then divide again into the Coquelles terminal where there are again ten tracks. The emergency track here is soon after trains leave the Tunnel.

To the north of the tracks and north of Calais Fréthun yard is Eurotunnel's Shuttle depot which includes F46, described as the biggest railway building in Europe. This has two through roads and is over 800 metres long in order to maintain complete Shuttle trains, with their locomotives, allowing them to be split into two halves if necessary.

At the southern exit from the terminal, the ten tracks quickly join to make two, then these pass under the Eurotunnel tracks from the Tunnel, then under the LGV, before joining the high speed lines into the Tunnel.

Below: Track diagram of the Coquelles terminal and depot area. *Courtesy TRACKmaps*

Above: Shuttle locomotive 9013 emerges from the French portal during celebrations of 250 million passengers being carried through the Tunnel on 13 October 2010. *David Haydock*

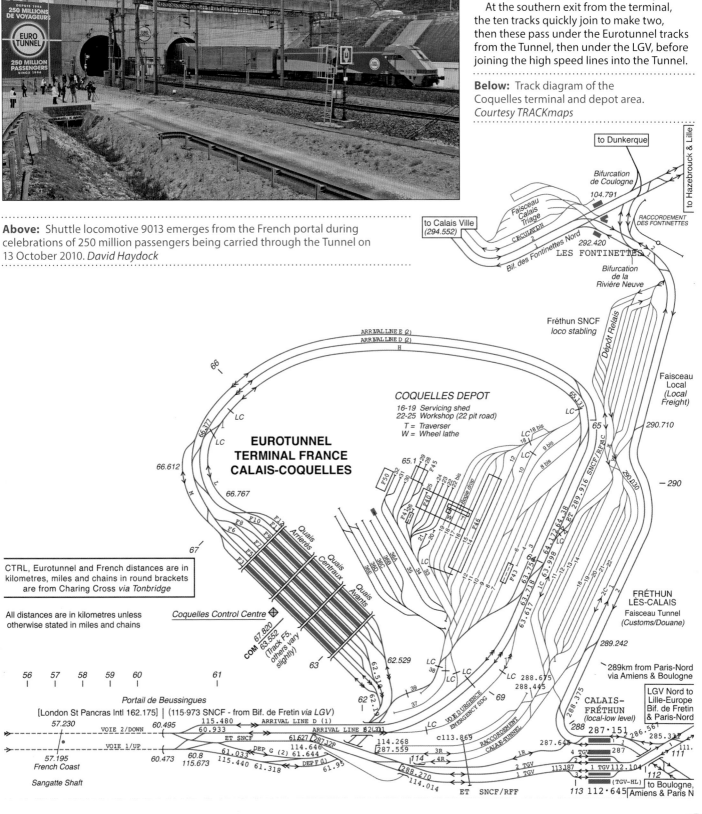

On a misty morning Eurostar set 3001/2 speeds past the village of Beaumont between Lille and Paris on the LGV Nord Europe on 24 May 2010. *David Haydock*

MORE THAN JUST A **TUNNEL**

On either side of the Channel Tunnel a whole network of lines needed building or modernising in order to take full advantage of the new international link. Unfortunately, plans for a new high speed line through Kent were nowhere near advanced enough to allow construction at the same time as the Tunnel.

On the other side of the Channel, in France, work was planned so that a high speed line all the way from the Tunnel to Paris would be completed on time. The first high speed line in France (*Ligne à Grande Vitesse* or LGV) opened in two stages between Paris and Lyon in 1981 and 1983. The second line, the LGV Atlantique, also opened in two stages from Paris to Le Mans and Tours in phases – in September 1989 and in late 1990.

The next line to open would be the one to be used by Channel Tunnel trains – the 333 km LGV Nord Europe – which opened on 23 May 1993 from Gonesse (16 km from Paris Nord) to Arras, then on 26 September 1993 from Croisilles, near Arras, to Lille and Calais (Tunnel and Calais Ville). The section to Calais was inaugurated with the Tunnel on 6 May 1994.

A key part of the LGV Nord Europe project was construction of the station at Lille Europe which is only a few hundred metres

from the historic Lille terminus which was renamed Lille Flandres. The original plan was for the LGV to pass to the south of Lille and for the "high speed station" for Lille to be built around 10 km from the centre, near the city's airport. However the city's Mayor Pierre Mauroy campaigned for the station to be built in the city centre and eventually

the city authorities paid the considerable extra cost (about €90 million at the time) this involved.

On the other hand, the controversy in Picardie was ignored. The high speed line from Lille to Paris is almost directly north–south but the burgers of Amiens feared that the city would be "left out" by economic development and campaigned for the LGV to be diverted their way. The original plan was for a station to be built halfway between Amiens and Saint Quentin near the town of Chaulnes, population 2000. TGV Haute Picardie station was nicknamed the "*gare des betteraves*" (sugar beet field station) by locals.

Above: A refurbished Eurostar set has just left the LGV Sud- Est at Pont de Veyle and is headed for Bourg St Maurice with the Saturday ski train from London on 16 March 2019. *Pierre Julien*

Despite a campaign of "civil disobedience" involving the purchase of land on the LGV route, no change was made to plans. Amiens was just promised a station on a putative LGV running more directly from Paris to Calais which would be built if and when the LGV to Lille was "saturated".

LGV Jonction and Rhône-Alpes

Just after the Channel Tunnel officially opened, on 29 May 1994, the French opened the 57 km LGV Jonction (also known as the Interconnexion Est) which skirted the east of the Paris conurbation, linking the Nord Europe and Sud-Est high speed lines, making it possible to run from Calais to Lyon without stopping in Paris, and with stations serving Roissy airport (opening 2 November 1994) and Disneyland Paris. Eurostar quickly took advantage of the latter by running a direct train from London for Disney fans from July 1996.

On 3 July 1994 the French also completed the second section of the 115 km LGV Rhône-Alpes, which bypassed Lyon and took high speed running to a point near Valence. Eurostar started using the Lyon bypass section in December 1997 for some of its trains to Bourg St Maurice.

LGV Méditerranée

This 250 km high speed line, which opened on 10 June 2001, completed the high speed line between Paris and Marseille, with new intermediate stations at Valence, Avignon and near Aix-en-Provence. This cut the timings for the 750 km from Paris to Marseille to around three hours non-stop. SNCF showed just how fast the TGV could cross the whole of France by organising a record run on 26 May 2001 from Calais Fréthun station to Marseille St Charles in just three hours, 29 minutes and 45 seconds for 1067 km, an average of over 305 km/h.

Eurostar started running to Avignon in summer 2002, but did not reach Marseille in service until May 2015. A branch of the LGV Med from the triangle at Angles, near

Above: The Calais to Hazebrouck line was electrified for freight trains from the Tunnel. This is Euro Cargo Rail 186 163 on this section soon after leaving Calais with the Scunthorpe–Ebange steel slabs on 19 September 2019. *David Haydock*

Avignon, to Manduel near Nîmes, reduced TGV journey times to Montpellier.

Belgian delay

All manner of disputes delayed the opening of a high speed line from Lille to Brussels until 14 December 1997. This meant that for the first three years Eurostars to Brussels left the high speed line just south of Lille Europe then ran over the conventional network from Lille to Tournai then on Line 94, under 3000 V DC, from Tournai via Ath to Brussels. The Lille–Tournai line had been electrified on 10 May 1993, in order to help speed Eurostar on its way, at 25 kV AC in France and 3000 V DC in Belgium.

The 71 km LGV Belge, from the triangle at Frétin east of Lille, to Lembeek on the Mons–Brussels classic line, immediately cut London–Brussels timings by about 40 minutes from 3h15 to 2h36. Later upgrading of the 17 km of classic line from Lembeek to Brussels Midi has since shaved a few more minutes from the schedule although the aim of increasing speeds to 200 km/h was dropped.

Modernisation for freight, too

At the same time there were more modest improvements to allow cross-Channel freight to operate efficiently. First and foremost was the electrification of the Calais–Hazebrouck line (energised on 15 June 1993) at the same time as Calais–Boulogne. In addition to this there was major work in the area just south of the Tunnel mouth in order to build a new international station at Fréthun. The Calais–Boulogne line was rebuilt on this site and Fréthun "local" station re-sited next to the latter. A freight yard (plus a small depot) to allow changes between Class 92 and SNCF locomotives was also created at Calais Fréthun, although initially known as Rivière Neuve.

HS1 and St Pancras

A significant handicap for Eurostar and freight trains in the first few years was the need to use the conventional line between London and the Tunnel. Not only was this very busy with suburban stopping trains, but it was also necessary for these very long, powerful, heavy trains to draw current from the third rail supply which was in no way designed to meet such requirements. Considerable modernisation of the Kent main line was made but the operators breathed sighs of relief when the two sections of the 110 km Channel Tunnel Rail Link (CTRL, later High Speed 1) opened on 28 September 2003 (74 km from Fawkham Junction to the Tunnel) and 14 November 2007 (36 km from Fawkham Junction to London St Pancras) respectively.

An additional "wing" of Waterloo station had been built for Eurostar, together with a flyover to take the train over multiple tracks south of Vauxhall, but this closed in 2007 as HS1 was built to serve St Pancras, which gained the suffix "International", north of the Thames.

High speed to Amsterdam

On 13 December 2009, the Dutch and Belgians opened the HSL Zuid which added high speed lines from Antwerpen in Belgium to the southern outskirts of Rotterdam and from northern Rotterdam to southern

Below: e300 sets 3218/7 are seen near Nashenden Crossover on HS1 with train 9084 07.15 London St Pancras to Marseille St Charles on 28 June 2019. *Jamie Squibbs*

Superlatives and records

The Channel Tunnel and its ecosystem can claim enough records to fill a page in the Guinness Book of Records. Eurotunnel itself is the biggest carrier of accompanied lorries in the world, with over 1.6 million a year.

The Tunnel is the busiest double track stretch of railway in the world – about 500 trains in 24 hours on heavy days.

Because of this, rails have to be replaced every 5–10 years and the need to keep the Tunnel open 24 hours a day, 365 days a year has led Eurotunnel to develop techniques to replace rail at the fastest possible rate, and to work with industry to extend the life of rails.

Eurotunnel Shuttle trains are amongst the largest, by loading gauge, in the world and amongst the longest and heaviest in Britain.

Eurotunnel's F46 840 metre building in Coquelles is thought to be the longest train maintenance building in Europe, if not the world.

Eurotunnel can even claim the biggest ever piece of land added to the UK – Samphire Hoe, near Dover, was created from spoil extracted from the Tunnel and is now a nature reserve.

Above right & right: Two views of the magnificent St Pancras International station. Top right with the DB ICE train on show in October 2007 and centre right in 2012 with the Olympic rings on show. *David Haydock (2)*

Amsterdam, a total of 130 km of new line. This cut journey times for Paris–Amsterdam Thalys high-speed trains by almost an hour to around 1h50 between Brussels Midi and Amsterdam. The Dutch were not able to use the new line until December 2012 due to the late delivery of Fyra trainsets, but this service was rapidly withdrawn as they were very unreliable. Eurostar did not take advantage of the new infrastructure for almost a decade, finally introducing a direct service in spring 2018.

Note that all of the high speed lines mentioned above were built for a maximum of 300 km/h. The most recent lines built in France mentioned below (LGV Est Européenne, LGV Rhin-Rhône and LGV l'Océane) have a maximum of 320 km/h, as has a section of the LGV Méditerranée.

Future opportunities

France

The LGV Sud Europe Atlantique (LGV SEA) high speed line (sometimes known as LGV L'Océane) in France, between Tours and Bordeaux (302 km) opened on 2 July 2017. This new line cut Paris–Bordeaux timings by about an hour from around three to around two hours. Eurostar seemed favourable to a London–Bordeaux service at the time but a year later said that traffic would be "too seasonal". However, the four infrastructure managers along the route are now offering "pre-planned paths" for such a service

and are aware that other operators may be interested if Eurostar is not. In the longer term it is expected that a high speed line will be built from Bordeaux to Toulouse (257 km). This will cut the journey time between the two cities from a current best of 2h07 to about 1h20 which would theoretically make London–Toulouse possible in just over six hours.

Following the construction of the new CNM high speed line extending from the LGV Méditerranée to Montpellier, the latter city could be reached in 6h30 from London but progress from there to Barcelona is still pretty slow, adding three hours and meaning an unattractive 9h30 from London. This could be reduced by about 30 minutes if France ever builds a Montpellier–Perpignan LGV.

France is now criss-crossed by high speed lines which would already allow attractive journey times from London, such as Strasbourg in 4h15 via the LGV Est Européenne line then Basel in 5h25 and Zürich in 6h25. An extension from Strasbourg to Stuttgart would allow a 5h40 journey time.

Dijon could be reached in 4h10 via the LGV Sud Est then Basel in 5h40 or Lausanne in 6h40. The Sud Est line would also give access to Genève in 5h50 from London.

A new high speed line from France to Italy via a new 54 km base tunnel is still some way off. At present, progress is very slow through Alpine France and it would take a high speed train 8h30 to reach Torino and 9h50 to Milano from London. It is currently faster to travel via Switzerland to reach Milano. A direct, limited-stop train from London over the route via Lausanne and Montreux would take just over nine hours to Milano.

Potential in Germany

In the light of worries over climate change and an increased interest in the train replacing the plane, and with a plan to merge Eurostar with Thalys, it looks likely that Eurostar will look again at serving Germany, for which e320 sets are pre-equipped.

On 15 December 2002, Belgian Railways opened the 66 km high speed line (known as HSL 2) from Leuven to Ans, near Liège. This was followed on 14 June 2009 by the 36 km HSL 3 from Chenée near Liège to Hergenrath on the border with Germany. The two lines, and a rebuild of the Aachen–Köln line cut Brussels–Köln timings considerably, Thalys and ICE services taking 1h50, with calls at Liège and Aachen, plus Brussels Nord for ICEs. This means that Köln would be easily reachable from London in 3h50, similar to the timing to Amsterdam.

On 1 August 2002 a new 180 km high speed line (NBS) was opened between Köln and Frankfurt in Germany. This cut the end-to-end journey time to just one hour compared with over double this via the scenic but winding route via the Rhine valley. German incumbent DB was able to introduce an ICE service from Frankfurt via Köln to Brussels taking under three hours which makes it competitive with air transport. The German NBS was built with steep gradients which means that only the more modern trains such as ICE 3 with power distributed over multiple bogies can be used. It seems quite clear that e320 sets could be used on this route and a London–Frankfurt journey of less than five hours would be easily obtainable.

Other possibilities (see map) by extending from Köln might be Dortmund in five hours, Hannover (6h20), Hamburg (7h40) or Berlin (8h00) while extensions from Frankfurt could reach München in seven hours, Leipzig (7h50) or Dresden (9h00).

High Speed 2

The other new high speed line which ought to interest Eurostar is HS2, the future line from London to Birmingham and Manchester, with all sorts of extensions possible in future. HS2 would open up the prospect of Birmingham–Paris journeys in just three hours, but the British government has not worked this sort of service into its plans and Eurostar, wisely, has said it will only consider the prospects once the new line is open.

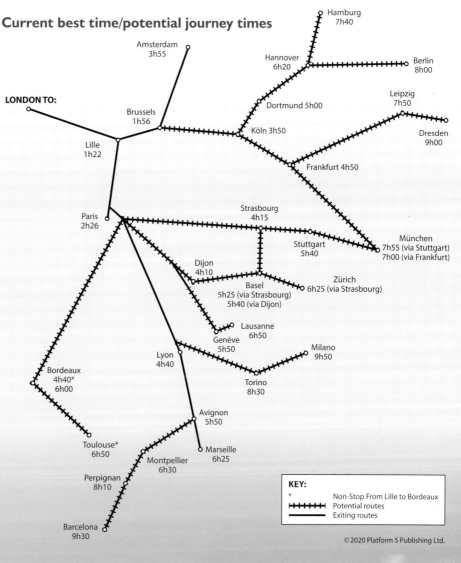

Current best time/potential journey times

LONDON TO:

Amsterdam 3h55
Brussels 1h56
Lille 1h22
Paris 2h26
Bordeaux 4h40* 6h00
Toulouse* 6h50
Perpignan 8h10
Barcelona 9h30
Montpellier 6h30
Avignon 5h50
Marseille 6h25
Lyon 4h40
Dijon 4h10
Genève 5h50
Lausanne 6h50
Torino 8h30
Milano 9h50
Basel 5h25 (via Strasbourg) 5h40 (via Dijon)
Zürich 6h25 (via Strasbourg)
Strasbourg 4h15
Stuttgart 5h40
München 7h55 (via Stuttgart) 7h00 (via Frankfurt)
Köln 3h50
Frankfurt 4h50
Dortmund 5h00
Hannover 6h20
Hamburg 7h40
Leipzig 7h50
Dresden 9h00
Berlin 8h00

KEY:
*   Non-Stop From Lille to Bordeaux
+++++ Potential routes
——— Exiting routes

e320 set 4020/19 is seen on the HSL Zuid line near Dordrecht with a train from London to Amsterdam on 13 September 2018. *Keith Fender*

EUROTUNNEL AND ITS SHUTTLE SERVICES

The Channel Tunnel "system" consists of a network of railways and terminals which allow the operation of three sorts of services:
- through high speed passenger services, between the UK and continental Europe, currently only operated by Eurostar
- through freight trains between the UK and almost anywhere in continental Europe, initially operated by national incumbents British Rail and SNCF but now mainly operated by DB Cargo
- a shuttle service between terminals at each end of the Tunnel carrying cars, coaches and lorries

At the stage of project assessment the British and French governments had rejected the idea of a fixed link across the Channel which allowed vehicle drivers to stay at the controls, for safety and security reasons. Instead all vehicles would have to be driven onto trains which would carry them through the Tunnel.

In fact the Channel Tunnel consists of three tunnels – two 7.6 metre diameter bore operating tunnels, plus a much smaller bore "service tunnel" to allow access for

Right: Cars slowly descend the ramp and drive onto the rear of a Passenger Shuttle at Cheriton on 12 May 2014.

maintenance and evacuation in the event of emergencies.

Train services which carry vehicles through long tunnels existed already in Europe, but on nowhere near the scale of the traffic expected to use Channel Tunnel. The only frequent services which remain today are those

Above: Eurotunnel locomotives 9803 and 9105 head Freight Shuttles at the Cheriton (UK) terminal on 11 March 2011. *David Haydock (2)*

through the Lötschberg and Simplon tunnels in Switzerland which are necessary in order

to avoid summit roads which wind over mountain passes and are usually closed in winter. These only carry cars and run every half hour at their most frequent.

In order to remove lorry traffic from the Swiss pass roads and today's motorway network and tunnels under the Alps, there are several services generally known as RoLa (*Rollende Landstrasse* or rolling motorway) which carry complete lorries over much longer distances. In particular, Switzerland finances services to remove lorries from its motorways and these run between Freiburg-im-Breisgau in southern Germany and Novara in northern Italy.

The wagons used on such services are generally completely open. Those used for RoLa services have very small wheels to allow complete lorries to be carried within the UIC loading gauge, although even this has had to be enlarged on most routes. As RoLa trains have journey times of several hours, lorry drivers leave their vehicles and are carried in a passenger coach where they can sleep. Wagons used on trains through the Lötschberg tunnel have open sides and rudimentary roofs. Passengers stay in their cars for the whole journey.

Massive loading gauge

In many ways the Channel Tunnel Shuttle operation resembles this existing practice in Europe but on a much bigger scale. The loading gauge within the Channel Tunnel is much bigger than on the European rail network so that a complete lorry can be carried inside an enclosed freight vehicle or a road coach inside a passenger vehicle, without the need for very small wheels. This massive vehicle size also means that all but the biggest cars can be carried in double-deck passenger vehicles.

However, the enormous size of these vehicles means that they are captive to a small system – the Tunnel itself plus the branches at each end connecting to the two terminals where vehicles can be transferred on and off trains. They therefore have to be maintained on site, too.

Half of capacity for Shuttles

From the beginning, half of the Channel Tunnel's capacity was allocated to Eurotunnel Shuttles. The TVM 430 cab signalling system allows trains to follow each other very closely – in principle, a train can operate every three minutes through the Tunnel, so maximum capacity is 20 trains per hour. However, this is theoretical and depends on all trains running at the same speed. All Shuttles operate at 140 km/h; Eurostars can operate through the Tunnel at 160 km/h but usually run at 140 (timed in 21 minutes for the almost exactly 50 km from portal to portal) so as not to catch up the Shuttles. Most through freights cannot manage more than 100 km/h due to restrictions on wagon speed.

Eurotunnel currently cannot run more than four Passenger Shuttle trains per hour with its current fleet, and demand currently does not justify higher frequencies. On the other hand, Freight Shuttles often run every ten minutes during peak periods – generally mid-week and before Christmas.

Channel Tunnel traffic 1995–2019

Year	Lorries	Cars	Coaches	Eurostar passengers	Freight train tonnes
1995	390 922	1 222 694	N/A	2 900 000	N/A
1996	519 003	2 077 000	N/A	4 867 000	2 361 000
1997	255 908	2 319 000	N/A	6 004 000	2 923 000
1998	704 666	3 351 000	N/A	6 308 000	3 141 000
1999	838 776	3 260 166	82 074	6 593 000	2 865 000
2000	1 133 146	2 784 000	79 460	7 130 000	2 947 000
2001	1 194 000	2 529 757	73 900	6 933 000	2 049 000
2002	1 231 100	2 335 625	71 911	6 602 817	1 463 580
2003	1 284 875	2 278 999	71 942	6 315 000	1 743 686
2004	1 281 207	2 101 323	63 467	7 276 675	1 889 175
2005	1 308 786	2 047 166	77 267	7 454 497	1 587 790
2006	1 296 269	2 021 543	67 201	7 858 337	1 569 429
2007	1 414 709	2 141 573	65 331	8 260 980	1 213 647
2008	1 254 282	1 907 484	55 751	9 113 371	1 233 445
2009	769 261	1 916 647	54 547	9 220 233	1 181 089
2010	1 089 051	2 125 259	56 507	9 528 558	1 128 079
2011	1 263 327	2 262 811	56 095	9 679 764	1 324 673
2012	1 464 880	2 424 342	58 966	9 911 649	1 227 139
2013	1 362 849	2 481 167	64 507	10 132 691	1 363 839
2014	1 440 214	2 572 263	63 059	10 397 894	1 648 047
2015	1 483 741	2 556 585	58 387	10 399 267	1 420 826
2016	1 641 638	2 610 242	53 623	10 011 337	1 041 294
2017	1 637 280	2 595 247	51 229	10 300 622	1 219 364
2018	1 693 462	2 660 414	51 300	10 976 500	1 256 000
2019	1 595 241	2 601 791	50 268	11 046 608	1 390 303

Note: N/A : figures not available

How have we done so far?

This book details the full story of the generally rising traffic through the Channel Tunnel but also points out the reasons for the ups and downs over time. The initial story was one of unconfined growth, but by 1998 two peaks were reached and have never been equalled since. The first is in the number of cars carried on the Shuttles. A massive 3.35 million were carried in 1998. The number dropped slightly in 1999 but then fell every year until 2008 when a low of 1.9 million was reached, a fall of almost a half. The reason was simple – the abolition of duty free sales, by then an anachronism in an EU where tariffs were abolished or harmonised, was planned for 1993 but was pushed back to the end of June 1999 to allow industry to adapt. Most of the massive number of cars carried in 1999 were Brits travelling to Calais to stock up on drinks and cigarettes. Eurotunnel's own retailing revenue plunged 74% after the 1999 change.

The other peak in 1998 was in through freight traffic. This had boomed in the first four years, with heavy investment in wagons and service launches and a remarkable quantity of finished cars, containers and wagonloads travelling via the Tunnel. This was a reflection of a "normal" European freight corridor, but was not to last. Both the UK and French freight partners were cutting back wagonload services, traffic was hit by strikes and a slight drop in traffic took place in 1999 and 2000. However, it was in 2000 that the first wave of migrants hit Calais, causing all Tunnel services to be disrupted. Eurotunnel quickly secured its operating areas and incursions hit SNCF traffic hardest. The national operator was slow to protect its trains, suspended services for a while and customers left in droves. Within two years traffic had halved, and never fully recovered. Traffic has even dropped below the 1.3 million tonnes carried by the train ferry before the Tunnel opened for most of the period since 2007.

Traffic on the Freight Shuttles grew gradually for most of the past 25 years but was hit badly in 2009 by the Tunnel fire. Since 2013 the company has invested in new wagons with the aim of reaching 2 million lorries a year by 2020 and seems well on the way to doing this, growth averaging 5% a year.

Apart from the odd hiccup due to Tunnel fires or economic slowdown, Eurostar has shown almost continuous growth since the Tunnel opened, the biggest boosts in traffic coming from the opening of high speed lines in Belgium and the UK which cut journey times. The most recent increases have come from the launch of services to Amsterdam.

The biggest challenge to Tunnel traffic at the time of writing is Brexit. After a boom in traffic due to stock building, lorry numbers have fallen and passenger numbers are down due to a lack of certainty on the future. In the longer term, the insatiable desire to travel cross-Channel will probably return. Lorry traffic will depend on how supply chain logistics are affected by Brexit. Eurostar's proposed merger with Thalys could lead to new routes being launched, especially to Germany, but this could take up to ten years to work through.

Although Eurotunnel is now close to using its half share of capacity, this is not the case for the other users. Eurostar reaches four trains an hour at certain times of the day or week but for most of the time there are only one or two trains per hour. There are no other high speed operators at present. As for freight traffic, there are currently only half a dozen trains per direction per day. As this book explains, the plans to run overnight trains and Eurostars north of London came to nothing.

Above: Lorry drivers board the Freight Shuttle Club Car on the same date.

Left: A lorry passes through the Passive Millimetre Wave Scanner on 11 March 2011.

Below: A lorry drives off a Freight Shuttle after arrival at Cheriton on the same date.

Right: Into the Tunnel! A driver's eye view of the Tunnel mouth on the French side of the Tunnel on 11 March 2011. The entrance to the service tunnel can be seen on the top right. *David Haydock (4)*

First revenue services

Revenue services through the Tunnel did not start until 1 June 1994. Eurotunnel had hoped to launch "Le Shuttle" (a shuttle service between Cheriton and Coquelles) carrying lorries on 9 May but this was eventually pushed back to 19 May. The trains were initially reduced to half size, carrying 14 lorries at a time. Those carried were by invitation only and trains ran only during the daytime. This was still the situation in July.

On 8 November 1994 Eurotunnel received consent from the Inter-Governmental Commission (IGC) for seven-day working of the Freight Shuttles and by May 1995 the company had become the market leader on the Dover–Calais route with 28 267 lorries or 35% of the market.

Passenger Shuttles

Eurotunnel gained its operating licence for the Passenger Shuttles on 29 July 1994 and started carrying staff and friends from 15 August. A shareholders' service started slightly later but it was not until 22 December 1994 that the revenue service started. The launch of Passenger Shuttles was actually hobbled by a car catching fire on 9 December which delayed obtaining an operating certificate.

The "tourist service", as it was named initially, only ran hourly from 09.00 to 21.00 seven days a week and was by reservation only. From 2 January 1995 this increased to 24 hours a day with hourly departures 07.00 to 23.00, and two-hourly trains during the night.

On 26 June 1995 Le Shuttle carried its first paying coaches, with one departure per hour programmed.

The single-deck wagons used to carry coaches, camper vans, tourist vehicles with trailers and cars higher than 1.85 metres were not introduced until spring 1995.

To reserve or not to reserve?

From April 1995 the service was increased and reservations abolished – Eurotunnel promoted this as "turn up and go" which, superficially, seemed a good selling point. The magazine **Today's Railways** argued, however, that this led to overcrowding and long waiting times at the terminals at peak times and that a clear departure time would be more attractive. In the end Eurotunnel did restore reservations and it is possible today to turn up 45 minutes before the reserved departure time (30 minutes until recently) pass through the entrance gate (which now reads the number plate and immediately issues a "hanger" carrying a departure letter) pass through security and customs (already taking longer pre-Brexit), wait a short time in the terminal building or in the waiting area, then drive onto the train. A timing of 1h30 from checking in to driving onto the motorway at the other end is still (just) possible.

Today the Passenger Shuttle service runs every quarter-hour at peak times, requiring eight of the fleet of nine trains, and half-hourly or less at quieter times.

In early 1995 tickets for a car plus all occupants cost from £49 for a day return to a maximum of £136 return. Today there are three tariffs; in March 2019 prices for a trip a month ahead were £133 to £156 return for a "short trip", £166 to £198 for the standard tariff and £388 in "Flexi Plus". So an increase of 271% for even the cheapest prices over the past 25 years.

Interestingly, in the same period the price for lorries has actually fallen. The price one way was quoted as £375 for a truck at the time of opening. The author found the price of £536 return (£268 each way) a month ahead for the Shuttle in March 2019, a fall of 28% and this was an open ticket found on the internet. Regular customers surely pay less. The cheapest fare for a truck by ferry cost £403 return. It is interesting to note that Eurotunnel has always refused to account the Shuttle services separately.

The Eurotunnel "system"

Operation of Eurotunnel Shuttle services is a well-planned "ballet" with operations as tightly-timed as Ryanair flights, and based on an endless circuit composed of the Tunnel itself plus loops at each terminal. The Folkestone terminal has tracks which turn clockwise after leaving the Tunnel, whereas the Coquelles terminal has an anti-clockwise loop. This has been carefully thought out to produce relatively even wheel wear on the trains. At each terminal vehicles (passenger and freight vehicles are separated) pass through ticket, customs and security checks then drive to waiting areas before being called for loading about 20 minutes before departure. They then drive down a ramp onto the loading platform then onto the train.

Over time, safety and security procedures have evolved to take into account the threat of fire and terrorism, and the pressure of migrants trying to reach the UK. The most visible evidence of this are the astonishing numbers and height of fences, usually double with barbed wire or electrified wires, which have been installed around the Coquelles terminal and all the way to the Tunnel after the two "migrant crises".

Operation of the Shuttles is tightly timed to an hourly sequence. A Shuttle train takes exactly 35 minutes between terminals. On arrival of a Passenger Shuttle, doors are opened and vehicles are driven out of the front of the train under the watchful eye of Eurotunnel staff. As soon as unloading has been completed, vehicles are called on from the waiting area and driven straight onto the rear of the train. Staff ensure that vehicles are close together then, once a Shuttle vehicle is full, close the fire doors between vehicles. Drivers and passengers stay in their vehicles during the crossing, although they can stretch their legs and use the toilets if they wish.

The procedure is different for Freight Shuttles as drivers do not stay in their cabs. In addition, safety and security checks before loading are much more extensive. There are banks of heat sensors where the lorry drivers check in. Eurotunnel staff then identify lorries with the least inflammable loads, such as fresh fruit and vegetables and direct them to the front of the train. This reduces the risk to drivers in the Club Car at the front but also the possibility of flames spreading to the whole train through fanning if there were ever a fire. Manual checks are also made before loading as well as other visual checks for smoke emanation as trains leave the loading terminal and again as they enter the Tunnel.

The installation of extra fences around the Tunnel and terminal area have led migrants to try to stow away on lorries so Eurotunnel has installed a series of devices to check for the presence of people inside HGV trailers. When lorries arrive at the check-in they first pass through a "Passive Millimetre Wave Scanner". This consists of sloping metal plates on either side of the lorry (see photo) which capture the atmosphere's natural radiation and project it through the lorry sides. From the reflected energy, the device is able create a three-dimensional image and distinguish a soft object, such as a person, from a load of hard wooden boxes, for example. This is the same technology used in airports to detect objects under a person's clothing.

The next stage is for a member of Eurotunnel staff to insert a "wand" inside the lorry trailer to detect suspiciously high levels of CO^2. This stage is voluntary but is accepted by most lorry drivers as they could face fines if they arrive in the UK with migrants on board. If this were not enough members of the French and British border agencies also have devices which can detect the heartbeat of a person inside a lorry trailer.

The proportion of lorry drivers who do not speak English well, or indeed at all, has risen over the past 25 years and Eurotunnel has reacted by providing instructions in the Club Car on what to do in case of fire in nine languages. There are also 60 smoke hoods stowed in the Club Car to give out if necessary.

When loading, drivers drive their lorries onto the rear of the train, with one vehicle per Shuttle wagon, turn off the engine and the trailer refrigeration unit if there is one, then descend from their cabs. They are then picked up in turn by a minibus and taken to the "Club Car" passenger coach at the front of the train. The relaxation allowed by this procedure is important as drivers can count this as a 45-minute mid-shift rest period under EU drivers' rules. On arrival at the destination terminal, the procedure is reversed – the lorry drivers are picked up by a bus and dropped next to their respective lorries, then drive them off the front of the train. As with the passenger procedures, the unloading then loading plus checks is normally carried out in just 25 minutes, so that a journey through the Tunnel plus unloading/loading takes exactly an hour.

PASSENGER SHUTTLES

The nine stainless-steel Passenger Shuttle trains were designed and built by Bombardier's Crespin factory in northern France to carry road passenger vehicles. They consist of double-deck vehicles for cars and motorcycles and single-deck vehicles which can carry coaches, minibuses, caravans and cars over 1.85 metres high, which is often the case for cars with roof racks.

Each 776 metre long train consists of a single-deck unloading vehicle at the front, 12 single deck coaches, a single-deck loading vehicle and a double-deck unloading vehicle in the middle, 12 double-deck coaches, and finally a double-deck loader vehicle at the rear.

The total fleet of 254 wagons is therefore:
- 18 single-deck loading/unloading wagons plus one spare
- 18 double-deck loading/unloading wagons plus one spare
- 108 single-deck wagons
- 108 double-deck wagons

The fleet of nine trains allows a 15-minute passenger service to operate at peak times, with one train spare. The trains were built by the Euroshuttle Wagons Consortium, consisting of GMT-Bombardier of Canada, La Brugeoise (Brugge, Belgium) and ANF Industrie (Crespin, France). These are all now parts of Bombardier Transportation. Construction of the 508 bogies was subcontracted to GEC-Alsthom's Le Creusot plant. The two spare loading wagons were ordered later, in 1990, by Eurotunnel.

Below: Eurotunnel locomotive 9033 heads a Passenger Shuttle out of the Tunnel on 7 October 1997. The form of the end loading wagon is very clear. *Chris Wilson*

Above: The front unloading wagon opens thanks to each section sliding over the other. *David Haydock*

"Largest in the world"

The Passenger Shuttle trains are said to be "the largest railway vehicles in the world". In order to carry complete passenger coaches they are 26 metres long, which is not unusual, but also 5.575 metres high (18 feet 3½ inches) above the rail and a maximum of 4.1 metres wide (13 feet 5½ inches). This is possible thanks to the 7.6 metre (22 feet 11½ inches) diameter bores of the Channel Tunnel. In fact, US rail vehicles are also very big; in particular on many lines the height of the loading gauge is such that "double stack" container trains – one container on top of another – can operate. The maximum height of the loading gauge is therefore higher in the USA, at a maximum of 6.147 metres. However, US trains are not so wide as those in the Tunnel, the maximum being 3.25 metres. This means that the overall "envelope" (height x width) is 22.85 m² in the Tunnel and 19.98 m² in the US. Of course, most freight trains in the USA are much

Right: The Passenger Shuttle unloading wagon (see left) is now fully open and the bridging plates have been lowered to allow cars to drive off. They will be on the motorway a couple of minutes later.

longer than the 800 metre Shuttles, the longest reaching around three kilometres. Trains from mines to ports in some parts of the world, such as Australia, are much longer again!

The Passenger Shuttle vehicles were designed for a maximum speed of 160 km/h, although they operate normally at 140 km/h. A trial with 160 km/h operation in 2012 in order to allow a slightly longer turnround during the London Olympics in 2012 and during busy holiday periods was inconclusive so was not continued.

Each single-deck wagon weighs 63 tonnes, while double-deck wagons weigh almost 67 tonnes due to the extra floor. Each single-deck wagon can carry up to 24 tonnes and each double-deck wagon 12 tonnes – in general the latter is equivalent to five conventional cars on each floor. Fully loaded trains are designed to weigh a maximum of 2400 tonnes.

All Passenger Shuttle vehicles are built from stainless steel throughout, to resist corrosion due to the damp, salty atmosphere in the Tunnel and surrounding areas, and are well insulated against fire, noise and thermal variations. Most are left unpainted but a few have advertising vinyls. There are no toilets in single deck vehicles due to width restrictions; instead passengers must walk forward to the toilets in the front unloading wagon. In double-deck vehicles there is a toilet on both decks, plus stairs between the decks, in the centre of every third vehicle. Trains are divided for maintenance purposes into three-car "units", with the toilets in the centre car, known as "*triplettes*". All vehicles are air conditioned, the system being particularly powerful as it needs to remove fumes during loading and unloading.

Loading and unloading vehicles have sliding doors and "bridging plates" which

Above: Two double-deck Passenger Shuttle vehicles at Coquelles depot on 19 September 2019, where work was starting on preparation for refurbishment. The massive size and arrangement of the interior fire doors are very clear.

Left: A driver's-eye interior view of the fire doors. *David Haydock (3)*

fold down over the gap between train and platform. Double-deck loading vehicles have ramps to allow access to the upper deck. Single-deck loading wagons are more complex, with four sections which can slide open over each other.

When vehicles are loaded onto Passenger Shuttle trains, all fire doors between wagons are opened, and drivers continue towards the front of the train until reaching the front or when they reach other cars stopped in front. A raised "pavement" on either side prevents vehicles from deviating from a straight course and touching the train walls. A member of staff ensures the vehicles are close together then the driver must cut the engine, put the vehicle in first gear and apply the handbrake. The driver must leave the front windows open to hear announcements. Once a vehicle is full, the member of staff closes the fire doors at the

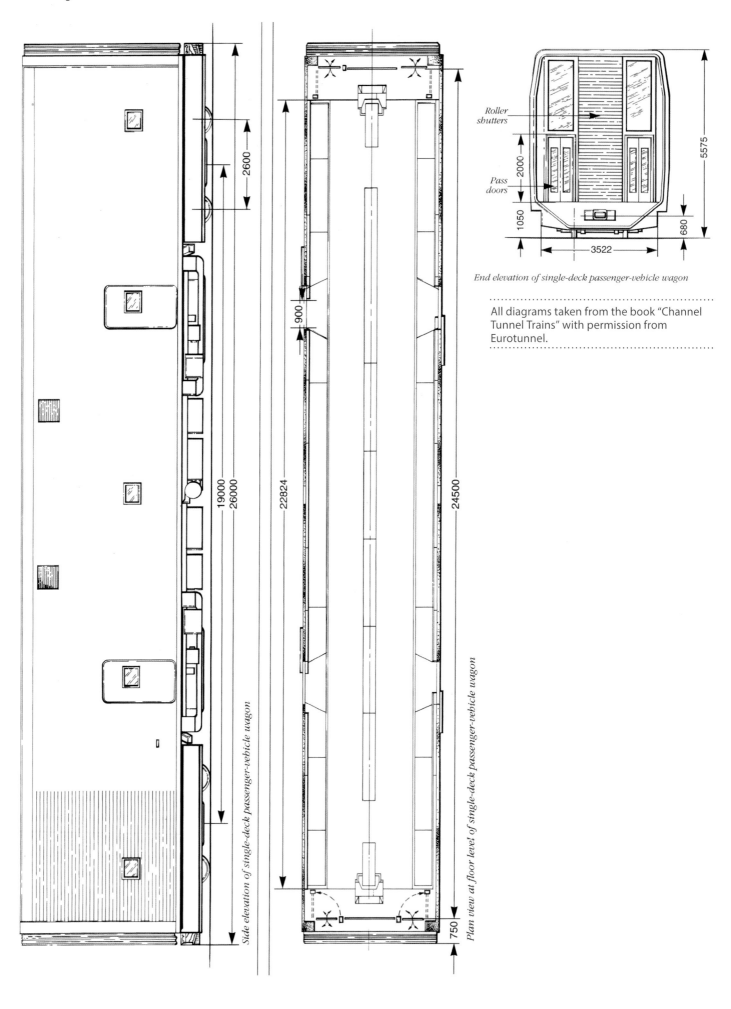

Side elevation of single-deck passenger-vehicle wagon

2600

19000
26000

Plan view at floor level of single-deck passenger-vehicle wagon

900

22824

24500

750

Roller
shutters

Pass
doors

2000

1050

680

5575

3522

End elevation of single-deck passenger-vehicle wagon

All diagrams taken from the book "Channel Tunnel Trains" with permission from Eurotunnel.

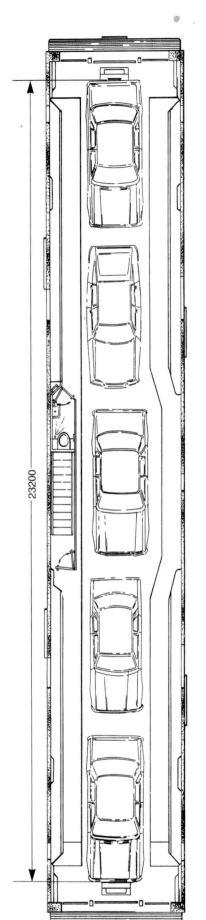

23200

Plan view of upper deck of double-deck passenger-vehicle wagon

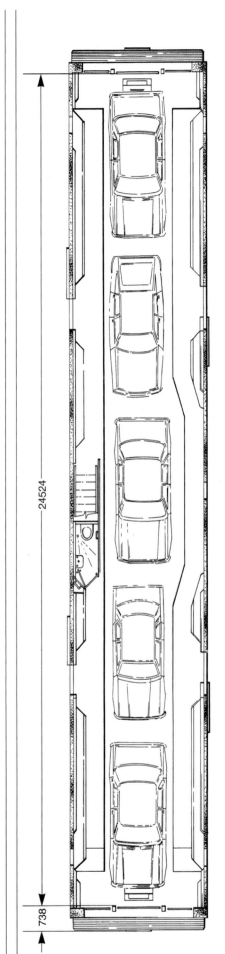

24524

738

Plan view of lower deck of double-deck passenger-vehicle wagon

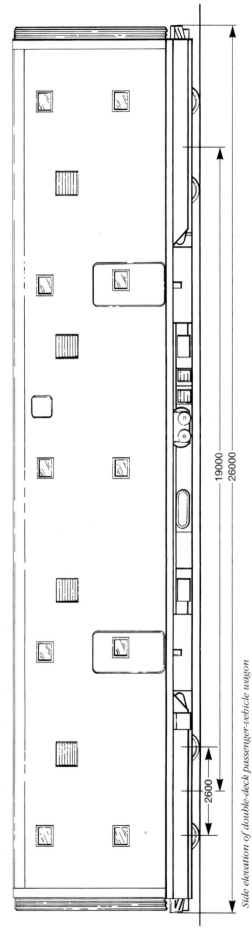

19000

26000

2600

Side elevation of double-deck passenger-vehicle wagon

Top to bottom: Before and after refurbishment views of the Passenger Shuttle interiors, the top four photos being double-deck and the bottom two single-deck Shuttles. The main visible difference will be the end doors which will slide along the vehicle sides after refurbishment rather than opening on hinges like conventional doors. *"Before" photos by David Haydock (3), artist's impressions of the "after" situation courtesy of Eurotunnel.*

end of each coach. Small swing doors in these fire doors allow passengers to move through the train, to reach the toilets, for example. The fire doors also form relatively air-tight seals which avoid major changes in air pressure.

In order to avoid heavy vehicles causing large deflections in the train suspension when loading and unloading, both Freight Shuttles and single-deck Passenger Shuttle vehicles were built with stabilising beams or jacks under the wagon which lower onto concrete beams by the track and lift the wagon slightly off its suspension. All loading wagons have retained these devices but it was found that they were not needed on other wagons and were decommissioned, making wagons lighter and easier to maintain.

Passenger Shuttles are, of course, equipped with a comprehensive fire detection and extinguishing system. No smoking or flash photography is allowed on board for this reason. There are even sensors which can detect a fuel leak and trigger a discharge of water and detergent to flush it away. In the event of evacuation being necessary there are two doors in the centre of each vehicle.

As the table in this chapter shows, passenger traffic on the Shuttle – both cars and coaches – rapidly built up to levels which are not equalled today. In 1998 over 3.3 million cars and well over 80 000 coaches were carried. However, a great deal of this traffic was on day trips or weekends away linked to the existence of duty free sales in Calais. When this was abolished traffic plunged.

With traffic stabilised at a lower level Eurotunnel put one of its nine Shuttles into store in 2005 and left it outside under a tarpaulin for seven years. In 2012, with the London Olympics and the Queen's Silver Jubilee likely to boost summer traffic, Eurotunnel reinstated the set after a heavy overhaul costing €10 million.

Passenger Shuttle refurbishment

Although the Passenger Shuttle vehicles spent their first 25 years without a refurbishment, Eurotunnel carried out a constant stream of minor modifications to take account of experience in service. When the ninth Shuttle was overhauled in 2012 modifications included LED lights replacing neon tubes and refurbished toilets. These were also being gradually applied to the other trains. All of the trains gradually had the stabilising jacks removed from coaches except the loading wagons themselves. Other new components have been tested on otherwise unchanged Passenger Shuttles, one of the most important being a more powerful air conditioning system.

On 20 March 2019 Eurotunnel announced that it had contracted Bombardier Transportation's Crespin plant, in northern France, about 120 km from Calais, to carry out a mid-life refurbishment of the Passenger Shuttle wagons. The nine trains have travelled an average of 300 return trips a month (30 000 km) since introduction and have carried 236 million passengers. The contract is valued at €150 million over a period of seven years, with delivery of refurbished Shuttles from mid 2022 to mid 2026. The work will not include the single-deck loading wagons which will be modernised by Eurotunnel itself.

The refurbishment work will be carried out by Bombardier in a dedicated area at Eurotunnel's depot in Coquelles. The engineering work necessary for the project will be carried out at Crespin, while a "platform" for meetings will be created in Lille, about halfway between Coquelles and Crespin. At its peak, Bombardier will be fielding up to 35 engineers and 150 other staff on the project.

The aim of the work, as well as to refresh the interiors, is to make the Shuttle wagons more reliable and therefore reduce maintenance costs by as much as 50%. This will be done by replacing troublesome components and adding modern diagnostic equipment to the wagons so that faults can be detected as early as possible. Eurotunnel will therefore be able to move from periodic to preventative maintenance.

Two points will receive particular attention. The air conditioning and ventilation systems in the Passenger Shuttles have been found to be insufficient, particularly in taking away all the heat generated by the vehicles plus their occupants. A new, more powerful HVAC system will be installed. All this will be possible using less energy than previously.

The second major change will be in the fire doors at the vehicle ends which will be replaced by a completely new design. The current doors consist of passenger doors on each side which fold inwards during unloading/loading and a central shutter which rolls down from the ceiling after loading. The new central shutters will be similar to the existing models, but the side doors will slide sideways during unloading instead of folding inwards. This means that they will leave an extra metre or so clear at each end of each wagon, leaving more room for vehicles. Over the past 25 years cars have become progressively bigger and longer, meaning that a Passenger Shuttle is able to carry fewer cars than before.

A final modification which is worth mentioning is the replacement of the Halon gas used to extinguish fires by an alternative which does not damage the climate.

FREIGHT SHUTTLES

The original Freight Shuttle vehicles were considerably simpler than the passenger vehicles but, with hindsight, more complicated than the market required. Each carrier wagon was designed to carry a complete lorry – tractor unit plus trailer – weighing up to 44 tonnes, a train consisting of two rakes each consisting of one loading and one unloading wagon plus 14 carrier wagons. One train would therefore carry 28 lorries. The lorry drivers would ride in a "Club Car" – basically a standard passenger coach – at the front of the train. The initial order was for eight complete trains:

- 32 loading/unloading wagons, plus one spare
- 224 carrier wagons, plus four spares
- Eight Club Cars, plus one spare

At an early stage it was decided that the carrier wagons could not be of a completely closed design with air conditioning and communications and fire doors like the Passenger Shuttles, with lorry drivers staying in their cabs – the weight of the wagon plus one of the heaviest lorries would exceed the imposed maximum axle weight of 22 tonnes. Instead the first generation of Freight Shuttle vehicles were semi-open, with a solid roof and trellis walls which would prevent anything loose on a lorry from blowing about and touching the overhead wires and so on. The ends are completely open and have bridging plates between wagons so that lorries can be driven from one end of the train to the other. Drivers leave and regain their lorries through an opening in the side and are taken by minibus to the Club Car at the front of the train.

Like the Passenger Shuttles, lorries enter the loading wagon from the side

then drive down the train until they reach the end of the train or another lorry in front. As on the Passenger Shuttles, a raised "pavement" on each side keeps the lorries in the middle. They are parked carefully in order to balance their weight then chocked in place. Once again the loading wagons have jacks to absorb weight during loading. Carrier wagons were built with an electricity supply which can be connected to trailer refrigeration units during the crossing but this was later decommissioned.

The loading/unloading wagons are relatively simple, consisting of an open flat wagon, with fold-down bridging plates on each side and a small "shelter" at the end to help shunting and the surveillance of loading. Total length of a train was initially 730 metres.

Above: Breda Freight Shuttle vehicles, including a loading wagon, at Coquelles depot in 1995.

Below: An early photo of a Breda Freight Shuttle entering the Channel Tunnel, while a Eurostar leaves the Tunnel in the background. This photo is no longer possible due to the many extra fences built to stop migrants from reaching the railway. *David Haydock (2)*

Italian company Breda-Fiat won the contract to build the Freight Shuttle wagons; the bogies were built by Fiat at Savigliano in Italy.

The "Club Cars" in which the drivers ride through the Tunnel were built by OMECA and based on the 300 km/h air-conditioned coaches built for ETR.500 high speed trains built for Italian State Railways (FS), although

Right: The much jollier exterior of the Freight Shuttle Club Car after refurbishment in 2014. Note the step to bridge the wide gap between the platform and coach.

Below & bottom: A Club Car before and after the 2014 interior refurbishment. *David Haydock (3)*

fitted with proven 160 km/h bogies. The lorry drivers were treated to first class-style 2+1 seating around tables (52 seats in all), and a toilet at each end of the coach. The main change to the ETR.500 design was the addition of a compartment for the train captain at one end. The coaches also have 67 cm flaps at doors to bridge the massive gap between the coach's UIC gauge and the Shuttle platforms.

Of the initial eight trains only six remain today. Breda wagons were involved in two serious fires and many were damaged. The original 28-wagon rakes have all been extended to 31 wagons, using spare wagons which survived the fires. The Breda rakes are only 31 wagons long, compared with 32 wagons for the others, due to their higher weight.

A second generation of wagons

As early as 5 March 1996 Eurotunnel announced an order for 72 new Freight Shuttle wagons worth FRF 106 million (€16.16 million), with an option for 144 more, from Arbel Fauvet Rail (AFR) in Douai, northern France. The new wagons would be delivered in March and April 1998. The first wagons were formed into two rakes of a new generation which were considerably simpler and cost a third as much per wagon than the Breda wagons. Their simplicity also reduced maintenance costs and improved reliability. They were basically similar to drive-on wagons used for "RoLa" through the Swiss Alps but with added "shelters" (known colloquially as "pagodas") over the top to stop lorry tarpaulins from touching the overhead wires if they came loose. At the same time Eurotunnel signed two more contracts for four locomotives, with an option for five more Club Cars to carry truck drivers (with an option for three more). The Club Cars were ordered on 15 March 1996 from Costamasnaga of Italy at a cost of

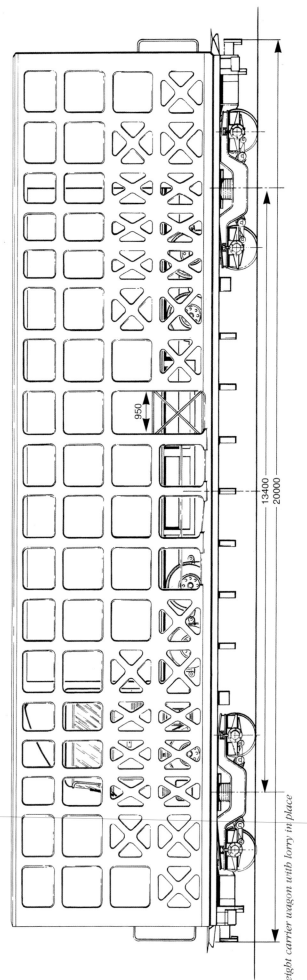

Freight carrier wagon with lorry in place

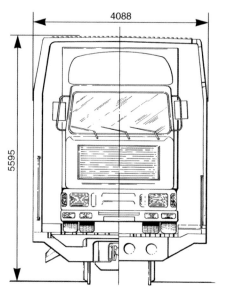

End elevation of freight carrier wagon

All diagrams taken from the book "Channel Tunnel Trains" with permission from Eurotunnel.

FRF 30 million (€4.57 million) for delivery in spring 1998. In the end, after the take up of options, Arbel built nine complete Freight Shuttles while Costamasnaga delivered 11 Club Cars.

The first prototype wagon was delivered by Arbel in early October 1997. Arbel described the new wagon as a "standard" design "upgraded" for Eurotunnel's needs, compared with the Breda wagons "downgraded passenger cars". The Arbel vehicles were based on a wagon built to carry French army tanks of which the company had built 200. The major change was the addition of a roof, supported by simple struts, in four sections. There was no electricity supply for refrigerated lorries, no lighting and no stabilising hydraulic rams along the train for loading. Only the loading wagons had a support system, and their design was simplified. As far as refrigerated lorries were concerned, the electricity supply on the original wagons stopped being used soon after the start of regular services – with a standing and journey time of well under an hour, a trailer's insulation is enough to keep a load cool enough. All semi-automatic couplings were replaced with LAF (now LAF-Lloyd) automatic devices.

The new wagons were formed into trains of 32 wagons plus loaders, allowing Eurotunnel to carry two more lorries per train.

In 2012 Eurotunnel asked the Intergovernmental Safety Commission for permission to remove the roofs from the Arbel wagons, after a prolonged period of trials during which some sections of roofs were removed. Eurotunnel argued that the roof was only likely to fan flames in the event of a fire and that roofs did not exist on such wagons anywhere else in Europe. They also added unnecessary weight and maintenance costs.

However, before all of the roofs could be removed a third fire occurred (see later chapter).

Club Cars refurbished

On 27 February 2014 Eurotunnel revealed an improved interior for the eleven Costamasnaga Club Cars at a cost of €1.2 million. The first batch of eight Club Cars, built at the same time as the Breda freight wagons, had received a light refurbishment previously. The previous layout had been copied directly from the Italian ETR.500 coaches from which the coaches were derived. The new layout was devised to take into account 20 years of operating experience. New slimmer, more ergonomic Compin seats were laid out in a 2+1 arrangement, all of them facing the front of the train. 54 new Compin seats plus six fold-down seats replaced the original 48 face-to-face 2+1 seats. Food and drink machines (since removed) were relocated to the front end of the coach and toilets redesigned. Eurotunnel had served hot meals in the first trains but demand declined to an extent that it was no longer worthwhile. Work was carried out by French company ADF at Eurotunnel's Coquelles depot. The upgrade also included video screens to give lorry drivers useful information, such as traffic and weather conditions, plus safety information.

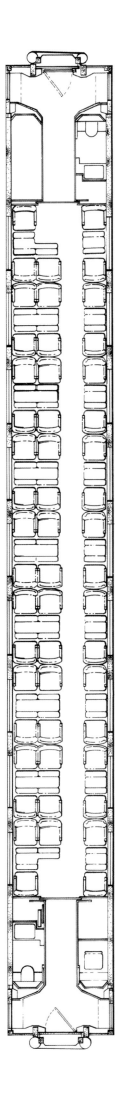

Plan section of club car

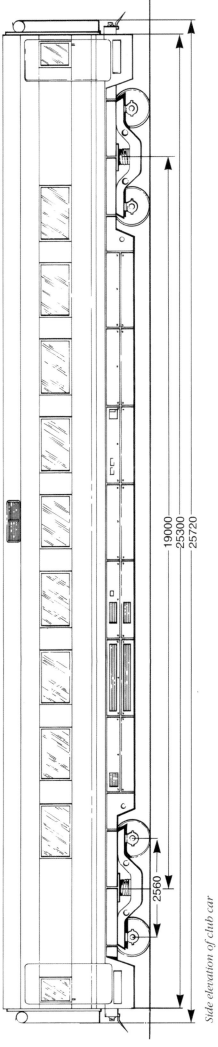

19000
25300
25720

2560

Side elevation of club car

More Freight Shuttle wagons

On 13 January 2015 Eurotunnel announced that it had ordered three new sets of Freight Shuttle wagons to add to the 15 it already had in its fleet – six of Breda wagons and nine of Arbel wagons. The aim of buying more wagons was Eurotunnel's strategy of carrying 2 million lorries between the UK and France by 2020. Despite the uncertainty caused by Brexit, traffic growth (almost 1.7 million trucks in 2018) means that the 2 million mark looks likely to be attained, if not in 2020 then relatively soon.

The new wagons, at a cost of €40 million and delivered in 2016/17, were to be built by WBN Waggonbau Niesky, a German company near Görlitz on the border with Poland. Each train would be formed of 32 carrier wagons, three loading wagons and a coach to carry lorry drivers.

A fleet of 18 trains would allow Eurotunnel to operate eight trains per hour, per direction at peak times, which are generally in the middle of the week – Tuesday to Thursday – and in the period coming up to Christmas. The maximum frequency at present is six trains per hour. The contract also included an option for enough wagons to form two extra trains, bringing the total to 20, plus a second option for six complete trains to replace the Breda wagons. No new Shuttle locomotives would be needed as the fleet was already big enough.

The Niesky wagons are, in fact, very similar to those built by Arbel, in an effort to standardise operations. Eurotunnel had argued, successfully up to the order date, that it should be dispensed of having "pagodas" on the Niesky wagons and would proceed to remove them from the Arbel wagons. This would make wagons lighter and easier to maintain.

However, only four days after the new order was announced, a new fire occurred on a Freight Shuttle in the Tunnel, and the eventual conclusions of the safety authorities included the retention of the "pagodas".

The first of the new wagons was inaugurated on 28 April 2017. The Niesky wagons, close up, are indeed very similar to those built by Arbel. Only two differences are clearly visible, and those only close up. The first is the addition of curved sections of metal to the "pagoda" roof supports, in order to reduce air resistance. The second is the addition of cable supports along the wagon solebars – control cables in the Arbel wagons were slung underneath the middle of the wagon chassis and this made cables difficult to inspect and maintain.

Above: A Freight Shuttle formed of Arbel wagons leaves Coquelles on 11 March 2011. On the first two wagons two of the four "pagodas" have been removed while they all remain in place on the wagons behind.

Below: The very similar WBN (Niessky, on left) and Arbel wagons (right) seen on 23 September 2019. Just visible on the WBN wagons are curved 'streamlining on the "pagoda" roof supports and the cable supports all the way along the solebar. *David Haydock (2)*

THE CHANNEL TUNNEL FIRES

Eurotunnel once said that it would not expect a fire to happen more than once every hundred years but the company has had to face the consequences of three serious fires inside Tunnel, all of them on Freight Shuttles, in the 25 years since it opened.

18 November 1996

The first occurred on 18 November 1996 – only two years after services started in earnest. A fire broke out on one of the rear lorries on a Freight Shuttle from Coquelles to Cheriton – two watchmen at the Tunnel entrance had seen flames two metres high, despite nothing untoward being noticed during loading. The watchmen immediately contacted Tunnel control which implemented the emergency procedure which was for the train to continue out of the Tunnel at low speed. However, within a few more minutes the train was immobilised in the centre of the Tunnel and the overhead

system's power circuit breakers then blew, cutting power to the train. After a 20-minute wait because of thick smoke the three Eurotunnel staff led the 31 lorry drivers to safety via an emergency connection to the service tunnel. They were then transferred to a Shuttle travelling in the opposite direction.

Eight hours were necessary to extinguish the fire which spread to 15 more lorries. The fire, which reached 1200° C, damaged about 800 metres of the Tunnel. All services through the Tunnel were suspended for three days before permission was granted to use the undamaged sections of Tunnel. Eurostar services did not restart for over two weeks and then with 20–30 minute delays due to restricted capacity in the Tunnel.

Reports later blamed a short circuit in the refrigeration unit of a lorry carrying pork fat. However, by spring 1998 the investigating judge had declared that the fire was started by "vandalism". This was thought to refer to a firework landing on the train, launched

by staff protesting in Coquelles at layoffs by Eurotunnel. However, 21 years later no definite cause for the fire has been proven.

The south running tunnel finally reopened on 13 May 1998, although Eurostar did not resume a normal service until 1 June – more than six months after the fire; repairs had cost £38 million but were paid for by insurance. Overall the fire was said to have caused £200 million in damage including lost revenue.

Four and a half months after the fire new procedures were put in place for HGV Shuttle services including more systematic checks of lorries during loading and surveillance of departure. Refrigeration units are now switched off and checked as such, while departures are now watched by a member of staff to check there is no smoke, or loose cords or tarpaulins flapping.

In addition, emergency procedures were revised – in the event of a fire a train would be brought to a controlled stop, with the Club Car next to an emergency exit door. Eurotunnel decided to centralise fire alarm monitors in its control centre, and installed new devices to detect more precisely where a train had stopped. Smoke hoods were

Top: The consequences of the 2008 fire, still visible on 11 March 2011: locomotive 9817 plus three Passenger Shuttle vehicles, damaged beyond repair, await a sign from the insurance company before they can be cut up.

Above left: Eurotunnel Krupp MaK diesel 0001 plus Genifer 182 586 (ex DB 212 221) head ex SNCB coach 42387 after a press visit to see repairs to the fire-damaged Tunnel on 1 December 2008. *David Haydock (2)*

Top left: A cement wagon inside the Tunnel during repairs after the 2008 fire.

Centre left: Scaffolding inside the Tunnel in order to allow repairs on two levels at the same time.

Bottom left: "Shotcreting" taking place during repairs to the Tunnel walls on 1 December 2008.

Right: The first public demonstration of a SAFE fire-fighting "station" inside the Tunnel on 1 February 2011. *David Haydock (4)*

deployed in the Club Cars for passengers and staff, and fire suppression systems using water sprays were to be installed every 15 km inside the rail tunnels.

11 September 2008

On the afternoon of Thursday 11 September 2008 a fire broke out on a lorry being carried on a Cheriton–Coquelles Freight Shuttle. The train was brought to a standstill 11.5 km from the French portal. 29 lorry drivers and three crew were evacuated into the service tunnel. 14 of them suffered minor injuries, including smoke inhalation. The fire spread to other lorries and the fire burned for 16 hours before being put out by the Kent and Pas-de-Calais fire services. Six wagons and one locomotive, 9817 "JOSÉ CARRERAS", were destroyed.

All traffic through the Tunnel was stopped for the rest of the day, then after inspections the following day the south tunnel was brought back into limited use. On 1 October the first third of the stricken train was removed from the northern tunnel and the reopening of the non-damaged "Intervals" of the latter allowed a nearer to normal service to operate with trains "flighted" through the Interval closest to France in the southern bore. Around 90% of Eurostars, 70% of Freight Shuttles and 60% of Passenger Shuttles were able to operate, even though limited to 100 km/h.

Within a month of the fire Eurotunnel announced that the 650 metre damaged section of the Tunnel would be repaired within four months – rather than six months for the 1996 fire – at a cost of €60 compared with €90 in 1996, despite the fire burning twice as long. However, this did not include the loss of revenue, which had already reached €22 million for September – about €1 million a day. With services being restored to a decent level more quickly Eurotunnel estimated lost revenue at around €100 million.

By November 2008 Eurotunnel had contracted a group of companies to repair the damaged bore and these were working 24 hours a day, seven days a week, despite the other five Intervals remaining open to traffic. At shift changeovers staff were moved between a temporary base in Coquelles in a former Belgian Railways (SNCB) coach (Type M2 open second 42387) pushed into the Tunnel by one or two diesel locos.

Following the restitution of Interval 6 to Eurotunnel in mid October 2008, damaged cables, cooling pipes and catenary were dismantled to assess the damage to the

tunnel lining. Core boring to take samples of the tunnel lining, the mortar behind it and the rock underneath showed that the construction had stood up very well to the 1000° C temperatures.

The next stage was to replace over a thousand bolts holding down concrete lining segments and re-grouting around them. Loose and damaged concrete was then removed using very high pressure water jets, much of the work being carried out by robots. Repairs were then made to the reinforcing steel mesh, after which, from the end of November, "shotcreting" was used to build up a 15 cm thick layer of concrete. This stage lasted into January, after which track, catenary, signalling, cooling pipes and safety equipment were renewed, while the rest of the Tunnel was cleaned of smoke deposits.

The repaired "Interval" eventually reopened on 9 February 2009, just in time for the ski season rush both on the Shuttle and on Eurostar.

SAFE makes Tunnel safer

After the 2008 fire Eurotunnel introduced a plan called "Salamander" designed to reduce the impact of any future incident. This had four main points:

- installation of the four SAFE installations.
- detection of lorries at risk before and during loading, carried out by six inspectors who check safety rules are being respected by drivers.
- signs and leaflets on safety in nine languages – 60% of the lorry drivers in the 2008 fire could understand little or no English or French.
- a modification of the safety rules in the Tunnel for Freight Shuttles. A train carrying a lorry on fire must now continue to the nearest point where a fire can be circumscribed and passengers plus staff evacuated – either out of the Tunnel or to the next SAFE point.

Eurotunnel invested €20 million in the four SAFE stations which became operational in 2012.

Following both of the first two fires, some experts and fire brigades called for the Freight Shuttle wagons to be enclosed and for them to be fitted with sprinklers. In the case of the (enclosed) Passenger Shuttles, there have been occasional cases of cars catching fire but these have never caused casualties or spread to cause serious damage as staff on board have managed to extinguish fires manually. The idea of having enclosed Freight Shuttles has been studied but it was found that their increased tare weight would make it impossible to carry any but the lightest of lorries.

The open-sided design of the Freight Shuttles has, at times, been defended as "helping reduce the spread" of any fire that breaks out but others claimed that any increased air flow over a fire would actually cause it to burn more strongly. Short of enclosing wagons, fire brigades requested that Eurotunnel equip the wagons with fire suppression systems. This was also rejected by the operator as impractical.

Instead Eurotunnel now relies on a system known as SAFE (*Stations d'Attaque du Feu* or fire attack points); although such a system had been mooted after the 1996 fire it was only after the 2008 fire that the plan was pushed ahead.

Each SAFE "station" is 870 m long – longer than longest Shuttles – and is divided into 30 metre sections. Once a train has been stopped within this area heat detectors determine the position of the fire and a mist of water is released under high pressure in the section or sections concerned. The system uses a relatively small quantity of water to create a fine mist of droplets which absorbs oxygen and stifles the fire. Tests have shown that the temperature of a fire can be reduced from 1100°C to 50°C in three minutes.

The aim is not so much to extinguish the fire but to give the fire services time to reach the fire and to improve visibility by preventing smoke release.

A close shave

At about 13.50 CET on 29 November 2012 the Eurotunnel control centre registered two successive fire alarms. The train concerned was a Freight Shuttle from the UK to France which had already passed both the SAFE stations, so the driver was told to continue out of the Tunnel and was routed into the emergency siding at Coquelles. Fire engines were quickly on the scene and put out the fire.

The fire had broken out on a lorry carrying cars but it was not clear if it started in the lorry itself or one of the cars.

17 January 2015

On this Saturday at 12.23 CET the on-board fire detector on a UK–France Freight Shuttle set off an alarm and this was followed by an alarm from a CO_2 detector. The Shuttle was brought to a controlled halt in Interval 4, the central section of the northern bore, after power was lost from the overhead. The 38 lorry drivers and four staff on board were evacuated by 12.37.

The emergency services arrived about an hour later and discovered that two lorries were on fire. The fire services took about two hours to put out the fire but continued to douse the lorries for several hours. The southern bore was reopened to traffic at 03.43 CET the following day, then Interval 2 and Interval 6 in the northern bore by Sunday evening.

The fire seriously damaged two lorries but the train was removed on the Sunday afternoon. Repairing the Tunnel took a further two days.

The report on the fire, released just under a year later found that the fire was caused by an over-height whip aerial on the lorry's cab roof causing an arc between the lorry and the overhead power line. The arc had activated devices which tripped the power supply and stopped the train, although control centre staff could not find the cause, and so restored power. The second power trip occurred just after the control centre received the fire alarm.

The RAIB investigating board found that sensors designed to detect over-height objects were not sensitive enough and that a member of staff who noticed the wayward aerial was assured that they would have detected it if it were a danger. The RAIB also found that CCTV had shown smoke within a lorry cab after the first power trip but that no attempt was made to direct the train to the first SAFE station.

A final report on the fire said that an opportunity was missed to stop the train at a SAFE station due to delays in obtaining information on the incident. It then took the fire services 3½ hours to tackle the blaze. Three vehicles had been used to recover passengers from the scene rather than conveying firefighters to the site of the incident.

The report recommended that Eurotunnel improve its detection of over-height objects and that the "pagodas" should be reinstated on carrier wagons. Eurotunnel had hoped to remove all "pagodas" from Arbel wagons and order new wagons without "pagodas", but this policy had to be reversed.

Eurotunnel changed its operating procedures so that any train involved in a power line trip with this sort of wagon at the tunnel portals will now be directed to a SAFE station for investigation.

EUROTUNNEL SHUTTLE
LOCOMOTIVES

At the development stage it was expected that each Shuttle train would be loaded up to 2400 tonnes and so two powerful locomotives were required for each train, with one at the front and one at the rear to allow rapid acceleration and rapid reversal of direction when necessary. In fact, as the Shuttle "system" is a one-way loop this is not usually necessary. However, Channel Tunnel safety rules mean that trains need to be able to exit the Tunnel in either direction in an emergency; this possibility is also useful for shunting or stabling a train.

The original order for the Shuttles was for 17 trains – nine passenger and eight Freight Shuttles – so a total of 34 locomotives was needed; four spare locos were then added, giving a total of 38 locomotives, to be known as Class 9/0. The specification was demanding – intensive use (up to 20 single journeys a day, totalling about 1200 km) hauling trains up to 2400 tonnes at 140 km/h over gradients up to 1.1% (1 in 91) in conditions which could change from well below freezing outside to a constant

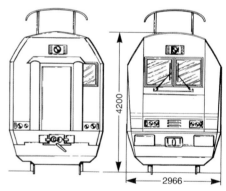

9704
Eurotunnel 2015

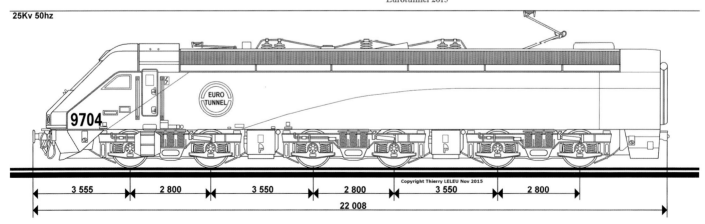

24°C inside the Tunnel with around 100% humidity. In addition, the locomotives would have to be able to restart a train on the steepest gradient with one bogie out of service, or restart and exit the tunnel at reduced speed if one of the two locos failed completely. If a complete Shuttle train breaks down, the next one must be able to push it out of the Tunnel. Shuttle locomotives have standard screw couplings and heavy duty buffers as complete Shuttle trains might also be called upon to pull or push a failed freight train.

The locos could be custom-built with a single driving cab as they would always work with a train, although there would be a small window at the other end for shunting movements. There was also a corridor connection at the non-cab end to allow access to the passenger coaches.

It was decided at an early stage that the locomotives would need to have six axles in order to spread the loco weight and increase adhesion. However, while the Class 92 locomotives built for through freight services would be Co-Co machines, it was decided to order a Bo-Bo-Bo design for Shuttle services because of the tight curvature at each terminal. The bogies would have a rigid wheelbase of 2.8 metres. An additional advantage of this configuration was that, if one bogie was out of action, this would mean only a third of the power, compared with half in a Co-Co arrangement.

Swiss technology

At an early stage, the designers turned to the Swiss locomotive construction industry, because the country already had Bo-Bo-Bo

9013
Eurotunnel 2014

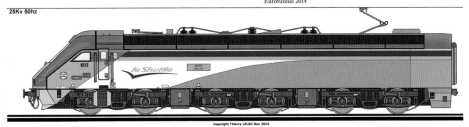

9005
Eurotunnel 2014

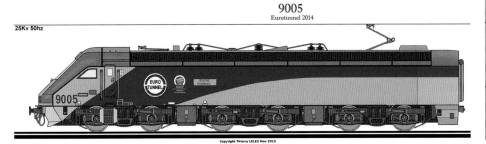

Shuttle locomotive fleet list

Unmodified locomotives (13)	
9005	JESSYE NORMAN
9007	DAME JOAN SUTHERLAND
9011	JOSÉ VAN DAM
9013	MARIA CALLAS
9015	LÖTSCHBERG 1913
9018	WILHELMENIA FERNANDEZ
9022	DAME JANET BAKER
9024	GOTTHARD 1882
9026	FURKATUNNEL 1982
9029	THOMAS ALLEN
9033	MONTSERRAT CABALLE
9036	ALAIN FONDARY
9037	GABRIEL BACQUIER

Increased power freight locomotives (20)	
9701	
9702	
9703	
9704	
9705	
9706	
9707	
9711 (9101)	
9712 (9102)	
9713 (9103)	
9714 (9104)	
9715 (9105)	
9716 (9106)	
9717 (9107)	
9718 (9108)	
9719 (9109)	
9720 (9110)	
9721 (9111)	
9722 (9112)	
9723 (9113)	

Rebuilt locomotives (24)	
Original locomotives uprated to 7000 kW.	
9801 (9001)	LESLEY GARRETT
9802 (9002)	STUART BURROWS
9803 (9003)	BENJAMIN LUXON
9804 (9004)	VICTORIA DE LOS ANGELES
9806 (9006)	RÉGINE CRESPIN
9808 (9008)	ELISABETH SODERSTROM
9809 (9009)	FRANÇOIS POLLET
9810 (9010)	JEAN-PHILIPPE COURTIS
9812 (9012)	LUCIANO PAVAROTTI
9814 (9014)	LUCIA POPP
9816 (9016)	WILLARD WHITE
9819 (9019)	MARIA EWING
9820 (9020)	NICOLAI GHIAROV
9821 (9021)	TERESA BERGANZA
9823 (9023)	DAME ELISABETH LEGGE-SCHWARZKOPF
9825 (9025)	JUNGFRAUJOCH 1912
9827 (9027)	BARBARA HENDRICKS
9828 (9028)	DAME KIRI TE KANAWA
9831 (9031)	PLACIDO DOMINGO
9832 (9032)	RENATA TEBALDI
9834 (9034)	MIRELLA FRENI
9835 (9035)	NICOLAI GEDDA
9838 (9038)	HILDEGARD BEHRENS
9840 (9040)	

9030 was withdrawn and scrapped after the fire in 1996 before it could be named "MONTSERRAT CABALLE". 9040 was built to replace 9030 and was never named. 9039 has never existed.

9817 (ex 9017 "JOSÉ CARRERAS") was damaged beyond repair in the 2008 fire and was scrapped on site by Eurotunnel.

electric locomotives which were used frequently in long tunnels such as those on the Gotthard and Lötschberg trans-Alpine lines. In addition, Switzerland was foremost in new traction developments at the time. The choice was eventually made to order locomotives from ASEA Brown Boveri (ABB), which had experience in Switzerland, for electrical equipment, and UK company Brush, which in 1986 had started delivery of Bo-Bo-Bo locomotives to New Zealand Railways, for mechanical parts and assembly. The locomotives would weigh 132 tonnes and have a continuous rating of 5600 kW. However, they were built to UIC loading gauge – much smaller than the Shuttle wagons they would power – to allow their movement over the conventional network if necessary.

ABB provided the locomotives with the very latest in electrical traction systems, using Gate Turn Off (GTO) thyristors and asynchronous three-phase traction motors. These also allowed an important feature for the Channel Tunnel – regenerative braking. This means that the traction motors "go into reverse" when braking, thus generating electricity which is fed back into the supply system. This not only saves energy but avoids the traditional mechanical systems which turn braking energy into heat as well as producing dust from brake pads or shoes, thus avoiding dirtying and heating the Tunnel. The driver's brake controller "blends" electro-pneumatic brakes and regenerative braking automatically.

The front locomotive controls the rear one through a Time Division Multiplex system. All locomotives and Shuttle wagons are coupled to each other by specialised Scharfenberg couplers.

Classes 9/0, 9/7 & 9/8

Technical details
Built: by Brush Traction, Loughborough.
Class 9/0 (original build): 1993/94.
Class 9/7: 9701–9707 built 2001/2.
9711–9723 built as 9101–9113 in 1998–2001, rebuilt 2010–12 as 9711–9723.
Class 9/8: Built 1993/94 as Class 9000; rebuilt as Class 9800 2003–2009. 9840 built as 9040 in 1998.
Wheel arrangement: Bo-Bo-Bo.
Electrical supply system: 25 kV AC 50 Hz overhead.
Traction motors:
Class 9/0: Six ABB Type 6FHA 7059 asynchronous three-phase of 960 kW each, fully suspended.
Classes 9/7 & 9/8: Six ABB Type 6FHA 7059A asynchronous three-phase of 1167 kW each, fully suspended.
Maximum tractive effort: 400 kN.
Continuous rating:
Class 9/0: 5760 kW.
Classes 9/7 & 9/8: 7000 kW.
Length: 22.008 metres.
Width: 2.97 metres.
Weight: 136 tonnes.
Wheel diameter: 1250 mm.
Design speed: 160 km/h.
Maximum speed: 140 km/h.

References:
Channel Tunnel Trains by Peter Semmens and Yves Machefert-Tassin, Eurotunnel 1994

It should be noted that locomotive cabs have two seats, the second being for the "train captain" although he or she normally rides in the rear cab of the train. The train captain supervises the Shuttle wagons and their passengers, passes messages to them and to staff, and deals with emergencies. Should a train need to reverse out of the Tunnel the train captain operates the train.

In normal service, the driver uses manual control to depart from and arrive at the two terminals but uses a "cruise control" set at 140 km/h in the Tunnel itself. On the downward gradient this automatically applies regenerative braking to avoid exceeding this speed.

Production

The welded monocoque body shells for the locomotives were built by Qualter Hall Engineering of Barnsley, South Yorkshire, and were fitted out by Brush at Loughborough. The transformer was mounted vertically in the centre of the loco as the third bogie made it impossible to place it between the bogies as in many designs. There are three sets of traction converters – one for each bogie. The rotary

Top: The rear cab window is clearly visible on this photo of Passenger Shuttle loco 9810.

Above: The rear of 9840 which was built to replace burnt-out 9030 and, like Class 97/0, has no back cab.

Right: A classic three-quarters view of 9810 at Coquelles depot on 27 February 2014. The loco has since lost its name plates.
David Haydock (3)

air compressor is larger than on a typical locomotive and has twin driers because the air in the Tunnel is extremely humid. The interior of the locomotive was divided into four zones, each fitted with its own heat- and fire-detection systems which activate the discharge of Halon 1301, an inert gas, in the event of fire. The gearbox and drive systems were derived from those supplied by ABB for Deutsche Bundesbahn Class 120 Bo-Bo electric locos. There are two Brecknell-Willis pantographs on each power car. However Shuttle trains normally operate with the rear pantograph raised on each loco.

First deliveries

The first Shuttle locomotive was delivered to Coquelles depot on 14 December 1993. It had travelled from Brush in England on a low loader, without its bogies, and had crossed the Channel on the Nord-Pas-de-Calais freight ferry. The locomotive was then lowered onto its three bogies on 16 December. The second locomotive arrived shortly after this.

However, dynamic testing with the first Shuttle locomotives did not start straight away. The late delivery of the locos had forced Eurotunnel to hire five Class BB 22200 electric locomotives from SNCF.

Shuttle locos 9003 and 9004 were sent to the Velim test track in the Czech Republic soon after delivery and were tested both singly and together from September 1993.

Additional locomotives

The first batch of Shuttle locomotives was numbered 9001 to 9038. Within only two years of the Tunnel opening, the continuous increase in freight traffic meant that Eurotunnel needed to buy more trains.

On 21 May 1996 the company ordered five more locomotives. These would be of a slightly simpler design (there is no second driving position or facilities for the train captain as he/she rides in the Club Car), as they would be dedicated to Freight Shuttles, but with improvements including IGBT instead of GTO thyristors and one inverter per traction motor instead of one per bogie. They were therefore numbered in a separate number series, from 9101 upwards. After the fire on 18 November 1996, which damaged loco 9006 and wrote off 9030, the last of the five was built to the original design for Passenger Shuttles – although without the rear cab – and numbered 9040. There was no 9039. Two additional sets of wagons were ordered at the same time.

The first loco was delivered on 28 February 1998 and the others by the end of 1998. They were all delivered in a simpler livery of blue and grey with a lack of white and green. In 1998 Eurotunnel ordered a further nine locos which were numbered 9105 to 9113.

More power

These were followed by a further seven locos for Freight Shuttles in 2001–3, numbered 9701 to 9707, which were considerably more powerful than the first order, with a maximum rating of 7000 kW. Eurotunnel portrayed 9701 as the "world's most powerful electric locomotive" when it was delivered by lorry on 5 December 2001. The more powerful locos were the key to running heavier Freight Shuttles – in principle up to 3000 tonnes, carrying 32 lorries per train. The last new locomotive arrived on 8 June 2003.

Upgrading for higher power

9101 to 9113 were rebuilt to the more powerful rating in 2010–2012 and renumbered 9711 to 9723. Then in late 2002 Brush Traction and Bombardier Transportation won a contract to upgrade the 37 remaining Class 9/0 locos, 9030 having been scrapped after the first Tunnel fire. This consisted of a €95 million contract for 25 locos and a follow-on contract for 13 more, worth €42 million.

In the end only 25 Class 9/0 were upgraded, being renumbered in the 9800 series, 9001 becoming 9801, 9014 becoming 9814 and so on. Work included raising the rating from 5600 to 7000 kW with installation of IGBT converters plus new traction motors and control equipment. Work was due to run from February 2003 to April 2009. The first to be modernised was 9025 which was moved to Brush Traction in summer 2003. The loco returned to Eurotunnel as 9825 in February 2004.

This left 13 locos still in the original configuration. Eurotunnel decided the expense of converting all locos was not worthwhile and the locos are generally used for the lighter Passenger Shuttles.

In November 2009 another fire damaged locos 9814 and 9817. Both were initially put into store but 9814 was revived to power the ninth passenger Shuttle in 2012. 9817 was too heavily damaged and was cut up once insurance claims had been investigated and compensation paid out.

Mid-life refurbishment

With the earliest locos over 25 years old, Eurotunnel is now mulling mid-life refurbishment for the whole fleet. It is thought that the first ones to be dealt with will be the 13 remaining unrebuilt Class 9/0 locomotives which will almost certainly be brought up to the same power as the others.

Names

Almost all of the 9/0 batch of locomotives were named after opera singers, in some cases the nameplate being revealed by the singers themselves in special ceremonies. Four locomotives received the names of famous tunnels on European railways during 1997 in "twinning ceremonies". In exchange SBB electric loco Re 460 077 is named "Chunnel", BLS electric locomotive Re 465 012 and Jungfraubahn EMU 209 are "EUROTUNNEL" and MGB (former FO) loco 108 is "CHANNEL TUNNEL".

Loco 9030 was allocated the name MONTSERRAT CABALLE but had not received plates when it was damaged beyond repair in the first Tunnel fire.

Other names which were never applied were CECILIA BARTOLI, DAME GWYNETH JONES, GHYSLAINE RAPHANEL, GRACE BUMBRY and MARILYN HORNE. Presumably four of these had been selected for the locomotives which received "tunnel names".

Neither 9040, the replacement for 9030, nor any of the dedicated freight locomotives ever received names.

Observers occasionally report that Shuttle locomotives have been "de-named". However, there have been no deliberate decisions to remove the names – instead they have actually fallen off in traffic.

EUROTUNNEL'S
"**KRUPP**" LOCOMOTIVES

Eurotunnel has a fleet of ten Krupp-MaK Bo-Bo diesel-electric locomotives to haul maintenance trains in and around the Tunnel, as well as rescuing broken down trains and, occasionally, moving trains over HS1 between the Tunnel and St Pancras International, or Eurostar's depot at Temple Mills.

It was Transmanche Link Construction, the company which built the Tunnel, which originally ordered the first five locos. They were then passed on to operator Eurotunnel when the latter took over the infrastructure in 1993. They were delivered in 1991/92 and were thus able to assist in some Tunnel construction work.

The locos were delivered by Krupp-MaK (now Vossloh Locomotives) of Kiel in Germany and known as Type DE 1004. The design was based on that of Type DE 6400 of which 120 locos were, at the time, being delivered to Dutch Railways (NS). The MTU 12-cylinder engine was the same as in

Class 6400 and this engine type had been used in other Krupp-MaK locos, including Type DE 1002, delivered from 1978 to 1993, mainly to Köln port operator HGK, and the G 1204 BB, of which 16 went to various German private operators. The engines in the Eurotunnel locos were originally downrated to 950 kW but have now been uprated to 1180 kW. The link with NS Class 6400 was clear – the five Eurotunnel locos were even outshopped in the same livery – dark grey with a yellow cab and yellow front ends.

The original five Krupp-MaK locomotives (0001 to 0005) were, of course, equipped with TVM 430 cab signalling which is installed in the Channel Tunnel but also all the way over the HS1 high speed line to London St Pancras and the Eurostar depot at Temple Mills. In the case of Eurostar trains being delivered, rescued or even taken for scrap, at least two MaK locos are used in multiple, and sometimes three.

In 2007 the five locos were modified with large particle filters by HUG (which made the filters) at the SBB depot in Biel/Bienne in Switzerland and received modified bonnets. This obviated the need to use them with "scrubber wagons" which were connected to the exhaust and cleaned the exhaust gases, when used inside the Tunnel.

Extra locomotives

Class 6400, on which Eurotunnel's locos were based, had only ever been used for freight in the Netherlands, by the national railway's freight subsidiary NS Cargo, which was later acquired by German Railways (DB) and later became DB Cargo Nederland. As DB Cargo lost traffic to new competitors in the Netherlands, many Class 6400 became surplus and a large number were put into store at Amersfoort. DB decided to redeploy or sell most of the surplus locos and several ended up in Poland and Norway. In 2011, Eurotunnel purchased two locos – 6456 and

Top: Ex NS locos 0009, 0010 and 0008 are seen at Antwerpen Noord yard in Belgium on 31 August 2016 while on delivery from Shunter in Rotterdam to Coquelles depot. *Carlo Hertogs*

Above left: Eurotunnel Type DE 1004 Krupp-MaK locomotives 0003 and 0002 sandwich ex NS Type DE 6400 0007 hauling Eurostar e320 set 4018 and 4017 as the 6K74 14.00 Calais Fréthun to Temple Mills Reception, seen passing under the A20 road near Hothfield on 4 August 2015. The Eurostar was on delivery from Siemens. The large bump in front of the cab housing the particle filter is visible on 0003. *Antony Christie*

Above: Krupp-MaK 0010 cannot operate in the Tunnel and is seen on 28 April 2017 at Coquelles depot where it is used for shunting. *Laurent Charlier*

6457 – which were modified by the company itself for use in the Tunnel, including a less obvious particle filter system and a fire protection system, and put into service as 0006 and 0007. These cost a total of €1.3 million. The purchase was the direct consequence of the simultaneous breakdown of five Eurostar sets in the Tunnel on 18 December 2009, and was jointly financed by Eurostar. The report into the incident had criticised Eurostar's lack of rescue locomotives and recommended a joint rescue fleet be set up. In fact the fleet is totally owned and managed by Eurotunnel and can

Fleet numbers

ET no.	Built	Works no.	Former NS no.
0001	1991	100867	-
0002	1992	100868	-
0003	1992	100869	-
0004	1992	100870	-
0005	1992	100871	-
0006	1991	1200056	6456
0007	1991	1200057	6457
0008	1991	1200050	6450
0009	1991	1200051	6451
0010	1990	1200047	6447

0001 to 0010 are registered as 21901 to 21910 in the British TOPS computer system and are known by staff as 901 to 910. They have also been allocated the European Vehicle Numbers (EVNs) 92 87 000 9901 to 9910 F-GB-ET. ET is the Eurotunnel Vehicle Keeper Marking. In principle, it is not possible to have both F and GB as part of the Vehicle Keeper Marking (VKM). The "87" in the number indicates France, but the locos are allocated to and maintained at Cheriton depot in England.

Technical details

	0001–0005	0006–0010
Built (by Krupp MaK of Kiel, Germany):	1991/92.	1990/91.
Model:	DE 1004.	DE 6400.
Power (MTU 12V396 TC 13 engine):	1180 kW (1580 hp)*	1180 kW (1580 hp).
Main alternator:	ABB.	ABB.
Traction motors:	ABB.	ABB.
Maximum tractive effort:	290 kN.	290 kN.
Continuous tractive effort:	140 kN.	140 kN.
Power at rail:	750 kW (1012 hp).	750 kW (1012 hp).
Brake force:	120 kN.	120 kN.
Length:	14.40 metres.	14.40 metres.
Weight:	85 tonnes.	85 tonnes.
Design speed:	120 km/h.	120 km/h.
Maximum speed:	100 km/h.	100 km/h.
Fuel capacity:	3500 litres.	3500 litres.

* uprated from 950 kW.

also be used to rescue Hitachi "Javelin". high speed trains operated by Southeastern between St Pancras and Kent.

In mid 2016, Eurotunnel acquired three more Class 6400 – 6450, 6451 and 6447. The first two locos were modified for Tunnel operation and became 0008 and 0009, while 6447 was renumbered 0010. The last has not been modified to operate in the Tunnel and is restricted to shunting at Coquelles depot. It is finished in Eurotunnel's blue and silver livery, partly in order to remind staff it cannot be used in the Tunnel. The others retain their grey and yellow colours.

In 2019, the original five locos started to be overhauled (with no significant modifications) by Shunter in Rotterdam, a private company which is also charged with the maintenance of all the original Class 6400 diesels still used by DB Cargo Nederland in the Netherlands. Locomotives 0006 and 0007 will also be overhauled in this programme; 0008 to 0010 have been overhauled only recently.

Following the overhauls, Eurotunnel is forming semi-permanent multiple pairs of locomotives. The company does not consider it cost effective to equip the former NS locomotives with expensive TVM 430 equipment. Instead the multiple pairs will

each consist of a "master" locomotive from the 0001–0005 batch and a "slave" loco from the 0006–0009 batch. The locos are coupled with their short noses outwards and the TVM display from the cab at the "long nose end" of the "master" loco is transferred to the cab at the "short nose end" of the "slave" loco. Two hefty cables (which need a lengthy coupling time, thus "semi-permanent") are strung between the two locos in order to carry the TVM 430 data from the "master" to the "slave".

At the time of writing loco 0002 was paired with 0006 while 0005 was with 0007, but these may change as further locos return from overhaul.

SCHÖMA LOCOMOTIVES

Construction of the Channel Tunnel was made possible by 900 mm gauge tracks laid inside the Tunnel bores – both the Service Tunnel and the main bores – on which trains brought in staff and materials. The locomotives were built by Hunslet but instead of moving to another project when construction was complete, some were rebuilt to standard gauge and converted to power Tunnel maintenance trains. At its peak the network had a fleet of no less than 60 Hunslet battery/overhead electric locos and 55 Schöma diesel locos.

The 900 mm gauge lines finished operation at Easter in 1993 and some of the diesel locomotives were transferred to Schöma in Germany for rebuilding into small diesel locomotives to be used for maintenance work inside the Tunnel. The result is unrecognisable compared with the Hunslet locomotives and it is difficult to identify any parts which may have been re-used.

Ten of the locomotives produced are known as Schöma Type CFL 200 and are relatively conventional small shunters. They have an end cab with excellent visibility thanks to large glazed areas. The pantograph on top of the cab is only for earthing.

The other two locomotives are Type CS 200 and are longer, with an overhead inspection platform at one end, an off-centre cab and a short bonnet at the other. There are two pantographs, one of them for earthing.

All of the locomotives have received girls' names and have cast plates at one end.

Above: 0039 "PACITA", a CS 200 loco with an inspection platform, is seen at Coquelles on 11 March 2011.

Below: The same locomotive seen from the other end on 19 September 2019. *David Haydock (2)*

Technical details

Ten locomotives are Type CFL 200; 0039 and 0041, with inspection platform, are Type CS 200*.
Built: 1989/90 by Hunslet Engine Company at Leeds for 900 mm gauge.
Rebuilt: 1993/94 by Schöma in Germany for 1435 mm gauge.
Wheel arrangement: B.
Engine: Deutz F10L 413 FW of 170 kW at 2300 rpm.
Transmission: Mechanical. Clark 5421-179.
Length: CFL 200 7.87 metres;
*CS 200 10.94 metres.
Weight: CFL 200 25 tonnes; *CS 200 28 tonnes.
Wheel diameter: 1010 mm.
Maximum speed: CFL 200 48 km/h; *CS 200 75 km/h.
Train brakes: Air.
Train supply: Not equipped.
Multiple working: Not equipped.

Above right: Hunslet/Schöma locomotive 0037 "LYDIE" is seen at Coquelles on 11 March 2011. *David Haydock*

BATTERY LOCOMOTIVES FROM **SOCOFER**

On 29 November 2018 Socofer announced that it had won an order for 19 two-axle locomotives, with an option for six more, from Eurotunnel. The battery locomotives will weigh a maximum of 40 tonnes and will be used to power maintenance trains in the Channel Tunnel. The Li-ion batteries will give a power of over 227 kW and the loco will also have a Volvo 129 kW Euro 6 diesel engine for recharging although this is not expected to be used very often as recharging will normally be from a ground supply. Batteries of Type NMC will come from French company Foresee Power. The locos should be able to operate eight hours between charges. The locos will also have a pantograph on top of the cab but this is only to earth the vehicles. Maximum speed will be 30 km/h.

The 12 metre long locos will replace all 12 of the Hunslet/Schöma locos currently in service (locos 0031–0042) which are significantly less powerful. The new locos will also shunt in Eurotunnel's yards outside the tunnel and may replace MaK diesel locos on lighter duties. Eurotunnel has ordered a large fleet in order to be able to concentrate weekend maintenance work into a single period rather than two at present, in order to avoid service reductions in peak periods. The first loco will be delivered in early 2021 for trials and once authorised the others will then be delivered at the rate of two per month.

Socofer is a well-established family firm based in Saint Pierre-des-Corps near Tours and specialises in track maintenance machines and shunters. Recent contracts include 19 track machines for Pakistan, three track machines for the Berlin S-Bahn and three 3-car "vacuum-cleaner" trains for the New York metro. In the past the company has also supplied French Railways (SNCF) with kits to modernise its shunter fleet.

Below: An artist's impression of one of the new locos. *David Haydock/Courtesy of Socofer*

EUROSTAR:
TAPPING A MASSIVE MARKET

In 1988, when a consortium was set up to design a high speed train to operate from London to Paris and Brussels, the only such train in regular operation in Europe was the French TGV. The first German ICEs were only delivered in 1989 and the first few did not enter full service until 1991. SNCF had almost ten years of operational experience with the TGV by then.

TGV sets can generally be described as being composed of a power car at each end, with eight articulated trailers in between, totalling 200 metres long. The first TGV Paris Sud-Est (PSE) trains, built from 1978, had tried and trusted DC traction motors, but in order to provide enough power there were not only two motor bogies under each power car at either end, but also a powered bogie at the outer end of each

outer "trailer" car. The total power rating was 6450 kW under 25 kV AC but only 3100 kW under 1500 V DC. These trains were still giving excellent service almost 40 years later but the last few, including set 01, were withdrawn in December 2019.

By the time trains were needed for the Channel Tunnel routes the second generation of TGV was already under construction. The TGV Atlantique took advantage of the rapid advances in traction technology by using synchronous traction motors which gave over double the power (1100 kW each) of those under TGV PSE sets. This removed the need for powered bogies

under the trailer cars. SNCF took advantage of this extra power and lengthened TGV Atlantique sets to ten trailers compared with eight for TGV PSE sets. However, for the next generation, TGV Réseau, SNCF reverted to eight cars and has stayed with this standard ever since. The TGV Duplex double-deck design which emerged in 1995 retained this standard.

The need to operate over the French high speed network, and to avoid creating a completely new design, made it almost

inevitable that the trains for the Channel Tunnel, initially known as the *Trans-Manche Super Train* or TMST, would be derived from the TGV.

The TMST design

The simplest way of designing the new train might have been to simply produce an 8-car "European" TGV which could operate in multiple. However, the safety rules put forward by the authorities for the Tunnel made multiple working impossible. Instead the TMST would be a version of the TGV with a power car at each end plus two identical rakes of nine articulated trailers between them. However, given the length of the trains and the need to operate over relatively steep gradients in the Tunnel and high speed lines it was necessary to imitate the TGV PSE sets by adding a powered bogie under the "trailers" next to the power cars – making a total of six powered bogies.

The trains needed to squeeze into the UK loading gauge as they would have to operate over the classic route through Kent until a high speed line was built. They are therefore slightly narrower than TGVs in France – 2.814 rather than 2.9 metres. In addition the

Below: Refurbished Eurostar set 3007/8 is captured at Allan, between Avignon and Valence, with the Marseille–London service on 13 July 2019. *Pierre Julien*

Top to bottom: Standard, First Class and bar car interiors in the original Eurostar sets.

Opposite: Original seating plan for each half set. *Courtesy Eurostar (4)*

power car had a completely different, more rounded, front end design. A livery of white and yellow was chosen, possibly to integrate the yellow front end, which was compulsory in the UK at the time.

Although the TMST was based on the TGV, the three countries involved all wanted their own railway industries to take advantage. TGV builder GEC-Alsthom headed the consortium but UK companies Brush and BREL were involved, mainly with the power cars, as were Belgian companies ACEC (power cars), BN (trailers) and French firms ANF and De Dietrich (trailers).

The order for the full-length trains was announced on 31 December 1989. Of the 31 trains, SNCF would own 16 (half sets numbered 3201 to 3232), British Rail 11 (3001 to 3022) and SNCB four (3101 to 3108) – at the last moment SNCF had added three sets and SNCB one due to more optimistic traffic forecasts. The total cost was £713 million, or £23 million per set. This would be about £50 million today. This seemed a lot at the time but looks more reasonable today. In 2010 the new e320 sets were estimated to cost €60 million each.

In early 1994 the three Eurostar operators decided to acquire an extra power car to replace any of the others suffering serious damage or failure. This was delivered in 1996 and numbered 3999.

The power cars were built by GEC-Alsthom's plants in Belfort and Birmingham (UK 1 to 15, and UN 1 to 4), while the trailers were built at Crespin (ANF), Brugge (BN) and Reichshoffen (De Dietrich). All of these were moved to Washwood Heath (Birmingham) or Belfort to be formed into complete sets.

Each final set was formed of two 197 metre half sets (these were occasionally swapped if there were problems but this was unusual; power cars were swapped more often) making a total length of 394 metres with an empty weight of 752 tonnes, the fully loaded weight being 816 tonnes. A complete set had seats for 210 first class and 584 second class passengers plus 52 fold-down seats in the entrance areas. When trains operate winter sports services to Bourg St Maurice a few seats in each coach are cordoned off to take extra baggage/skis.

Maintenance of the sets was initially carried out at North Pole (west London), Forest (Brussels) and Le Landy (Paris). North Pole was replaced by Temple Mills when the HS1 high speed line opened in 2007. At the same time the heaviest work on Eurostar sets gravitated towards Temple Mills and the other two depots only carried out lighter work.

Eurostar interiors

The nine cars of a Eurostar half set were known as R1 to R9, R standing for *Remorque* (trailer) in French. R1 to R5 were second class, R6 was the buffet car then R7 to R9 were the first class vehicles. For first class passengers this had the benefit that second

e300 SEATING PLAN COACHES 1-9

KEY

Seats	
Priority seats	
Single table	
Double table	
Window	
Door	
WC	
Baby changing facility	
Wheelchair space	
Luggage rack	
Train Manager's office	
UK and European power points available at all seats	
USB sockets available in Business Premier and Standard Premier	
Access door	
Automatic door	

All our trains are non-smoking

POWER CAR

COACH **1** STANDARD/52 SEATS

COACH **5** STANDARD/52 SEATS

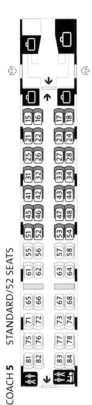

BUFFET BAR

BAR

COACH **2** STANDARD/56 SEATS

COACH **7** BUSINESS PREMIER/STANDARD PREMIER/39 SEATS

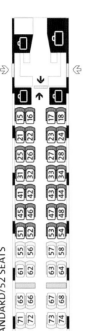

COACH **3** STANDARD/56 SEATS

COACH **8** BUSINESS PREMIER/STANDARD PREMIER/39 SEATS

COACH **4** STANDARD/56 SEATS

COACH **9** BUSINESS PREMIER/STANDARD PREMIER/25 SEATS + 2 COMPANION SEATS

TOWARDS BRUSSELS ↗

← TOWARDS LONDON

Top right: On 10 December 1992 power car 3202 was shown off to the press for the first time at SNCF's new Le Landy (Paris) depot.

Centre right: Eurostar set PS1 (3001/2) is seen at Strasbourg in the company of DB dual-voltage loco 181 213 "SAAR" on 27 January 1993.

Bottom right: SNCF electric BB 15058 heads set PS2 (3201/2) on 9 June 1993 through Le Bourget on its way to Le Landy depot. *David Haydock (3)*

class passengers did not need to walk through to reach the buffet car. R1 (which was not actually a trailer as it had a power bogie at the outer end) had a "family area" with eight seats while at the other end of the half set first class R9 had a disabled toilet, two customs/security compartments and a baggage compartment.

On 10 December 1992 the first Eurostar power car was revealed to the press, with 3202 on show inside SNCF's new Le Landy depot. Also that month the first Eurostar train (set PS1 – Pre-Series 1, 3001/2) was delivered by Alstom to SNCF and in January 1993 it started tests between Mulhouse and Strasbourg. This line is often used by Alstom for new high speed trains because it is not far from the company's Belfort plant, is pretty straight and flat and is passed for regular operation at 200 km/h, with the possibility of adding 10–20% for special runs. Set PS1 was initially shortened for the test runs. For its first tests PS1 was configured with just seven trailers – R1 + R2 + R3 + R4 + R9 + R10 + R18 – total length was 188.2 metres and weight was 389 tonnes.

Set PS1 continued tests in France through spring 1993 then on Sunday 20 June was hauled through the Tunnel by SNCF diesel loco A1AA1A 68041 (with BB 66275 on the rear), taking more than two hours. Both diesels were the only members of their classes ever to visit the UK. PS1 was then taken forward by BR locos 73118, 83301 (an ex Class 33) and 73205. PS1 rapidly started making test runs at night over the third rail-electrified line between Ashford and Dollands Moor. The tests of third rail pickup went fine but there were immediate problems with interference with the signalling system and it took many months before these were resolved.

The first full length Eurostar, PS2, left Belfort on 8 June 1993, hauled by SNCF BB 15058 to Le Landy depot. The train was then used to prove the TVM 430 cab signalling on the energised sections of the LGV Nord towards Lille at up to 300 km/h. This full weight train was used to check braking characteristics. Tests went well and PS2 was quickly running all the way from Paris Nord to Fréthun (Calais).

Also in late spring 1993, power car 3101 from the third TMST set was coupled to SNCF test coaches to carry out braking tests on the Metz–Thionville line

Meanwhile set F1 (3203/4) arrived at Le Landy in September 1993 then left for tests around Nantes in October. Tests of the pantographs were carried out on the

Top right: SNCF diesel A1AA1A 68041 hauls Eurostar PS1 (3001/02) out of the UK portal of the Channel Tunnel on 20 June 1993, en route to North Pole depot. The SNCF loco operated only as far as the crossover by the portal from where two Class 73s, a Class 33 and a barrier wagon took over. This was the first time a Eurostar set had been hauled through the Channel Tunnel. *Colin J Marsden*

Centre right: Belgian power car 3101 is seen with three test coaches at Thionville, France, in September 1993. *Jean-Marie Vaillant*

Bottom right: Set F2 (3205/6) is seen at Arras with a press special from Paris Nord on 13 April 1994. *David Haydock*

Nantes–Angers line which has some of the highest wire heights in France and was by then passed for 220 km/h operation.

Next to arrive was the first Eurostar set assembled at Washwood Heath (Birmingham) in the UK, coded UK1, which was tested from 16 October between Lichfield and Erdington. UK2, actually the second Belgian train set 3103/4, was delivered to North Pole depot on 23 December 1993, while around the same time PS1 moved from the UK back to Belfort after test equipment was removed. On the way, the train exceptionally ran into Coquelles Eurotunnel loading terminal for a photo call.

Into service

By early 1994 many of the main tests had been carried out, the high speed lines were open in France and European Passenger Services (EPS) was gearing up for services to be introduced in the autumn. By September 1994 24 sets would be delivered, of which 17 would be ready for service.

On 13 April 1994 journalists had their first chance of riding on a Eurostar between Paris and Arras in northern France on set F2 (3205/6) which is still in service today. In France tests went particularly well, probably a reflection of the 15 years or so of experience with high speed lines and trains, the Eurostar being "just" a very long TGV. The biggest change to previous TGV designs – the British-built asynchronous drive – caused no significant problems. It was in Kent where the main problems had occurred and the only solution found for the potential interference was to insulate all signalling.

Tests in Belgium under 3000 V DC overhead had started in November 1993 with set F1 (3203/4) on the Mouscron–Tournai–Enghien line (SNCB Line 94) plus Tournai–Lille to test the changeover between 3000 V DC and 25 kV AC (the line had gone live on 25 May 1993). The high point during tests in Belgium was a run at up to 215 km/h on the Gent–Brugge line during the night of 19/20 March 1994.

On 6 May 1994 the Channel Tunnel was officially inaugurated with set 3003/4 carrying H.M. the Queen and the Duke of Edinburgh plus Prime Minister John Major from London, while set 3211/12 brought President François Mitterrand and his wife plus Prime Minister Edouard Balladur from Paris Nord,

Above: The two inaugural Eurostars – 3004/3 from London and 3211/12 from Paris – meet in the Eurotunnel terminal at Coquelles for the official inauguration of the Channel Tunnel on 6 May 1994.

Below: H. M. the Queen and French President François Mitterrand, with Prime Ministers Edouard Balladur and John Major are seen at the opening ceremony. *Philippe Morel (2)*

the two trains meeting nose-to-nose in the Eurotunnel Shuttle terminal at Coquelles.

Following permission from the Inter-governmental (safety) Commission (IGC) passenger-carrying test runs (mainly staff and their families) with Eurostar started on 17 August 1994 with both London–Paris and London–Brussels services each day in order to run in the trains and practise safety procedures. Brussels services were allowed 3h20 while Paris trains were timed in about 3h05. Several London–Paris runs were completed in less than three hours despite restrictions between London and the Tunnel. Signalling was still being immunised and Eurostar sets were restricted to drawing 4500 amps – the same as a Networker EMU – instead of the required maximum of 6800 amps. In order to detect interference, the trains were fitted with an Interference Current Monitoring Unit or ICMU which cut the power to the train if tripped. This happened frequently.

High hopes

At the time of the service launch in 1994 the plan was to reach a full Eurostar service of 15 train pairs a day on both the Paris and Brussels line. As a comparison, 25 years on, the actual service is 16 train pairs to Paris on a typical weekday and just ten to Brussels. There are now three trains which carry on from Brussels to Amsterdam, with more to come.

Following the go-ahead from the IGC on 6 October, the initial "Discovery" service, launched at last on Monday 14 November 1994, consisted of just one morning and one evening train on each route. Trains from London to Paris Gare du Nord took exactly three hours non-stop – today's best time is 2h16 – from Waterloo International via Bromley South, Sevenoaks and Ashford operating off the third rail, then as today via the Tunnel and the LGV Nord high speed line. There was some slack in this schedule, several press runs completing the journey in 2h50, and one late train arrived in 2h48½.

Trains to Brussels took 3h15 non-stop (one train pair stopped at Lille Europe) compared with 1h55 today non-stop. Trains had the double handicap of operating off the third rail in Kent, then after passing through the Tunnel and using the high speed line for less than

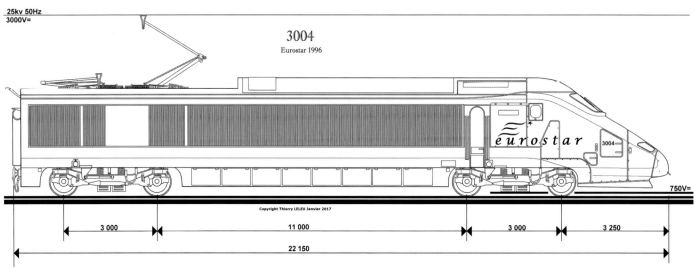

25kv 50Hz
3000V=

3004
Eurostar 1996

Copyright Thierry LELEU Janvier 2017

750V=

3 000   11 000   3 000   3 250

22 150

Set 3223/24 is seen at Waterloo International on 19 January 1996. *Chris Wilson*

30 minutes, turning onto the conventional network after Lille Europe and operating via Tournai, Ath and Halle. This continued until the LGV Belge opened in 1997.

"Discovery" fares were £47.50 to Brussels or Paris (£40 to Lille) for a budget "Special" ticket, £77.50 (£66) for "Discovery" in second class with change of reservation possible or £97.50 (£83) in "Gold" with a meal served at the seat. The fares seemed rather high in second class for the time and rather low in first class. As a comparison, in mid 2019 on a Wednesday one month ahead the cheapest fares on both routes were £44 in Standard, £112 in Standard Premier and £276 in Business Premier, the last with meal, free newspapers etc. £276 was the only price in this class, on all trains. Booking just a few days ahead on a Saturday cheapest prices were £123, £202 and £276 to Paris and £179, £192 and £276 to Brussels. So close to departure Business Premier starts to look a good option! The cheapest fares, booked well ahead, in limited numbers and with no refunds in spring 2019 were £29.

The general opinion of press and pundits at the time of launch was that Eurostar was a very classy train, with a wonderful ride and that the catering was excellent. Eurostar has successfully retained this image for the last 25 years, albeit with the proviso that the ride on the newer Velaro trains is much inferior and sometimes even alarming.

Remember... before Eurostar?

A train plus ferry service between London and Paris continued to operate, via both Calais and Boulogne, until Eurostar became fully functional. Timings in the last winter before this was withdrawn (on 21 January 1995) were as follows:

London Victoria	08.33	08.55
Folkestone Harbour a.		10.55
Folkestone Harbour d.		11.15
Dover Western Docks a.	10.20	
Dover Eastern Docks d.	11.30	
Calais Maritime a.	14.00	
Calais Maritime d.	15.14	
Boulogne Maritime a.		13.15
Boulogne Maritime d.		13.54
Amiens	16.55	15.09
Paris Nord	18.21	16.26

Paris Nord	09.28	10.56
Amiens	10.54	12.09
Boulogne Maritime a.		13.22
Boulogne Maritime. d.		14.00
Calais Maritime a.	12.31	
Calais Maritime d.	13.15	
Dover Eastern Docks a .	13.45	
Dover Western Docks d.	14.40	
Folkestone Harbour a.		14.05
Folkestone Harbour d.		14.35
London Victoria	16.11	16.35

Below: BB 67439 and another Class BB 67400 are seen at Calais Maritime with a train to Paris in 1992. *David Haydock*

Goodbye boat train

Eurostar was a big success from the very start and on 23 January 1995 the service was doubled to four train pairs a day on the Paris route and three to Brussels – it was already very clear that the Paris route with an average 85% occupancy was more popular than Brussels (29%). At the same time the first Eurostar stops at Calais Fréthun, 10 km from the town centre, were introduced. Expansion could have been faster but only 15 Eurostar sets were available compared with the programmed 25. It could therefore be said that the withdrawal of "boat train""services from Calais and Boulogne. Maritime to Paris on 21 January 1995 (see box) was a little

HSTs connect with Eurostar

In order to provide connections with Eurostar before the North of London services started, European Passenger Services (EPS) decided to run two "Eurostar Link" services into Waterloo from the West Coast Main Line and the East Coast Main Line operated by HSTs. At one point it had been thought that connecting trains would run at hourly intervals. From 3 July 1995 services operated as follows:

Edinburgh	v 08.30	19.27 ^
Newcastle	v 09.59	17.04 ^
Darlington	v 10.26	16.33 ^
York	v 10.58	16.04 ^
Doncaster	v 11.22	15.41 ^
Newark	v 11.45	15.11 ^
Peterborough	v 12.14	14.24 ^
Waterloo	v 13.47	12.46 ^

Southbound timings slightly different, northbound an hour later, on Saturdays. No service on Sundays

Manchester Piccadilly	v 07.37	19.40 ^
Stockport	v 07.45	19.30 ^
Crewe	v 08.13	19.00 ^
Stafford	v 08.34	18.32 ^
Wolverhampton	v 08.59	18.13 ^
Birmingham New St	v 09.27	17.44 ^
Birmingham Int.	v 09.50	17.31 ^
Coventry	v 10.04	17.19 ^
Rugby	v 10.21	16.56 ^
Milton Keynes	v 10.45	16.28 ^
Waterloo	v 11.46	15.42 ^

Northbound timings slightly later on Saturdays. No service on Sundays.

It was not long before EPS was reporting poor loadings although commentators noted that publicity for the service was poor, especially to French and Belgian passengers coming to the UK. Fares were also often higher than parallel InterCity services. The services were withdrawn on 4 January 1997.

Above: An HST set led by power car 43151 is seen at Waterloo on 9 October 1995 with the connecting "Eurostar Link" service to Manchester. *Colin J Marsden*

Eurodisney, Lyon and Marseille, for example, with a change in Lille.

In May 1995 Eurostar carried 208 000 passengers. This compared with 322 000 travelling by plane in May 1994, before Eurostar was launched, meaning that Eurostar had already captured 65% of the market. On the Brussels route, Eurostar only carried 47 000 passengers but this was 44% of the market. Altogether airlines estimated they had lost 50 000 passengers a month to Eurostar.

By 22 October 1995 the service was approaching the full timetable which exists today, with 11 trains to Paris but just six to Brussels.

On 8 January 1996 Ashford International station opened and the Paris service was boosted to 13 trains on Fridays. The new station put Ashford at just two hours from Paris and had cost €100 million to build, with almost 2000 parking spaces. The station would be served by five trains a day to Paris and four to Brussels on weekdays. By July 1996 the station was being used by 4000 passengers a week. Traffic was so good that Eurostar increased the number of trains stopping in the Kent town on 1 June 1997.

In summer 1996 the Paris service reached 16 trains a day, the same frequency as today. In September 1996 fares to Paris were raised to reflect the popularity of the service.

London to Disneyland Paris

On 1 July 1996 Eurostar launched its first trains not serving either Paris Nord or Brussels with a direct service from Waterloo International to Marne-la-Vallée-Chessy station which is situated by the gates of Disneyland Paris. Initially there was a special check-in for passengers travelling to Disneyland. The initial service left Waterloo daily at 09.23 (09.10 on Sundays) serving Ashford at 10.23 then running non-stop to MLV-Chessy, arriving at 13.28. The return was at 18.35, serving Ashford at 19.38 and arriving in Waterloo at 20.39. It is not really possible to visit Disneyland in a day (let

alone six hours) and most journeys are sold in a package including a hotel stay. In 1996 the service ran until 28 September then restarted in April 1997. In 2002 Eurostar started to operate the service all the year round, albeit with lower frequencies in winter.

Today the service leaves St Pancras at 10.14, calling at Ebbsfleet, Ashford and Lille Europe and arriving in MLV-Chessy at 14.03. The return is at 16.55 or 18.01 arriving in London at 18.47 or 19.46. The service now runs four or five times a week for most of the year, but daily during certain peak holiday periods such as Easter. The service is only suspended from early January to early February.

As the train does not attract as many passengers as the main Paris service, it is still operated by the original e300 Eurostar sets, although now refurbished.

1500 V DC for the Alps and the Midi

Within a year of Eurostar operations starting, the operators were already looking at the modifications needed for the trains to operate off 1500 V DC overhead, the system used both in the Netherlands and south of Paris on classic lines. In principle it was thought that the modifications would not be too complicated because the trains could already operate off 750 V DC third rail and 3000 V DC from the overhead. Tests on both the French 1500 V DC network plus the Paris–Lyon high speed line were thus planned by SNCF in spring 1996. Modifications to operate in the Netherlands were expected to be more complicated, with a new pantograph and ATB signalling necessary. This was later rejected by Eurostar as too costly.

In 1996 tests took place with modified Eurostar set 3203/4 but it was not possible to complete them in time to launch the through service from London to Bourg Saint Maurice which was due to start on 28/29 November. Over that weekend

premature. A train/catamaran service was restored briefly via Boulogne Maritime but this did not last.

The Eurostar service to Paris was again boosted on 27 February and 3 April 1995 but the Brussels service remained at three train pairs. Meanwhile the range of fares was considerably widened, the highest fare still being £97.50 single – those were the days! Brussels fares started to be reduced relative to Paris and through fares to other Belgian destinations added. On 11 May Eurostar also launched a deal with one fare to any Dutch station, by connecting with Thalys or the Benelux service between Brussels and Amsterdam.

The summer Eurostar service which started on 28 May 1995 brought a considerable boost, to nine train pairs on the Paris service (with extras on peak days) and five train pairs on the Brussels route. The fastest timings to Paris were reduced to 2h53, although one enthusiast had recorded 2h41 by this time. The increased service led Eurostar to start advertising connections, to Antwerpen and Liège in Belgium and to

3203/4 did make the first direct run, over the Lyon avoiding line via Lyon Satolas (now Lyon Saint Exupéry), St André-le-Gaz and Chambéry (25 kV AC, single track), Chambéry–Albertville (1500 V DC) then 25 kV AC to Bourg St Maurice. The second run, on 2/3 December, during heavy snow, was via the LGV Sud Est to Mâcon (25 kV AC), then via Bourg-en-Bresse, Ambérieu, Culoz and Chambéry (1500 V DC) then as before. The service still varies between these routes according to pathing requirements.

The tests went very well but services did not start until winter 1997. The next sets to be modified for 1500 V DC operation were 3225/6 and 3227/8. The first train to carry passengers on this route ran on 16 March 1997 for the travel trade and journalists. At this event it was announced that the service would start on 27 December 1997 running to April 1998. Timings would be:

London Waterloo	v 07.53	16.43 ∧
Ashford	v 08.53	15.43 ∧
Albertville	v 15.55	10.50 ∧
Moutiers S-B.	v 16.25	10.20 ∧
Bourg S. M.	v 17.00	09.45 ∧

At 1127 km this would be the longest ever continuous rail journey from a British station, and although the journey took eight hours, some journalists reckoned this was only 15 minutes longer than a charter flight plus road transfers. This record stood until Eurostar started serving Avignon which is about 1160 km from London then Marseille in 2015 which is 1253 km from London. London–Marseille is currently completed in 6h28 outwards (an average of almost 194 km/h) with stops in Ashford,

Lille, Lyon and Avignon, the return journey being broken for 75 minutes for a customs check in Lille.

At the time the British were taking 800 000 ski holidays a year, of which 300 000 were in France and two-thirds of these in the Tarantaise valley served by Eurostar.

It is of note that the operation of both trains during the daytime on Saturdays meant a great deal of empty running – from Paris Nord to Bourg St Maurice on Friday afternoon and Bourg St Maurice to Paris Nord on Sunday mornings. This inefficiency was corrected after only one winter's operation – Eurostar realised that keen skiers would settle for overnight runs to maximise time on the *pistes*, so started running a Friday evening departure from London and a Saturday evening return from Bourg St Maurice. Although some of this involves the rare use of the LGVs at night (usually closed for maintenance) the trains also use classic lines at lower speeds as time is less of the essence when the skiers are asleep. Timings from December 1998 were:

Waterloo International	v 19.57	07.42 ∧
Ashford	v 21.07	06.37 ∧
Bourg St. Maurice	v 06.45	22.08 ∧

Another point of interest is that the train changes drivers in Lille (service-only stop) and the Lille staff (there are two) take the train all the way to Bourg St Maurice, a journey of about ten hours. The same arrangement exists in the opposite direction.

By the time the "Ski Train" was launched on 13 December 1998, two more sets had been modified for 1500 V DC operation – 3207/8 and 3215/6. A further five sets were then converted during 1998 in order to work extra services expected during the football World Cup, which France went on to win.

Above: Set 3227/8 is seen near Aubagne, east of Marseille, with the Brussels–Nice service on 23 August 1999. *Gilles Lefranc*

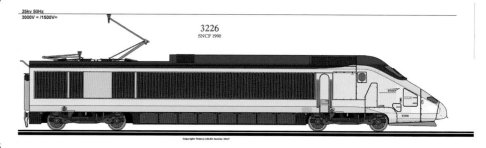

Belgian high speed line cuts Brussels timings

On 14 December 1997 the high speed line from Frétin near Lille to Lembeek, on the outskirts of Brussels, opened to traffic, allowing London–Brussels timings to be cut from 3h15 to 2h36. Eurostar took the opportunity to add extra early and late trains, boosting the service to ten train pairs a day, all of them calling at Lille Europe. The new high speed line branched off the Calais–Paris LGV Nord at the Frétin triangle east of Lille then headed roughly east, then later east-north-east. The new line passes just south of Tournai and Ath on classic Line 94 then runs alongside the latter for around 10 km from Coucou (where there is a connection between the two lines and a maintenance base) to a point north-east of Silly. The LGV then parallels the A8 motorway and joins Line 96 just south of Halle.

Lille to Brussels Midi from a standing start was timed at 38 minutes for 104.5 km (average 165 km/h) from the beginning, although it is now routinely completed in

35 minutes by Eurostars from Lille (179 km/h) and 34 minutes from Brussels (184 km/h), thanks to the complete rebuilding of the Halle–Brussels section.

Within six months of this acceleration Eurostar revenue was up 60% on the Brussels route.

Eurostar to Marseille

On 11 March 1998 Eurostar marked another advance when set 3225/6 ran all the way to Valence, south of Lyon. This was seen as preparation for special trains organised for the football World Cup – England played their first match of the campaign against Tunisia in Marseille in June 1998, although a Eurostar did not run there.

By 2000 Eurostar was talking of launching direct services from London to Avignon and Bordeaux. Meanwhile Eurostar ran three excursions that year – on 15 January from Tours to London, on 13 May from Orléans to London and on 16 September a day return from London to La Rochelle (1006 km) with set 3201/2.

In summer 2002 Eurostar launched a new service running out and back on Saturdays

Above: Set 3225/6 passes Corbehem with a Paris Nord–Valenciennes service on 3 March 2011. *David Haydock*

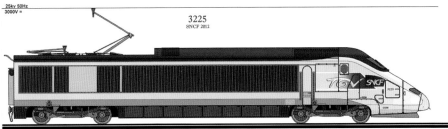

in summer from London to Avignon Ville (as opposed to Avignon TGV). The service was an immediate success and Eurostar extended the operating period in 2003. On 23 May that year Eurostar ran a special to Bordeaux leaving London at 07.53 and arriving at 15.32. The train returned to London on Monday 26 May at 15.57 arriving at 22.50, the extra hour because the train ran via Paris where passengers disembarked and passed through customs.

Too many trains

Although traffic was booming on Eurostar trains, by the end of 1998 it became clear to the company that the "Three Capitals" fleet – 31 18-car sets – was over-provided. Even today, with 11 million passengers carried, compared with 6.3 million in 1998, Eurostar needs only 25 sets: 17 e320s plus eight refurbished e300 sets.

The first sign that the fleet was too big was in late 1998 when it was reported that SNCF and SNCB were considering running four spare sets on the Paris–Brussels route to relieve the Thalys fleet. This never happened but in spring 1999 it was announced that two French Eurostar sets would be used from 30 May to replace four TGV Réseau sets working the Brussels–Nice service. Units to be used were 3203/4, 3225/6 and 3227/8 which had been removed from the "Three Capitals" pool and had already been used on weekend Paris–Dunkerque and Valenciennes–Paris services. By now the three trains had lost their Eurostar markings in favour of the SNCF logo but retained their original livery. They were never returned to the main pool and their third rail equipment

was removed before High Speed 1 opened. Timings were:

9532 09.25 Brussels Midi–Nice Ville 18.46
9573 09.24 Nice Ville–Brussels Midi 18.36

This is a distance of 1431 km – about 880 miles – a shade further than Land's End to John O'Groats!!!

The three sets were withdrawn from Brussels–Nice on 10 June 2001 then were employed for several years on the Paris Nord–Lille service, with incursions to Dunkerque, Calais, Boulogne, Rang-de-Fliers and Valenciennes. There were slight changes to their livery, with a silver front end, the addition of a TGV logo and TGV colours by the doors.

Meanwhile SNCF modified another set, 3209/10, for 1500 V DC operation in early 2001 and by the beginning of 2002 the following sets were modified for 1500 V DC: 3201/2, **3203/4**, 3207/8, 3209/10, 3215/6, 3223/4, **3225/6, 3227/8** and 3229/30. The sets marked in bold were the first to be withdrawn, in December 2014, once SNCF introduced Duplex sets on the Lille service. These three sets had spent less than five years doing what they were designed to do.

Remarkably, given that 3203/4, 3225/6 and 3227/8 were equipped for 1500 V DC but were never used off the 25 kV AC Paris–Lille corridor, in 2006 SNCF decided to expand the 1500 V DC fleet by adding three more sets. In the end only 3213/4 was converted.

Then with the LGV Méditerranée high speed line completing the Paris–Marseille route in 2001, SNCF announced that a London–Marseille direct service would be launched shortly. SNCF investigated the possibility of running day and night services like those to Bourg Saint Maurice, but initially said that the trains were not reliable enough to run "so far from home". Indeed in mid 2001 Eurostar had stock shortages, its trains reaching only 65% availability. In the end a London–Avignon service was launched first and it was not until 2015 that London–Marseille started.

Near disaster

The most serious accident to befall a Eurostar was on 5 June 2000 when set 3101/2 derailed at almost 300 km/h at Croisilles junction near Arras on the Paris–Lille high speed line. The train jumped the track and came to a standstill upright. None of the 501 passengers or 16 staff was seriously hurt. 12 people were treated for shock and bruises.

Eurostar set 3003/4 has just left Ashford for London and passes the CTRL under construction at Tutt Hill on 17 May 2002. *Chris Wilson*

In the few derailments of TGVs the train has always stayed upright and in a straight line, certainly due to the articulated arrangement with close-coupled coaches (the author does not include the TGV accident due to a massive overspeed through a curve during testing at Eckwersheim when the train plunged down an embankment). However, in the Croisilles derailment, by good fortune the train jumped to the left and did not foul the track in the opposite direction, on which all trains were rapidly halted.

The cause of the accident was the gearbox on the rear bogie of the leading power car which had come loose and dropped onto the track. SNCF reluctantly admitted that a similar failure had happened only six days before in Kent on the approaches to the Channel Tunnel with set 3007/8. Five sets with similar problems were found during inspections immediately after the accident. A report on the accident blamed a lack of communication between the three Eurostar operators.

3101/2 cursed?

Set 3101/2 never seemed to fully recover from the shock. Although repaired, the "Belgian" set then suffered a second major problem with its transmission on 17 October 2001. After languishing at Forest depot since this problem Belgian politicians discovered the long disused set and accused Belgian Railways of waste. SNCB promptly promised to return to service, although it missed being refurbished. The set was eventually slated for refurbishment in 2010. It was split in half in early 2012 in order to be used to test options for interior refurbishment, half going to Hellemmes works and half to Thouars in western France. However, Eurostar then ordered more Velaro sets, cut the refurbishment programme from 28 to eight sets and the trailers from 3101/2 went for scrap. The consolation is that both power cars have been preserved and can be found in the National Colleges for High Speed Rail in Doncaster (3101) and Birmingham (3102).

CTRL opens

On 28 September 2003 the first section of the Channel Tunnel Rail Link (CTRL, now known as High Speed 1) opened to traffic from Fawkham Junction to the Tunnel (74 km), lopping 20 minutes off Eurostar journey times and bringing the London–Paris journey time down to 2h35 and London–Brussels to 2h20. On special runs on 27 September set 3107/8 ran from Brussels to London Waterloo in a record 1h58 and set 3005/6 clocked up a record 2h18 from Waterloo to Paris Nord. For these runs the trains were allowed to operate at higher-than-normal speeds of 170 km/h in the Tunnel (normal limit 160 km/h) and 320 km/h in France (300 km/h).

From 5 January 2004 Eurostar took advantage of the shorter journey times by launching a pair of non-stop services between London and Brussels taking 2h20 outbound and 2h15 inbound to London.

Eurostar set 3214/13 is seen at Nashenden on HS1 with the Marne-la-Vallée (Disneyland) to London St Pancras on 9 April 2017. *Jamie Squibbs*

London to Cannes!

On 16 May 2006 set 3209/10 was named *"THE DA VINCI CODE"* by the film's stars Tom Hanks and Audrey Tautou at Waterloo International then ran non-stop to Cannes for the film's premiere at the city's film festival. The train departed at 09.40 and arrived in Cannes at 18.03, a time of 7h23 for 1421 km, certified by the Guinness Book of Records as the longest ever non-stop international train journey, at an average of 192.46 km/h.

Right: Set 3209/10 is seen at Brussels Midi in the special livery for the film on 29 June 2006. *Didier Delattre*

Shortly after this Eurostar announced that revenue on the Brussels route had risen 41% and that the company had achieved a 57% share of the market. Traffic grew 15% in the year after the CTRL opened and continued to grow well in the following year.

On Eurostar's tenth birthday in late 2004 the company had reached 63% of the market between London and Paris but the total traffic (Paris and Brussels) of 7 million passengers was only 40% of what was forecast and the company was still making big losses.

CTRL becomes HS1

The second section of the CTRL from Fawkham Junction to St Pancras International opened on 14 November 2007 and by then the whole high speed line was known as High Speed 1 or HS1. St Pancras station was completely redeveloped at a cost of £800 million.

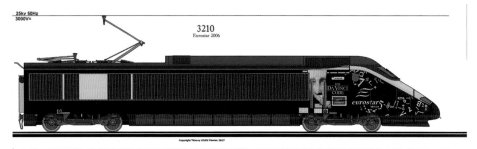

Below: As well as Eurostars, HS1 is used by Hitachi "Javelin" EMUs operating fast suburban services from Kent to London. These are 395 022 and 395 011 with a service from Margate to St Pancras at Lenham Heath on 9 April 2017. *Jamie Squibbs*

The Starck refurbishment

The first interior refurbishment for Eurostar was launched less than seven years after the trains started running, in 2001, and was timed to coincide with the opening of the first phase of High Speed 1 in 2003. A total of £35 million was spent over three years upgrading train interiors, terminals, ticket offices, lounges and staff uniforms. Eurostar chose Philippe Starck as artistic director for the project.

The new second class seats were little changed except for a new grey and brown striped design. The first class seats however received a complete makeover, the new ones being a flat grey with unusual orange headrests which "surrounded" the head. These were intended to help passengers "snooze". The highlight of the refurbishment was a new "premium class" in one coach next to the bar vehicle. This featured very large, high-backed seats with wide wings at head level. Two seats were removed from each coach to make space for an extra luggage rack. The bar was also redesigned.

From 1 September 2005 Eurostar introduced new classes of travel. Replacing Premium, First and Second Class, were Business Premier, with a ten-minute check-in, Leisure Select and Standard. Ticket prices would be based on advanced booking and the level of flexibility required. At the same time Eurostar introduced new cut-price advance fares.

Above, below left & below right: The Second Class (above), Premium Class (below left) and First Class (below right) seating proposed by Philippe Starck. In the event, the high-backed winged seats were not installed in the trains, but were used in Premium Class waiting areas. *Courtesy Eurostar*

The exterior Eurostar livery remained unchanged, despite a different shade of yellow being used for publicity. Toilets were also unchanged.

The first set to be turned out with the new interior was 3219/20 in September 2004. Refurbishment of the 27 sets was completed in December 2005. The project cost £25 million or about £900 000 per set. Belgian set 3101/2 was not included (see above). Nor were SNCF sets 3203/4, 3225/6 and 3227/8 which were taken out of the "Three Capitals" pool.

The first Eurostar to enter St Pancras was North of London set 3313/4 on 6 March. This set was used for all the tests of HS1.

On 4 September a special run from Paris to St Pancras set a new record of 2h03 and 39 seconds by set 3223/4. The train was allowed to run at higher-than-normal speeds.

On 20 September the same unit, 3223/4, set a new record of 1h43 and 53 seconds from Brussels Midi to St Pancras, an average of 215.4 km/h.

During the night of 13/14 November 2007 Eurostar moved all of its services to St Pancras International and from then on operated via HS1. On the new high speed line were two new stations: Stratford International and Ebbsfleet International. The station at Stratford had been built as an interchange with the London Underground, the Docklands Light Railway and various suburban rail services. The station is close to St Pancras and was only

Highlights from 25 years of Eurostar

14 November 1994	First international trains leave London Waterloo to Paris, Brussels and Lille
29 June 1996	Launch of direct Disneyland Paris route
13 December 1997	Launch of ski train to the French Alps
20 July 2002	New route to Avignon in the south of France
28 August 2007	Eurostar carries it's 100 millionth traveller
6 November 2007	St Pancras becomes Eurostar's new home
31 October 2012	World renowned Michelin starred chef, Raymond Blanc OBE is announced as the new Business Premier Culinary Director
14 November 2014	Eurostar celebrates its 20th anniversary by unveiling its new fleet of state-of-the-art trains at St Pancras International
1 May 2015	Eurostar introduces London to Lyon and Marseille "Provence" service
28 December 2016	On-board entertainment and Wi-Fi introduced on trains
3 February 2017	State-of-the-art business lounge unveiled in Paris
4 April 2018	Eurostar's first commercial service to Rotterdam and Amsterdam

Below: In June 2010 Eurostar set 3017/8 was given special vinyls to celebrate the 70th anniversary of General de Gaulle's 1940 radio address from London calling for resistance to the German occupation. *All line drawings by Thierry Leleu*

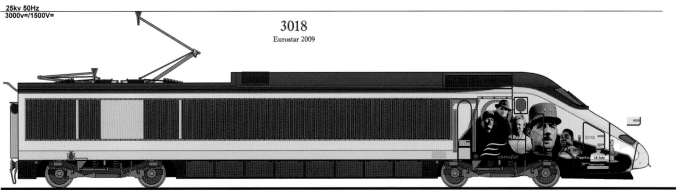

25kv 50Hz
3000v=/1500V=

3018
Eurostar 2009

Copyright Thierry LELEU Février 2017

Eurostar sets construction and scrapping

Power car 1	Power car 2	Set no.	Delivered	For scrap or refurb.	Names (now removed)	1500 V DC
"Three Capitals" sets						
UK sets						
3001	3002	PS 1/F 15	22/01/1993	16/03/2018	Tread Lightly / Voyage Vert	
3003	3004	UK 3	07/01/1994	14/12/2016	Tri-City-Athlon 2010	
3005	3006	UK 4	04/02/1994	26/10/2016		
3007	3008	UK 5	18/03/1994	Refurbished	Waterloo Sunset	x
3009	3010	UK 10	22/04/1994	19/01/2018	REMEMBERING FROMELLES	
3011	3012	UK 11	27/05/1994	16/02/2018		
3013	3014	UK 8	01/07/1994	17/03/2017	LONDON 2012	
3015	3016	UK 9	07/10/1994	Refurbished		x
3017	3018	UK 12	07/10/1994	31/03/2018		
3019	3020	UK 14	11/11/1994	02/12/2016		
3021	3022	UK 15	11/11/1994	04/09/2018		
Belgian sets						
3101	3102	UK 1	31/10/1993	28/02/2018 †		
3103	3104	UK 2	17/12/1993	25/11/2017		
3105	3106	UK 6	22/04/1994	06/11/2018 +		
3107	3108	UK 7	27/05/1994	01/02/2017		
French sets						
3201	3202	PS 2/F 16	08/06/1993	25/05/2018		x
3203	3204	F 1	24/09/1993	19/12/14 ¶		x
3205	3206	F 2	02/11/1993	Refurbished		x
3207	3208	F 3	10/12/1993	09/10/18 §	MICHEL HOLLARD	x
3209	3210	F 4	14/01/1994	Refurbished	THE DA VINCI CODE	x
3211	3212	F 5	25/02/1994	Refurbished ¶		x
3213	3214	F 6	18/03/1994	In service 02/20*		x
3215	3216	F 7	01/04/1994	Stored 02/20		x
3217	3218	F 8	06/05/1994	Stored 02/20		x
3219	3220	F 9	27/05/1994	Refurbished		x
3221	3222	F 10	24/06/1994	Refurbished		x
3223	3224	F 11	12/08/1994	In service 02/20*		x
3225	3226	F 12	09/09/1994	13/12/2014		x
3227	3228	F 13	30/09/1994	13/12/2014		x
3229	3230	F 14	28/10/1994	Refurbished		x
3231	3232	UK 13	28/10/1994	23/09/2017		
Spare power car						
3999		M62	02/09/1996	Refurbished		x
North of London sets						
3301	3302	FN 1		Stored 09/19		
3303	3304	FN 2		$		
3305	3306	UN 1		Stored 02/20		
3307	3308	FN 3		‡ $		
3309	3310	UN 2		Stored 02/20		
3311	3312	UN 3		Stored 02/20		
3313	3314	UN 4		¤	ENTENTE CORDIALE	

Eurostar sets, continued

Notes

† 3101 trailers; 3102 trailers 29/07/15. Power cars 3101 and 3102 donated to National Colleges for High Speed Rail at Doncaster and Birmingham.

+ Power car 3106 and one trailer preserved in Belgium.

¶ Powers cars 3203 and 3204 plus trailers 3211/3212 were sent for scrap on 7 December 2016. The power cars from 3211/12 have been combined with the trailers from 3203/4 to form the refurbished set 3211/12.

§ Power car 3207 scrapped separately

* These two sets were "mixed" in 2018. 3213/24 are hired to Thalys for Izy services. 3214/23 are not refurbished.

$ 3304 preserved in Derby. Mixed set 3303/3307 for scrap separately 06/19

‡ 3308 trailers for scrap 09/10/17

¤ For scrap 06/19. Power car 3314 saved for preservation at Temple Mills.

e320 sets		
Half set number	**Half set number**	**Delivered**
4001	4002	01/03/2016
4003	4004	01/03/2016
4005	4006	01/01/2016
4007	4008	01/12/2015
4009	4010	01/12/2015
4011	4012	01/12/2015
4013	4014	01/07/2018
4015	4016	01/11/2015
4017	4018	01/11/2015
4019	4020	01/12/2015
4021	4022	01/09/2016
4023	4024	01/01/2017
4025	4026	01/04/2017
4027	4028	01/06/2017
4029	4030	01/10/2017
4031	4032	01/11/2017
4033	4034	01/07/2018

Below: Eurostar set 3209/10 passes Ashford International station on the classic lines on 24 October 1996. *Chris Wilson*

expected to be used by Regional Eurostar services – which never materialised. So Stratford "International" is only served by domestic high speed services to Kent. Indeed Stratford International was not even served by Eurostar during the 2012 Olympic Games despite the station being surrounded by Olympic venues.

Ebbsfleet International on the other hand serves a wide area of north Kent and has connections with local rail services as well as 2500 car parking spaces.

Waterloo International was closed after only 13 years in use when the second section of HS1 opened in 2007, but reopened in two phases in December 2018 and May 2019 to allow expansion of suburban services at Waterloo.

Eurostar moved its train maintenance from North Pole in 2007 to a new depot at Temple Mills which is served by a single track link from Stratford International. North Pole lay empty for around a decade but is now used by Hitachi.

In the first six months after the move to St Pancras, Eurostar recorded traffic growth of over 18% and revenue growth of nearly a quarter. In 2008 overall Eurostar carried 9.1 million passengers, an increase of 10.3% over 2007 but not as much as expected due to the Tunnel fire on 11 September 2008.

One of the less publicised benefits of HS1 was that Eurostar was able to remove all of the third rail collection gear from its sets, reducing maintenance costs considerably. This of course means that trains cannot be diverted off HS1 if there is any serious problem, but in fact such incidents are extremely rare.

It was announced in late 2008 that Eurostar was seeking "expressions of interest" in the mid-life refurbishment of the 28 18-car sets (not the three SNCF sets or the seven NoL sets) to be carried out by 2014. At the time it was reported that Eurostar was considering buying Alstom's new AGV train to replace part of the fleet instead of carrying out the overhauls. As we know now, two years later Eurostar announced it would buy new sets (from Siemens) and refurbish the old ones.

In March 2009 Eurostar announced that it had chosen Pininfarina to design the refurbishment and the French press reported that the company was looking for new trains. One of the reasons for ordering new trains was Eurostar's desire to serve new destinations, especially Amsterdam. The latter would involve the addition of ETCS signalling; retrofitting the system to, and authorisation of, existing trains was expected to be very expensive – DB had paid €8 million per set to equip its ICE 3s.

The 2009 Eurostar debacle

Eurostar has suffered several high profile breakdowns which left large numbers of people in sufferance, but Friday 18 December 2009 will be remembered as catastrophic. On that evening no less than five Eurostar sets heading for London broke down in the Channel Tunnel, leaving over 2000 people stranded there all night. All trains were already late due to snow and ice in France. The first

stopped with traction problems about three-quarters of the way through the Tunnel in Interval 1. After about 2½ hours the train was hauled out by Eurotunnel's diesel rescue locos. However, in the meantime, a second train stopped behind the first and eventually lost all power. After about five hours passengers were evacuated. A third train, from Disneyland and full of families, stopped behind the first two and when given the all-clear over four hours later, also broke down and was later evacuated.

The other two trains were diverted into the south tunnel in order to avoid the first breakdowns, but the first one then failed and the second one broke down when it tried to push the previous one out of the Tunnel. Several other Eurostars were affected by the chaos and thousands of people spent the night in the trains or back at their origin stations.

Operator Eurostar was well aware of the risks to its trains in winter. The main problem is that snow and ice can be sucked into the power cars only to melt in the Tunnel and cause problems to electrical equipment. The company therefore had a plan for "winterisation" of all sets when winter approached. The most important aspect of this was to fit special membranes inside the power cars, covering the air intake grilles, thus letting in air but not snow.

In the aftermath of this incident Eurostar said that the weather conditions were "exceptional" and the snow was "fluffy" but that it had protected its trains as usual. In fact, sources inside the company revealed that the "winterisation" had been delayed and had only been very partially completed.

An independent review recommended, amongst other things, that Eurostar should acquire rescue locomotives. In the end the company jointly financed the purchase of two Krupp-Mak diesels which are managed by Eurotunnel as part of a fleet of ten.

TGV Duplex run aborted

History has largely forgotten that a special run was scheduled to take place in March 2010 with a TGV Duplex double-deck set over HS1 with the aim of beating the speed record set by Eurostar NoL set 3313/4 in 2007. The train was due to be presented at St Pancras to mark the publication of the UK government report on the building of HS2. The run never happened due to "bureaucratic problems".

Safety rules change

In late 2012 officials from the British and French governments agreed new joint regulations for the Channel Tunnel which came into force in March 2013. The new rules were that any vehicles complying with European Union TSI (Technical Specifications for Interoperability) would be authorised to use the Channel Tunnel. This removed many of the barriers to using new designs of trains or locos in the Tunnel if they are already approved in one EU country and conform to TSI standards. The IGC may only check those aspects which are relevant to operating in the Tunnel.

Sample Eurostar running times September 2019

Fastest London–Paris timings

Train 9004	arr.	pass	dep.
London St Pancras			07.01
Stratford West Jn.		07.06	
Ebbsfleet West Jn.		07.13½	
Ashford International		07.27	
Tunnel UK portal		07.33	
Tunnel FR portal		08.54	
Calais Fréthun		08.55	
Lille Europe		09.19½	
TGV Haute Picardie		09.43	
Paris Nord	10.17		
Train 9009			
Paris Nord			07.43
TGV Haute Picardie		08.17	
Lille Europe		08.41½	
Calais Fréthun		09.06	
Tunnel FR portal		09.07	
Tunnel UK portal		08.28	
Ashford International		08.34½	
Ebbsfleet East Jn.		08.46½	
Stratford East Jn.		08.53½	
London St Pancras	09.00		
London–Marseille			
Train 9084/5			
London St Pancras			07.19
Ashford	07.51		07.54
Calais Fréthun		09.28	
Lille Europe	09.54		09.58
TGV Haute Picardie		10.23½	
Roissy-CDG 2		10.47	
Marne-la-Vallée-Ch.	10.57 s		11.07 s
Le Creusot TGV		12.21½	
Mâcon-Loché TGV		12.36	
Lyon Part Dieu	13.00		13.06
Valence TGV		13.39	
Avignon TGV	14.07½		14.10½
Aix TGV		14.37	
Marseille St Charles	14.47½		
Train 9086/87			
Marseille St Charles			15.22
Aix TGV		15.34	
Avignon TGV	15.57½		15.59½
Valence TGV		16.32	
Lyon Part Dieu	17.14		17.25
Mâcon-Loché TGV		17.49	
Le Creusot TGV		18.03	
Marne-la-Vallée-Ch.	19.19		19.22
Roissy-CDG 2		19.30	
TGV Haute Picardie		19.53	
Lille Europe	20.20		21.36
Calais Fréthun		22.02½	
Ashford	21.34		21.36
London St Pancras	22.12		
s service stop			
in *italics*: UK time			

REGIONAL EUROSTARS:
THE NORTH OF LONDON SETS

It was not until the "Three Capitals" Eurostar sets had been operating regularly for a year that the first 14-car "North of London" (NoL) sets started testing in late 1995. By this time EPS had started to call them "Regional Eurostars" although "NoL" is still used by many people to this day. It was hoped that the first units would enter service in the "first half of 1996".

The "NoLs" had been conceived to allow the benefit of the Channel Tunnel to be felt by the whole of the UK and not just London. Trains would run from Paris or Brussels, serving Stratford International in east London, then would turn northwards, running at up to 200 km/h over the East Coast Main Line to York, Newcastle and Edinburgh, for example, or via the West Coast Main Line to Birmingham, Manchester and, possibly, Glasgow.

The trains were almost identical to the "Three Capitals" Eurostar sets but had only seven trailers instead of nine in each half set, a complete train being 14 coaches (318.70 metres) long. This gave less First Class accommodation for routes with more leisure traffic. The Three Capitals half sets have trailers numbered R1 to R9 from the power car end; NoL sets had trailers R1/3/2/5/6/7/9.

By mid 1996 Eurostar, despite delivery of the seven trains being complete, was unable or unwilling to name a start date, deadlines of summer then autumn 1996 having slipped. Introduction was said to be wholly dependent on obtaining authorisation for the trains to use the West and East Coast Main Lines.

In late 1996, after months of night time running, set 3301/2 started day time trials on the ECML between Newark and Welwyn Garden City.

Although Eurostar was no longer willing to put forward a date for the service launch, the initial timetable was published in the Thomas Cook European Timetable in spring 1997. The service consisted of a daily train pair between Glasgow and Paris via Edinburgh and the East Coast Main Line (in 9h23) and a daily train pair between Manchester and Paris (6h02). On Monday–Saturday this would be supplemented by a Manchester–Birmingham–Paris train pair (6h41, Birmingham 4h58). All trains were to stop at Lille Europe and the Manchester train at Ashford. On 4/5 June 1997 Eurostar set 3307/8 visited Glasgow for clearance trials, the set being hauled up the ECML by a pair of Class 37s.

Set 3301/2 was tested to Manchester in August 1997 and it seemed that all was going well for a launch in October of that year with staff training under way and customs facilities being installed in

places as unlikely as Stockport. However, the following month the service launch was again postponed when infrastructure manager Railtrack found that the trains were producing voltage surges in the overhead.

The first use of Regional Eurostars in revenue service occurred in early 1998 when the trains ran on a few occasions on the London–Brussels service. This took place due to problems with the transformers on some "Three Capitals" sets. In October 1998, set

3303/4 reached Berlin, when it was exhibited in an early version of the Innotrans trade fair.

In spring 1999 there was still no sign of the trains entering service and UK Transport Minister John Prescott announced a new study by consultants into Regional Eurostar services after a company called Inter-Capital and Regional Rail Limited proposed abandoning the plan and using the seven sets for a Heathrow–Paris service! The Virgin Group had also put forward

Left: Platform clearance testing of Eurostar sets at Glasgow Central using sets 3307 and 3308 took place over several nights in the first week of June 1997, with the set propelled into various platforms of the station by a Class 37/6 and barrier vehicle. A Eurostar driver was on the footplate of the Class 373 and had control of the brake. The Eurostar set was not authorised to take power in the area. This is the view at Glasgow Central station recorded late on 5 June 1997. Power car 3308 never ran in service and is now in York museum.

Top right: On the first day of GNER 'White Rose' operations, 30 May 2000, set 3304/03 arrives at London King's Cross with the 09.23 service from York, the first advertised Class 373 passenger train on the East Coast Main Line.

Centre right: On the launch day of 'White Rose' services, two GNER-liveried sets pose side by side at York. On the left, set 3302/01 has just arrived with the 14.34 service from King's Cross, while on the right, set 3304/3 makes ready to depart with the 17.43 to King's Cross. *Colin J Marsden (3)*

Bottom right: NoL set 3305/6 zooms through Doncaster with a London King's Cross–Leeds service on 24 July 2002. *Ernest Godward*

proposals to take on the trains and operate revised services.

By July 1999 Regional Eurostars were being tested on the East Coast Main Line between Kings Cross and York. After initially denying all knowledge of involvement, franchised operator GNER hired sets 3301/2 and 3303/4 from May 2000 and put them into service on the "White Rose" service from London Kings Cross to York. Set 3303/4 was named "White Rose" on 30 May. Maximum speed was initially restricted to 110 mph but was later raised to 125 mph (200 km/h). These two sets received GNER's dark blue livery. Set 3309/10 was the reserve set.

Although all plans to operate these sets on through London–France services had been dropped, set 3303/4 in GNER livery was tested in France in February 2002 in order to check that the NoL sets could run on high speed lines. This was a precursor to the NoL sets being used to test HS1 (at the time known as the CTRL: Channel Tunnel Rail Link).

In mid 2002 it was reported that all Regional Eurostars would be returned to service. 3301/2 and 3303/4 were joined by 3305/6 in GNER livery on the "White Rose". 3309/10 and 3311/2 in Eurostar livery were in reserve and 3313/4 was taken out of reserve to be used for tests on the CTRL. Set 3307/8 was also expected to be used for CTRL testing.

UK rail speed record holder

The first section of the CTRL from Fawkham Junction (Southfleet) to the Tunnel (74 km) went live on 9 February and tests at up to 330 km/h started in mid April with set 3313/4. On 30 July 2003 this set a new British rail speed record of 334.7 km/h (208 mph) which still stands.

The new line was inaugurated on 28 September 2003.

In December 2005 Eurostar recovered the five NoL sets it had been leasing to GNER and put them into store at North Pole depot. Eurostar said at the time they would be used to start Brussels–Amsterdam services when the HSL Zuid high speed line opened in 2007 as the trains ordered were late. This never happened as the cost of equipping them with ETCS and for 1500 V DC operation was found to be too high.

In early 2006 Eurostar said they would be used to test the CTRL 2 to St Pancras and for the "occasional charter" but later that year SNCF announced it would hire the sets to operate on services from Paris Nord from June 2007. All seven of the trains, except half set 3308, were transferred to Hellemmes works (Lille) for minor modifications. Half set 3307, which had never previously run in revenue service, eventually entered service with half set 3303 to replace half set 3304 around 2010. 3308 remained at North Pole depot as a spares bank. However, initially sets 3309/10 and 3313/4 were used to test HS1 before opening in November 2007.

The lease on the NoL Eurostars came to an end at the end of 2011 but SNCF renewed it. However, by 2012 half set 3304 was in store at Le Landy depot (it went for scrap in mid 2019). Half sets 3303 and 3307, which had worked together for a year or two, were stored at SNCF's Romilly works. Initial plans were to lease them to DB which wanted to operate a service from Brussels to London with them during the 2012 London Olympics. This fell through however.

The other NoL Eurostars were used on services from Paris Nord to Lille, Valenciennes, Dunkerque and Calais until December 2014 when SNCF deployed a full fleet of TGV Duplex sets on these services. The six sets which had been operating regularly were taken for storage at a former army base at Ambronay, near Ambérieu which is east of Lyon. The choice of this high security location led to speculation that there might still be the possibility of them operating again but in the end this did not happen. Half set 3304 (3303 had been paired with 3307 after a serious problem with 3304), which had been stored at Paris Le Landy depot, was finally moved to Valenciennes in July 2019. As for half set 3308, which had never operated in regular service

and had been used for various tests, and was stored at Temple Mills, power car 373 308 was donated for preservation at York's National Railway Museum, possibly the only item there which has never run in service. The trailers were sent for scrap in October 2017.

It was not until June 2019 that the first two NoL sets were despatched from Ambronay, to SME in Culoz, some 60 km to the south. The two units concerned were "mixed" set 3303/7 and 3313/4 which holds the UK rail speed record.

After magazine **Today's Railways Europe** pointed out the importance of the train, Eurostar decided to preserve power car 3314 which will now be plinthed at Temple Mills depot.

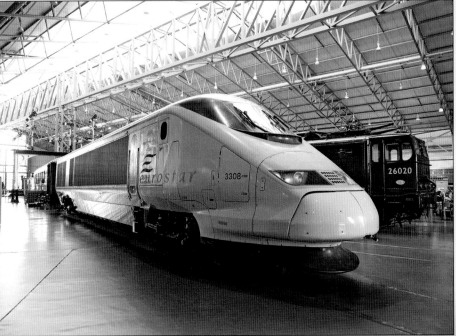

Opposite: At Waterloo International Eurostar staff celebrate the UK speed record of 334.7 km/h on 30 July 2003. Power car 3314 will now be preserved.

Above: NoL set 3312/11, with SNCF markings, forms the 07.52 Paris Nord–Valenciennes at Vitry-en-Artois on 8 March 2011. *David Haydock (2)*

Left: Preserved Class 373 power car 3308 is seen inside the National Railway Museum at York on 28 March 2018. *Antony Christie*

Below: SNCF diesels BB 67556 and 67511 are seen at Ambronay with NoL set 3307/4 which was being towed from the storage site at Ambronay to Culoz for scrapping. *Alex Vassal*

DEUTSCHE BAHN'S ICE IN LONDON

It was as early as 1997 that DB first said it wanted to operate trains through the Tunnel, announcing that the company would like to operate trains through London from 2003, once the Tunnel–London high speed line was open. In the event, nothing then happened for a dozen years.

The tail end of 2010 was an exciting period for the Channel Tunnel operators as it seemed that competition and expansion was on the horizon. On 28 July DB announced that an ICE 3 set would be tested in the Channel Tunnel. Then on 7 October Eurostar announced its order for new Siemens Velaro trains and that it was looking closely at new services to Marseille, Amsterdam, Genève and, possibly, Germany.

Just 12 days later, on 19 October 2010 German Railways (Deutsche Bahn or DB) brought ICE 3M set 4685 "Schwäbisch Hall" to London and announced plans to operate a through Frankfurt–Köln–Brussels–London service, as well as an Amsterdam–London service. The idea was to operate three train pairs a day from London, each formed of two ICEs in multiple (new Class 407) which would split in Brussels, one going forward to Rotterdam and Amsterdam, the other to Köln and Frankfurt.

The President of DB, Rüdiger Grube, in person, said that this would be possible by the December 2013 timetable change, and earlier if everything went well. Not long after this Deutsche Bahn said it was aiming to launch a direct service in time for the London Olympics in June 2012.

Unfortunately the plan did not work out. The plan was to operate these trains with new Class 407 (Velaro D) ICE sets on order (not the Class 406 displayed in London). DB gave the impression that extending its popular existing Frankfurt–Köln–Brussels ICE service through the Tunnel to London would be simple. Eurotunnel reckoned that this service could eventually carry an extra 3 to 4 million passengers a year through the Tunnel.

Above: Deutsche Bahn ICE 3M set 4685 is seen at London St Pancras International on 19 October 2010.

Below: Euro Cargo Rail (part of DB) TRAXX electric loco 186 168 passes through Douai in northern France on 11 October 2010 hauling ICE 4685 on the way to Calais then London. *David Haydock (2)*

DB was forced to admit that it would not be able to operate a direct service in time for the Olympics and came up with an alternative of hiring some of the North of London Eurostars and operating a Brussels–London shuttle connecting with its Frankfurt–Brussels ICEs. However, this plan was dropped.

The longer term plan depended on the Channel Tunnel safety rules being changed to allow operation of two sets in multiple and it seemed that this was likely to be the main sticking point. On 14 June 2013 it was announced that DB had received a safety certificate to operate through the Tunnel.

However, it also depended on the Class 407 "Velaro D" multi-voltage trains being delivered and authorised on time, and on them being equipped to operate through the Tunnel. In fact, the new trains did not perform well in Germany at the beginning and neither did the Class 406 trains they would replace. The period concerned was one of increasing discontent with DB's services and the German government put pressure on DB to "sort out" domestic ICE services before embarking on "foreign adventures". Class 407 took longer than expected to be authorised for Germany and once they had been accepted they were deployed on German internal services.

At the same time trials of use in multiple through the Tunnel could certainly not start until Class 407 could operate in multiple in Germany – authorisation for this became the main sticking point in getting the units into full service in Germany.

In mid 2013, DB started to "notice" challenges to its business case for a service to London. The UK Border Agency decided it would not set up any more facilities in continental Europe and DB would not be able to carry any *cabotage* traffic – such as Frankfurt–Köln or Frankfurt–Brussels on such a service.

Above & below: On 13 October 2010 ICE set 4685 ran into and out of the Channel Tunnel for press photographers... but never returned again! *David Haydock (2)*

Once the situation in Germany had been stabilised, Class 407 was then authorised for use in France and replaced Class 406 on Frankfurt–Paris services, the latter being redeployed on Frankfurt–Brussels/Amsterdam. DB retained one Class 407 set for tests in Belgium with a view to authorisation but this had still not been received in 2019!

The idea of extending Frankfurt–Brussels services to London was quietly shelved. It is clear that DB had completely underestimated the time, effort and finance needed to retrofit Class 407 for use via the Tunnel to London and set up expensive security facilities at German stations. At one point DB was suggesting that it might instead extend the Frankfurt–Köln–Brussels ICE service to Paris but even this is not seriously considered any more.

By early 2014 DB was saying it had "no immediate intention" of approving its Class 407 in the Netherlands and would not commit to a date for London services. In fact DB had not even ordered safety equipment for retrofitting to Class 407 sets.

By 2018 DB told "The Independent" that it had given up the idea of a service to London "in the foreseeable future" for both technical and economic reasons, one of the latter being the growth of low-cost airlines. However, the latter has not stopped DB building up a successful two-hourly ICE service between Frankfurt and Brussels.

On 7 October 2010, after 16 years of operations, Eurostar announced that it had ordered ten new 320 km/h trains as part of investment worth a total of €800 million which would also include refurbishment of the whole fleet of Trans-Manche Super Train (TMST) sets (this had been trailed for several years). Our sources put the cost of the new Siemens sets at around €600 million, or €60 million apiece. The new sets would be known as e320 reflecting their maximum speed, while the TMSTs were re-branded e300.

The new sets would be built by Siemens in Germany and based on the Velaro high speed "platform". The company was, at the time, delivering an 8-car version known as Velaro D (Class 407) to Deutsche Bahn. The

e320 would be 16 coaches long – just under 400 metres – and would be able to carry 894 passengers – 20% more than on an e300 which can carry 750.

The design of the Velaro is quite different from the e300 sets. Instead of having a power car at each end the train has traction equipment distributed throughout the train with a total of 16 axles out of 32 powered – all of the 16 coaches are supported by two bogies, compared with the e300 which has the two power cars with two bogies but with 18 articulated trailers on 20 bogies.

The power rating would be 16 000 kW compared with 12 240 kW for an e300 set. Under 1500 and 3000 V DC this falls to 8400 kW compared with 5700 kW for an e300. Like the e300 sets, the new Velaros consist of two identical half-sets coupled back-to-back. However, whereas the e300 sets have second class accommodation next to the power cars, a buffet car in the middle of each half set and all the first class in the middle of the train, e320s have the first class seats at the cab ends, the second class just behind and the two buffet cars

EUROSTAR,
SECOND GENERATION

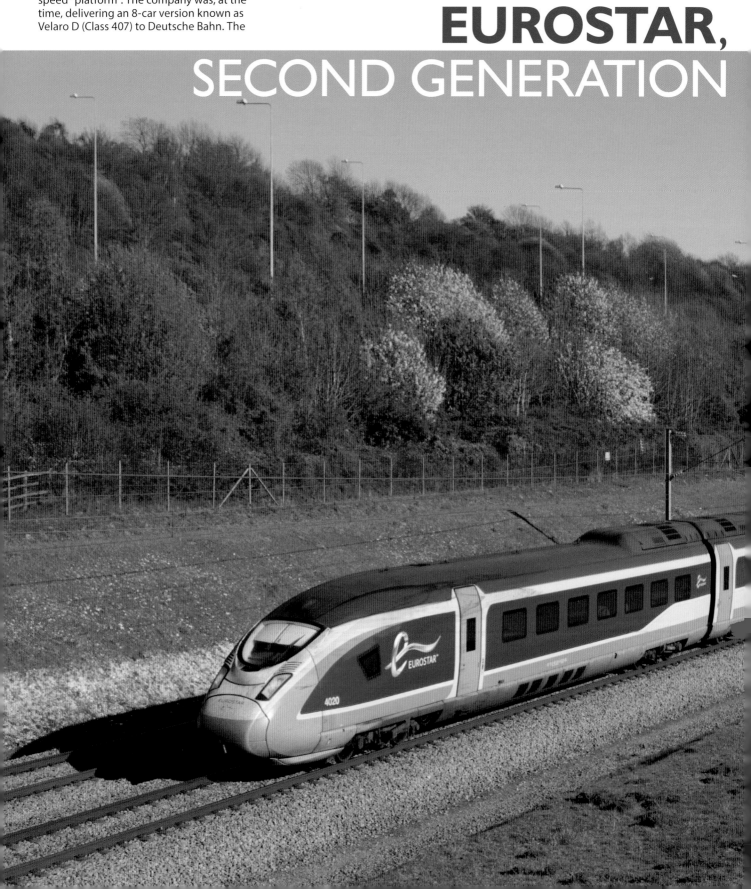

back-to-back in the middle. The e320s are significantly wider than the earlier Eurostars as they take full advantage of the European loading gauge as trains do not need to operate on the UK classic network with its restricted loading gauge.

Alstom and the French government were outraged that Eurostar (majority owned by SNCF) should order a German train. However, Alstom was offering a version of its new-at-the-time AGV articulated design which had not turned a wheel in service, whilst the Velaro platform was operating well already in Spain, Russia and China. Some sources suggested that the AGV could not be fitted with all the extra equipment needed for Channel Tunnel without pushing it over the 17 tonne axle load limit in force on French high speed lines.

New destinations?

Eurostar said at the time that the new trains would allow the company to serve new destinations such as Amsterdam and Genève, but also mentioned Köln and Frankfurt in Germany plus Marseille in France. Marseille is now served, but only by e300 sets while it took until 2018 for the Amsterdam service to be launched.

Incidentally, although the e320 sets can operate at 320 km/h this is not actually possible on the current routes either in the UK, France, Belgium or the Netherlands at present. There is a short stretch of 320 km/h track between Lyon and Marseille but e320 sets are not used on this route. Other 320 km/h-capable routes in France are not used by Eurostar at present. A putative London–Bordeaux service could run at 320 km/h south of Tours, but Eurostar usually deploys the smaller e300 sets on such routes, leaving the more capacious e320s for the flagship Paris route.

Eurostar to Germany?

In the case of the German destinations, these are still theoretical. The e320 sets are designed to operate off the 15 kV AC overhead in Germany but are not actually fitted with all the equipment necessary. At the time of the order, Eurostar was

e320 set 4020/19 is seen at Nashenden on HS1 with train 9043 Paris Nord–St Pancras on 9 April 2017. *Jamie Squibbs*

Delays and more delays

Construction of the new trains was to start in 2012 with the first sets entering service in 2014. Part of the first set was first spotted on its way to Siemens' test circuit at Wildenrath in Germany in September 2012. There then started to be reports that the DB Class 407 Velaro D sets, on which the new Eurostars were based, were having problems obtaining approval in Germany. Siemens assured the press that the first e320 would be delivered in mid-2014, but this was somewhat later than the sets **entering service** in 2014 as forecast in 2010. In addition, in early 2013 refurbishment of the e300 sets had not begun – this was supposed to have started in 2011 and be completed in 2014. Then in April 2013 Siemens admitted that the e320 sets would be late as it had "underestimated the complexity of the contract", blaming the time taken by the approval process after its experience with Velaro D.

The first e320 set to be tested away from the Siemens circuit in Germany was 4001/2 which arrived in Belgium on 25 June 2013. The second, 4003/4, was sent to Brittany to check track circuit activation in late 2013. 4005/6 had appeared in France by June 2014 and was based at Le Landy for endurance tests across the French LGV network. When the train eventually ran into Paris Nord, in late 2014, it was found that the train was too long for the driver to read the signals at the northern end of the platforms. e320 sets are about five metres longer than e300 sets and this had not been considered. In the end modifications – including a "high tech" mirror which showed the driver how close the train is to the buffers – allowed the sets to stop closer to the concourse, thus solving the problem.

e320 Eurostars were finally authorised to operate in France in October 2015, paving the way for introduction in December of that year.

The first set to be delivered to the UK was 4007/8 on 30/31 January 2014.

probably mulling over the London–Brussels–Köln–Frankfurt route because Deutsche Bahn was proposing to launch services on this route at the time. DB already operated an ICE high speed service from Frankfurt via Köln to Brussels and had announced in 2010 that it wished to run a through service to London in time for the Olympic Games in summer 2012 using its own newly-delivered Class 407 Velaros. This date slipped to 2013 then the Velaros suffered problems over authorisation in Germany, then again in Belgium. See "ICE in London" below.

At the time of writing, the "Green Speed" project looked like reviving the idea of services to Germany.

Top to bottom: First class seating, second class seating and the bar vehicle in the e320 train. *David Haydock (3)*

Opposite: Seating plan for an e320 half set. *Courtesy Eurostar*

EUROSTAR

e320 SEATING PLAN COACHES 1-8

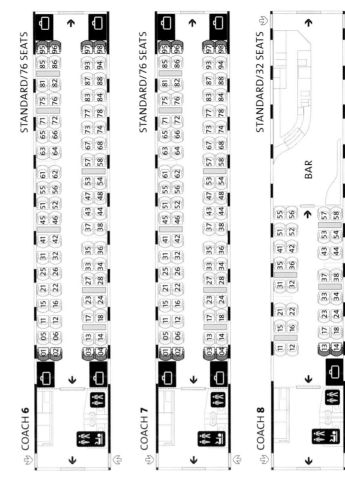

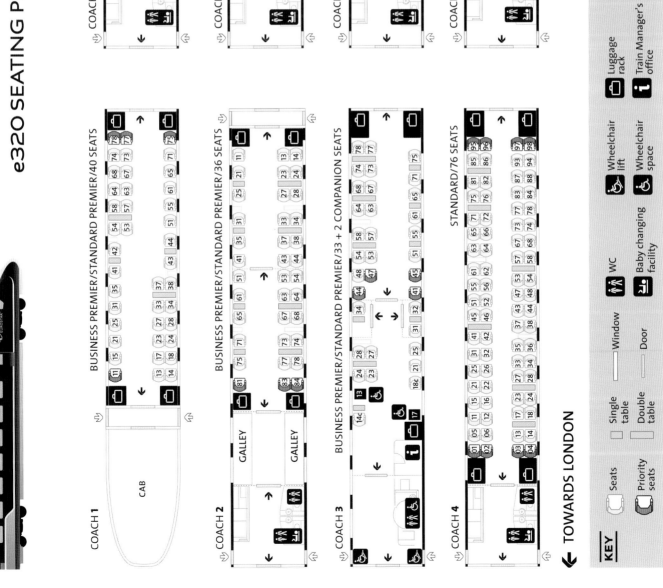

COACH 1 — BUSINESS PREMIER/STANDARD PREMIER/40 SEATS

CAB

COACH 2 — BUSINESS PREMIER/STANDARD PREMIER/36 SEATS

GALLEY

GALLEY

COACH 3 — BUSINESS PREMIER/STANDARD PREMIER/33 + 2 COMPANION SEATS

COACH 4 — STANDARD/76 SEATS

COACH 5 — STANDARD/76 SEATS

COACH 6 — STANDARD/76 SEATS

COACH 7 — STANDARD/76 SEATS

COACH 8 — STANDARD/32 SEATS

BAR

← TOWARDS LONDON

TOWARDS PARIS/BRUSSELS →

KEY

- Seats
- Priority seats
- Single table
- Double table
- —— Window
- ---- Door
- WC
- Baby changing facility
- Wheelchair lift
- Wheelchair space
- Luggage rack
- Train Manager's office
- UK and European power points available at all seats
- USB sockets available in Business Premier and Standard Premier
- All our trains are non-smoking
- ⇧ Access door
- ⬆ Automatic door

Eurostar e320 set 4022/21 heads towards Brussels on the HSL Zuid near Lage Zwaluwe (Netherlands) on 19 August 2019. The classic line with an NS VIRM EMU forming an IC Vlissingen–Amsterdam service is in the background.
Richard Latten

Comparison of e300 and e320 Eurostar half sets

e300

Built: 1992–1994
Builders: GEC-Alsthom, Brush, ANF, De-Dietrich, BN, ACEC.
Systems: 1500 V DC§ / 3000 V DC / 25 kV AC
Maximum speed: 300 km/h (200 km/h under DC).

e320

2012–2017
Siemens
1500 V DC / 3000 V DC / 25 kV AC (pre-equipped for 15 kV AC)
320 km/h (220 km/h under DC).

Statistics for half sets:

Accommodation: 0 + –/48 2T + –/56 1T + –/56 2T + –/56 1T + –/56 2T + bar/kitchen + 39/– 1T + 39/– 1T + 25/– 1T.   40/– + 36/– 2T + 34/– 1TD 2W + –/76 2T + –/76 2T + –/76 2T + –/76 2T + bar –/32 2T.

Weight: 68.5 + 44.6 + 28.1 + 29.7 + 28.3 + 29.2 + 31.1 + 29.6 + 32.2 + 39.4 tonnes.   58 + 59 + 59 + 53 + 53 + 58 + 57 + 58 tonnes.

Length: 22.15 + 21.845 + 7 x 18.70 + 21.845 metres.   26.035 + 7 x 24.775 metres.

Axle arrangement: Bo-Bo + Bo-2-2-2-2-2-2-2-2-2.   Bo-Bo + 2-2 + Bo-Bo + 2-2 + 2-2 + Bo-Bo + 2-2 + Bo-Bo.

Continuous rating: 6120 kW (25 kV AC); 2850 kW (1500 and 3000 V DC).   8000 kW (25 kV AC); 4200 kW (1500 and 3000 V DC)

§ Retro-fitted.

-/48 2T means no first class, 48 second class seats, two toilets. TD: universal access toilet. 2W: two wheelchair spaces.

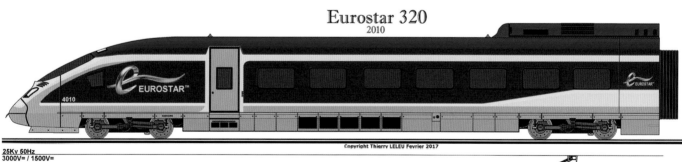

Eurostar 320
2010

4010 EUROSTAR

25Kv 50Hz
3000V= / 1500V=

Copyright Thierry LELEU Fevrier 2017

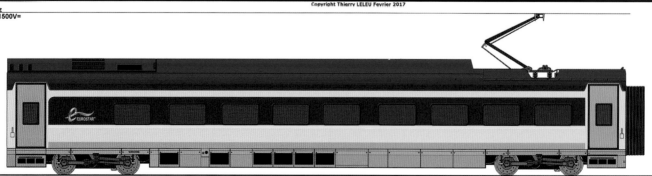

Copyright Thierry LELEU Fevrier 2017

In summer 2016 Eurostar was obliged to halt deliveries from Siemens because the overall reliability of the trains was not good enough. Although deliveries later restarted, reliability was still far from perfect in 2019, and was terrible in winter 2018/19 despite the conditions being milder than for many years. Even in 2019, random checks showed that a least four sets were out of action – almost a quarter of the fleet.

e320 sets were authorised to operate in Belgium during 2016, except for Brussels Midi where there was a similar problem to that at Paris Nord – no space for the longer sets, Brussels Midi having security gates at the western end which are closed behind the trains. Minor modifications at the station were carried out and authorisation was gained by the end of 2016, allowing e320s to operate to Brussels from May 2017.

It was with some dismay that the good people of Ashford and East Kent in general learned that the e320 sets would not be equipped with the UK signalling system and could therefore not serve Ashford. Initially this was not a problem as e300 sets were still deployed on services stopping in Ashford but as the number of e320 sets grew it was necessary to miss out Ashford for a short time. However, the conundrum was solved by equipping the section of line via Ashford with the French KVB beacon speed control system which was inaugurated on 4 April 2018. However, there were problems and e300 sets had to be put back on this service. From 16 December 2019, e320 sets started to serve Ashford on a regular basis.

Refurbishments cut back

In October 2010 Eurostar said it would refurbish all of its existing 28 e300 trains starting in 2011, with the first re-entering service in 2012 and all trains completed in 2014. Work would be carried out mainly at SNCF's workshops at Hellemmes in the suburbs of Lille. The work would include a complete technical overhaul and the installation of a similar interior to that in the e320s designed by Pininfarina. All trains would have the latest Wi-Fi and an infotainment system. The units would also receive a new livery similar to the e320s. The total of 28 trains quoted by Eurostar included set 3101/2 which had been languishing out of use for several years (see above).

However, in 2014 Eurostar intimated that it would only refurbish half of its old sets – just 14 sets. The process took far longer than expected for several reasons. During the process of stripping the old sets down it was found that rust was a serious problem. The trailers from Belgian set 3101/3102, which had been stored for several years after a shunting accident at Brussels Forest depot, were divided and sent to two sites in France in order to develop the internal refurbishment. It was hoped that standard "one size fits all" components could be developed. In fact, during this process it was found that the internal dimensions of the trailers were not exactly the same, this being the result of work being carried out by several different companies.

In the light of these problems, and of Eurostar's failure to develop as many new routes as hoped (the idea of a direct service to Genève was quickly dropped), the company announced that it would order a further seven e320 sets in November 2014 and that only eight e300 sets would be refurbished. Even this process took a very long time, the last refurbished set 3209/10 re-entering service in spring 2019, almost nine years after the work was announced. Most of the sets which were chosen for refurbishment were built in France. Of those built in the UK, only two survive.

The first power cars to be refurbished were 3015 and 3016 which were outshopped from Hellemmes works in April 2014. Apart from being given a thorough overhaul the power cars were equipped to operate off 1500 V DC. All of the refurbished power cars have been equipped for 1500 V DC if not already fitted. This is because loadings on services to Bourg St Maurice and Marseille are generally lower than those on the Paris route, where e320 sets normally work all services except the odd early morning and late evening services. e300 sets also operate the Marne-la-Vallée Disneyland service.

By June 2014 refurbished power cars 3015/16 had been paired with a set of non-refurbished stock for test runs. The lack of progress on the trailers was a theme which accompanied the whole refurbishment plan, because of the difficulties cited above. It was not until July 2015 that the set was completed, with refurbished trailers.

International? Set 4005/06 passes Stratford International station without stopping with the 15.03 Paris Nord–St Pancras International on 5 April 2019. *Robert Pritchard*

Above: Refurbished e300 set 3220/19 forms train 9094 Bourg St Maurice–London St Pancras, operating under 1500 V DC, at Pont de Veyle between Ambérieu and Mâcon on 16 March 2019. *Pierre Julien*

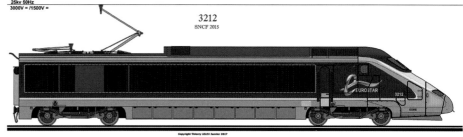

A little push... to Marseille

The Avignon service introduced in 2002 had a pretty stable timetable from year to year, leaving London at around 07.15 and arriving at Avignon Ville at 13.45 then returning around 16.30 and reaching London at 21.15. Customs checks were carried out on an isolated platform at Avignon Ville for the return.

From May to June 2013 Eurostar tested a new weekly "Provence" service via Lyon Part Dieu to Aix-en-Provence TGV station with stops at Valence TGV and Avignon TGV station. In order to avoid setting up customs and security checks at all three stations, Eurostar introduced a stop at Lille Europe on the return journey where all passengers had to alight with their luggage and pass through these checks. The stop lasted about 90 minutes and passenger numbers were limited to 350 (all carried in one half set) in order to check how practical this arrangement was.

Right: Non-refurbished set 3217/8 and refurbished set 3206/5 are seen at Brussels Midi on 23 July 2019. *Didier Delattre*

e300 SEATING PLAN COACHES 1-9

EUROSTAR™

KEY

	Seats
	Priority seats
	Single table
	Double table
	Window
	Door
	WC
	Baby changing facility
	Wheelchair space
	Luggage rack
	Train Manager's office
	UK and European power points available at all seats
	USB sockets available in Business Premier and Standard Premier
	Access door
	Automatic door

All our trains are non-smoking

POWER CAR

COACH 1 STANDARD/52 SEATS

COACH 2 STANDARD/56 SEATS

COACH 3 STANDARD/56 SEATS

COACH 4 STANDARD/56 SEATS

COACH 5 STANDARD/52 SEATS

BUFFET BAR

BAR

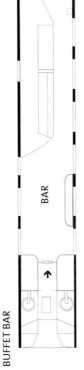

COACH 7 BUSINESS PREMIER/STANDARD PREMIER/39 SEATS

COACH 8 BUSINESS PREMIER/STANDARD PREMIER/39 SEATS

COACH 9 BUSINESS PREMIER/STANDARD PREMIER/25 SEATS + 2 COMPANION SEATS

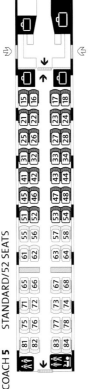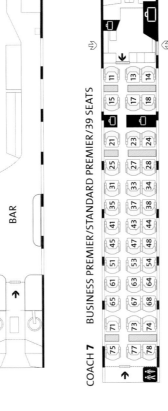

TOWARDS BRUSSELS →

← TOWARDS LONDON

Above: Siemens' Velaros have not been very reliable so far. Set 4024/23 is seen being hauled out of Paris Nord by SNCF Class BB 67200 rescue locomotives on 25 June 2018. *David Haydock*

Timings were:

London St Pancras	07.17 v	22.39 ^
Ashford International	07.55 v	22.09 ^
Lille Europe	-	22.04 ^
Lille Europe	-	20.30 ^§
Lyon Part Dieu	13.00 v	17.38 ^
Avignon TGV	14.09 v	16.21 ^
Aix en Provence TGV	14.34 v	15.57 ^
§ approximately		

The train actually ran through to Marseille, just 15 minutes further on, for servicing! The usual Avignon Ville service ran that summer.

Eurostar declared the Aix-en-Provence test a success and announced that a new service would run all year round from May 2015 all the way to Marseille, calling at Lyon Part Dieu and Avignon TGV, but not Valence or Aix-en-Provence. In order to deal with a larger number of passengers Eurostar doubled the passenger handling capacity at Lille Europe.

This service still operates, Friday to Monday in the high summer season, Friday, Saturday and Sunday in pre- and post-summer and just weekly in the depths of winter. Operation is with an e300 set. Insider information is that most southbound trains

Right: For scrap. Europorte loco E 37515 passes the former marshalling yard at Lille La Délivrance on 27 June 2012 with the trailers of Eurostar half set 3102, on the way to Hellemmes works. After stripping the interior 3102 was moved to Valenciennes for scrapping on 29 July 2015. *Patrick Verbaere*

carry 500–600 people, while returns are always more lightly loaded, with 300–400. Clearly customers do not like the stop in Lille!

Timings in 2019 were:

London St Pancras	07.19 v	22.12 ^
Lille Europe	-	20.21/21.36 ^
Lyon Part Dieu	13.00 v	17.25 ^
Avignon TGV	14.08 v	15.59 ^
Marseille St Ch.	14.45 v	15.22 ^

First Eurostar withdrawals and scrapping

Eurostar sets 3203/4, 3225/6 and 3227/8, which had been taken out of the "pool" by owner SNCF after less than five years in service were the first to be withdrawn. Having been used on the Paris–Lille line for a decade in a non-refurbished state, they were taken out of service in December 2014 after SNCF introduced TGV Duplex sets on the Lille route.

The first complete TMST to go for scrap was 3005/6 which left Temple Mills for Kingsbury, near Birmingham, on 26 October 2016. All movements are carried out under the cover of darkness. These trains need to run from Stratford International into St Pancras before running round and heading north. All of the sets dispatched from Temple Mills have been scrapped at Kingsbury near Birmingham. Those in France have mainly gone to Saint Saulve (Valenciennes).

In early 2020, Eurostar still had two non-refurbished e300 sets on its books.

Right: When Eurostar moved to London St Pancras the company also moved its trains from North Pole to a new depot at Temple Mills, north-east London. e320 set 4008/7 is seen there on 2 March 2015.

Below right: Le Landy (Paris) still carries out major work on Eurostar sets. This is set 3221/2 (left) and set 3007/8 with spare power car 3999 on 3 January 2019. *Keith Fender (2)*

3214/3223 was busy on "normal" services while 3213/3224 was in daily service with Izy (see below).

Amsterdam... at last

Well before the company ordered the new Velaro trains in 2010 Eurostar had spoken regularly of running trains from London to Amsterdam. The route is one of the busiest in Europe for the airlines with 6 million passengers a year. Eurostar was already carrying a decent number of passengers who were willing to change trains in Brussels, the fastest option, by using Thalys high speed trains, taking 4½ hours – just over two hours London–Brussels, time to change trains, then about 1h45 Brussels–Amsterdam. A through service would lop nearly an hour off this; a journey of about 3½ hours would certainly be attractive to passengers who wished to avoid air travel and all the hassle it involves. The London–Rotterdam journey time would be even shorter, at around 3¼ hours.

Eurostar announced in September 2015 that it would launch a direct service from

Below: e300 set 3209/10 was the last to be refurbished and left Hellemmes works (Lille) in March 2019. Before handover all sets have to be tested under both 25 kV AC and 1500 V DC; the latter usually taking place with a Lille–Les Aubrais (Orléans) run. As train 806886, the set crosses the flat Beauce plain at 160 km/h near Angerville on 3 March 2019. *Romain Vergnères*

London to Amsterdam in December 2017 in partnership with Dutch Railways (NS). Both NS and the Dutch government had been very keen on the idea ever since the Channel Tunnel project had been confirmed. Project documents for the time showed a two-hourly Amsterdam–London service running on the route. The Dutch also favoured Eurostar as it would add extra high speed services on the busy Amsterdam–Brussels route. Tests with e320 set 4013/14 in the Netherlands first started in April 2016.

Initially Eurostar stated that passengers from the Netherlands would be required to alight at Brussels Midi, pass through customs, then re-board the same train. However, within six months security requirements had become stricter and Eurostar decided that this solution would not be possible. Although NS was building new facilities for Eurostar passengers at Amsterdam Centraal and Rotterdam Centraal, the UK customs facilities there would not be ready until "late 2019". When the direct London–Amsterdam service started on 4 April 2018 there was no direct return working. Instead Eurostar e320 sets operated additional Amsterdam–Brussels Midi services and all passengers for London were required to pass through customs and board a new train. At time of writing direct services from Amsterdam to London were expected to start on 30 April 2020.

Record journey time... for one year

The initial Amsterdam service was of two trains a day, departing from London at 08.31 and 17.31, taking a record 1h48 non-stop from London to Brussels Midi, a saving of 17 minutes on the previous timetable when all trains stopped in Lille. The overall end-to-end journey time was 3h41. A third departure was added in June 2019 and in

mid 2019 departures from London were at 07.16 Mon–Sat, 11.04 daily and 17.16 Mon–Fri/Sun with a shortest journey time of 3h55. This 14 minute increase in journey time was "for pathing reasons" and saw London–Brussels rise to 1h56 and the time standing at Brussels Midi rising from four to ten minutes.

The Amsterdam trains were initially operated only by the seven sets in the second batch – 4021/22 to 4033/34 – which were delivered with ETCS Level 2 Version 3.5.4. The other e320 trains have now been modified to allow their use. Trains are driven by Eurostar's own staff between London and Brussels and by Netherlands Railways (NS) staff between Brussels and Amsterdam.

The carriage of Amsterdam/Rotterdam–Brussels passengers goes somewhat against Eurostar's credo but seems to have been a condition on which NS would invest in station security facilities. However, the Dutch government is also encouraging Eurostar to introduce a faster service, without a long stop in Brussels. The Dutch have talked of a 3h30 journey time which suggests that a commercial stop in Brussels might even be omitted.

A stop at Antwerpen may be added to the Amsterdam trains some time in the future. The authorities in the Belgian city would love Eurostar to stop there, and this would certainly generate much extra traffic, but it will probably be up to the city to pay for new security facilities to allow this. The initial plans for the Amsterdam service also showed a stop at Schiphol airport but this was later dropped.

Eurostar intends to add a fourth and fifth Amsterdam service once the customs issue is sorted out and will at last operate direct back from Amsterdam to London. The new traffic generated by the Amsterdam route helped Eurostar reach almost 11 million passengers

Above: e320 set 4013/14 runs empty from Amsterdam to Brussels, passing Rotterdam-Zuid on 7 May 2018 with the Rotterdam skyline in the background. *Richard Latten*

in 2018. The extra boosts to the service could well take traffic to 12 million and even 13 million – a significant step towards the 15 million predicted when the Channel Tunnel opened.

However, much will depend on the type of exit the UK organises from the EU. Once the situation is resolved, a Bordeaux service may look attractive and other destinations might follow.

As for journey times, the current timings are a little generous due to slow passage through Antwerpen and the need to share the Dutch high speed line with loco-hauled trains limited to 160 km/h. These will be replaced within five years with 200 km/h EMUs and it must be hoped that timings can be tightened a little then. In addition the northwards extension of Line 25N in Belgium to a point north of Mechelen station, slated for December 2020, should help. One must also hope that the extra 14 minutes added in 2019 can be removed again.

London–Genève flop

One of the potential destinations mentioned by Eurostar in 2010, when the e320 order was announced, was Genève. The Swiss city is popular with British tourists and business travellers, and is a gateway to the rest of Switzerland, in particular for skiing in winter. However, instead of a direct service being launched, Eurostar combined with SNCF/SBB subsidiary Lyria, which operates TGVs from Paris to Switzerland, to launch a Lille Europe–Genève direct service with good connections with Eurostar in Lille. The service, initially extended to Montreux, Aigle, Sion and Brig for skiers

Next stop Bordeaux?

One of the new destinations for Eurostar which has been mooted several times in the past is Bordeaux. Not only is the city itself an attractive destination for both tourism and business (gourmet food and wine), but a service from London could also call at Tours (Saint Pierre-des-Corps), for the Loire valley, and Angoulême, which is close to the Dordogne, an area very popular with Brits, and Poitiers.

Serious proposals for a service started to emerge in early 2016 in the run-up to the opening of the Tours–Bordeaux high speed line which was to take place in July 2017. Around this time Eurostar itself suggested that the route looked like a realistic proposition, in a similar way to the Marseille service, but a year later said that traffic would be "too seasonal".

However, the new line is operated by a private company, Lisea, which is keen to drum up additional business. The company, together with SNCF Réseau, Eurotunnel and HS1, is still talking up the idea of a Bordeaux service, whether operated by Eurostar or not. The grouping has "pre-planned" available timetable slots and is waiting to find an operator.

The fastest journey possible by train in 2019 is about 5h25: 2h16 non-stop London–Paris, 2h04 non-stop Paris–Bordeaux and just over an hour to cross Paris by metro.

Many projects, few realised

Over the years Eurostar itself and other parties have talked about running other services than the London to Paris and Brussels core routes. It took over 20 years

Above: TGV POS set 4410 forms train TGV 9796 Lille Europe–Brig on 30 March 2013 and is seen at Ronchin just after leaving Lille. *Didier Delattre*

(and with no Genève stop on the return journey), ran every Saturday from 22 December 2012 to 6 April 2013 with the following timings:

London St Pancras		06.57
Lille Europe	09.26	10.02
Brig	17.08	

Brig		12.51
Lille Europe	18.55	20.30
London St Pancras	21.09	

The service was obviously not a great success as it was cut back to just five Saturdays in 2013/2014.

However, the outlook for the Genève service looked good as Lyria announced a four times weekly service, between Lille and Genève from December 2014. Combined with Eurostar timings were as little as 6h18 in the outbound direction. The train also served Bellegarde, Marne-la-Vallée-Chessy and Charles-de-Gaulle TGV. Unfortunately, this service only lasted a year then was completely withdrawn, Lyria saying it would "concentrate on its core routes" in future.

Eurostar 4031/4032 forms train 9171 Amsterdam–Brussels Midi passing Mechelen station on 9 May 2018. The train is travelling at much reduced speed as the station is the last bottleneck on the Belgian high speed network. From December 2020 Eurostars will be able to pass the station at 160 km/h on the new line being built on the left of the photo (east of the station) where the photographer is standing. *Carlo Hertogs*

to launch an Amsterdam service but many other projects or simple proposals did not get off the drawing board.

In late 1999 Eurostar dropped plans to operate a Heathrow–Paris service which had been proposed to replace short haul connecting flights. The project was extremely complicated and involved adapting lines to Heathrow, electrifying a section of line and splitting Eurostar sets to make shorter formations.

There have been many suggestions that Germany would be a lucrative market, and Eurostar did say in 2010 that its new e320 trains would be pre-equipped for Germany. The most likely destinations would be Köln and Frankfurt, especially as Deutsche Bahn had seemed so keen to launch such a service, and the author assumes this was on the back of traffic forecasts. Köln is a popular tourist destination while Frankfurt is a big business centre.

However, Eurostar seems at best lukewarm on Germany and probably noted that DB decided that a London service was in the "too difficult" category. The British requirements on customs and security always make the launch of new services difficult, as is still apparent in the Netherlands. Despite a national government which is keen on the through service, and willing to finance new facilities, the service will have taken over two years to introduce in both directions.

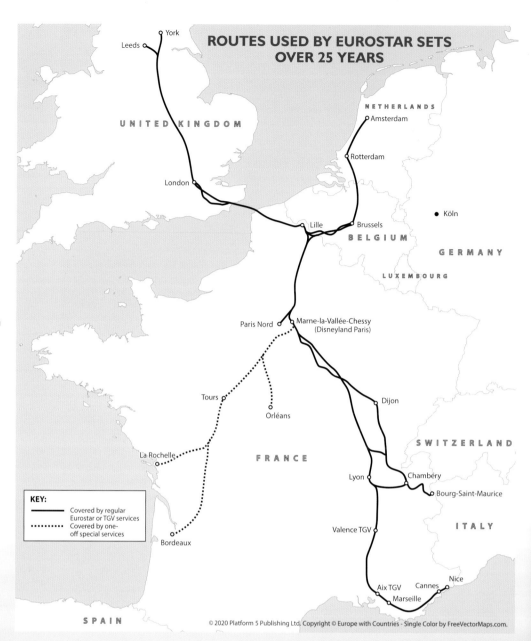

ROUTES USED BY EUROSTAR SETS OVER 25 YEARS

KEY:
— Covered by regular Eurostar or TGV services
···· Covered by one-off special services

© 2020 Platform 5 Publishing Ltd. Copyright © Europe with Countries - Single Color by FreeVectorMaps.com.

Below: On 25 February 2019 the photographer was lucky (and skilful) enough to snap two trains closing at almost 600 km/h on Belgian high speed Line 1 near Roosbeek. e320 set 4024/23 was on the way from Brussels to London as train 9331 and met Thalys PBKA unit 4304 running from Paris Nord to Essen (Germany) as train 9437. *Carlo Hertogs*

TGV POSTAL IN LONDON

On 21 March 2012 a French TGV Postal set was shown off to the press at London St Pancras in order to publicise a plan to introduce high speed postal services across Europe put forward by Euro Carex (Carex: Cargo Rail Express), which involved Air France-KLM, Chronopost (part of the French post office), TNT, UPS, Fedex and WFS, an airport freight handler. The idea was to run services between "railports", in many cases at airports on the high speed rail network such as Schiphol (Amsterdam), Bierset (Liège), Roissy-Charles-de-Gaulle (Paris) and Saint Exupéry (Lyon). London was also included, but not linked to a specific airport. SNCF and Eurotunnel were also sponsors.

The Euro Carex plan was the latest of several, including an early project to build a parcels version of Eurostar. This was killed off because of the astronomical cost of building such a specialised train. In principle, the climate for such services was very favourable in 2012. The European high speed network was growing fast, with Barcelona and Madrid shortly to be linked to Paris, and with Torino and Milano in Italy on the horizon.

A special demonstration run was made with TGV Postal set 951 on 20/21 March 2012 to show what might be achieved by a Carex service. The train started from Lyon Saint Exupéry at 16.42, stopped at Mâcon from 17.06 to 17.44, then at Roissy TGV station from 19.21 to 20.21 then finally ran non-stop to Calais Fréthun, arriving at 21.50. As the TGV set was not authorised to operate through the Tunnel or in the UK it was hauled forward by Eurotunnel rescue locos 0004 and 0005 at 23.25 (22.25 UK time) and arrived at St Pancras International at 00.45, nine hours after leaving Lyon. There seemed no reason why the TGV Postal sets could not be authorised to operate in the Tunnel or over HS1 so that a six hour through timing might be possible. Such a train could carry 120 tonnes of freight (the equivalent of seven Jumbo Jets) at up to 300 km/h.

However, in order to fully take advantage of loading gauge both Alstom and Siemens put forward draft plans for parcels versions of their TGV Duplex and Velaro high speed trains with a view to an order for up to 25 trains.

Euro Carex informed the press of its plans to operate trains from London to Amsterdam, Frankfurt and Lyon by 2015–2017, with extensions to Bordeaux, Aix/Marseille and Frankfurt via Strasbourg by 2018/19 then Hannover, Berlin, Barcelona and Madrid some time after 2020. The portents were good – the price of oil (and therefore airline kerosene) was rising and congestion at airports getting worse. However, unlike the planes themselves, the Carex project never got off the ground.

Above, below left & below right: TGV 951 at London St Pancras on 21 March 2012, plus photos of loading and the interior. *David Haydock (3)*

IZY: A EUROSTAR FOR PARIS–BRUSSELS

In December 2018, Thalys, a subsidiary of SNCF and SNCB which operates high speed trains mainly from Paris to Brussels, Amsterdam and Dortmund via Köln, hired a non-refurbished Eurostar set to operate the company's Izy (pronounced "easy") low-cost service between Paris and Brussels, replacing TGV Réseau sets. In autumn 2018 Eurostar inspected the non-refurbished e300 sets still in service and chose half sets 3213 and 3224 as in the best condition for hire to Thalys. The hybrid set was given a light clean and service by Temple Mills depot then was turned out in the Izy livery of white with a lime green window band and front end plus purple doors.

The unit went into service with Izy from 9 December 2018 and operates one return trip Brussels Midi–Paris Nord–Brussels Midi on Mondays to Thursdays and Saturdays, and two return trips on Fridays and Sundays, albeit to different timings. The trains operate from Brussels Midi over the LGV Belge and LGV Nord high speed line as far as Bifurcation d'Arras, then over the conventional line from there, via Arras, Longueau (near Amiens), and Creil to Paris Nord. This reduces track usage charges but still allows a Brussels–Paris timing of about 2¼ hours on most trains, compared with 1h25 by Thalys trains using the LGV Nord high speed line throughout.

Despite there being sufficient time to maintain the single set on weekdays, the hybrid set failed in January 2019 and had to be replaced with a standard e300 set. So in some cases, passengers who had paid only €16 from Brussels to Paris or return were treated to a refurbished e300 set.

Soldiering on

In autumn 2018 it was understood that Eurostar would withdraw the remaining half

Above: Soon after leaving the high speed line, Izy set 3224/3213 passes Boisleux, south of Arras, with train 9606 15.41 Brussels Midi–Paris Nord on 5 September 2019.

Below: On 22 April 2019 the Izy set traverses Fresnes-les-Montauban, just before leaving the LGV, with train 9602 10.28 Brussels Midi–Paris Nord. *David Haydock (2)*

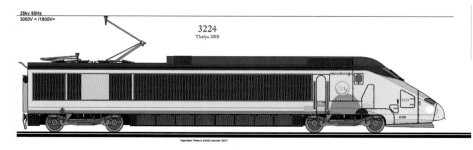

25kv 50Hz
3000V = /1500V=

3224
Thalys 2018

Copyright Thierry LELEU Janvier 2017

sets 3214 and 3223 following the formation of the Izy set, but instead they were paired and returned to service. It was also stated that the other two non-refurbished sets, 3215/6 and 3217/8, would be withdrawn by spring 2019 by which time the last two e300 sets to be refurbished would be outshopped from Hellemmes works. However, this did not take place. In February 2019, a period of wintry weather (although not particularly severe) knocked out up to eight e320 sets on some days, due to damage to windows (cracks) and under-body safety equipment. Eurostar was forced to cancel some services every day due to a shortage of trains and disruption continued until the end of March. These problems led Eurostar to stop the scrapping programme and retain the three non-refurbished sets mentioned above. 3215/6 and 3217/8 were taken out of use in 2019 but were not immediately scrapped.

25 years on

In February 2020, the Eurostar fleet consisted of the following sets:
- e300 (refurbished, all equipped for 1500 V DC): 3007/8, 3015/16, 3205/6, 3209/10, 3211/12*, 3219/20, 3221/22, 3229/30, spare power car 3999. All nameplates have been removed.
- e300 (non-refurbished): 3213/24, on hire to Thalys for Izy services, 3214/23.
- e320 (17): 4001/2 to 4033/34
* formed during refurbishment of power cars 3211/12 plus the trailers from 3203/4
A few "Three Capitals" sets were still stored, awaiting scrapping.

Above: Names and other plates removed from Eurostars, some still in service, at Temple Mills depot. *DAH Collection*

In early 2020, North of London sets 3301/2, 3305/6, 3309/10 and 3311/12 were still stored at a former army base at Ambronay, near Ambérieu, east of Lyon or had been moved to Culoz for scrapping. 3303/7 and 3313/14 (the world record holder) plus 3304 went for scrap in July 2019. 3314 was later saved for preservation.

Power car 3308 is preserved at the National Railway Museum in York. It is thought that the trailers from half set 3308 are still at Temple Mills depot. Also preserved are power cars 3101 in Doncaster and 3102 in Birmingham, both at High Speed Rail Colleges. Power car 3106, together with inner end first class trailer 373 3106 9 from the same set, are earmarked for the Train World museum at Schaarbeek near Brussels, but initially stored at Brugge in Belgium. These were chosen as the King of Belgium rode on set 3105/6 during the inaugural run from Brussels to London. The Cité du Train in Mulhouse chose power car 3208 to preserve but it was in too poor a state so another one was being sought in 2019. Finally, for now, 3304 has been preserved at the Hornby Musuem in Ramsgate.

Below: Non-refurbished set 3217/8 slows for the Tunnel on the approach to Calais Fréthun station on 3 September 2019 with train 9043 16.13 Paris Nord–St Pancras. *David Haydock*

CLASS 92:
POWER IN EXCESS

by David Haydock and Chris Booth

46 powerful Class 92 Co-Co electric locomotives were built to haul freight through the Channel but also to power these trains from the Tunnel along the main routes in the UK as well as Nightstar overnight trains from UK cities to Brussels and Paris as far as Calais. Things worked out very differently. 25 years on a very small proportion haul trains through the Tunnel while the rest power a few freights and sleeper trains in the UK, a significant number operate in Eastern Europe and the rest are just in store.

92 019 is seen at Elvanfoot, between Abington and Beattock summit, with 6V15 car empties from Mossend to Didcot on 3 June 2011. **Robin Ralston**

When the Channel Tunnel was being planned around half the capacity was expected to be used by Shuttle trains carrying cars, coaches and lorries between the Folkestone and Calais terminals, while the rest of the capacity would be shared between:

- Eurostar high speed services between London and Paris/Brussels
- European Night Services (later branded Nightstar) overnight passenger services
- through conventional freight trains between parts of the UK and the rest of Europe

Both the latter categories of train would be loco-hauled, and the locomotives which took the trains through the Tunnel would need to be specially equipped. They would need to be able to operate off the Tunnel's 25 kV AC 50 Hz overhead electrification system (with higher-than-normal wires to allow the very high Shuttle trains to pass under), to be equipped with TVM 430 cab signalling (there is no conventional signalling in the Tunnel) and be equipped for the Tunnel's strict fire prevention standards (Halon fire extinguishers). They would also have to be able to haul heavy loads over the 1.1% (1 in 91) gradients, and restart those trains from a standstill, even in degraded mode. 25 kV AC would also be needed for operation in the UK north of London and to Calais in northern France and the locos

Above: 92003 (left) and 92004 (right) in the main erecting shop Brush Traction, Loughborough on 18 August 1993. 92004 was being transported from one shop to another within the works by road vehicle.

Below left: 92004's body being moved by crane at Brush Traction, Loughborough on the same date.

Below: On 10 December 1993, body shells of 92010, 92012 and 92011 (left to right) inside the main fitting out bay at Brush Loughborough. In the background further Class 92s and Eurotunnel Shuttle locos can be seen. *Colin J Marsden (3)*

would be equipped with the British AWS (Automatic Warning System) safety system.

At an early stage both the British and French operators (British Rail and SNCF at the time) rejected the idea of changing locomotives at both ends of the Tunnel. It was also decided to order a single design, with locomotives operating in a single pool. It had been calculated that 18 locos would be needed just to shuttle freight and night trains through the Tunnel, as double-heading would be needed for most trains.

The locos would have to, at least, be able to operate through the Tunnel itself and continue to/from the London area (almost all forecast traffic would pass that way) over the existing 750 V DC third rail-electrified line via Ashford and Tonbridge, and to cope with even steeper gradients, of up to 2% (1 in 50), even when the voltage fell as low as 625 Volts as it does sometimes. This capability would also be needed for a promised high speed line, with freight capacity, between the Tunnel and London, which would have some 2.5% (1 in 40) gradients.

SNCF had considered adapting its latest standard electric locomotive, the Class BB 26000 "Sybic" built by GEC-Alsthom, for the Tunnel. These are 200 km/h dual-voltage (1500 V DC/ 25 kV AC) B-B "universal" locomotives which can operate almost anywhere in France and were already hauling trains all the way across France from the Lille area to the Italian border, for example. However the fact that the SNCF

contribution would only be nine locomotives (half the 18 needed for the Tunnel itself), and the complexity of adapting an existing design, led SNCF to decide to throw its lot into a joint order.

In the end, with the British in the driving seat, it was decided that a powerful Co-Co design was necessary to provide enough power and adhesion for the expected traffic. The partnership with SNCF allowed the order to be more substantial, thus spreading the cost of designing a very specialist locomotive. The final number ordered was 46: the nine needed to shuttle freights through the Tunnel to be owned by SNCF, seven for European Passenger Services (EPS) which would operate Nightstar services, and the other 30 for British Rail's Railfreight Distribution (RfD) freight activity in the UK which covered less-than-trainload services including traffic to the continent. The 30 locos would be able to cover the Tunnel itself, the section to London, and then the various routes to the north of England and Scotland.

The order was put out to tender and was won by Brush/ABB (ASEA Brown Boveri), which beat off competitor GEC-Alsthom. One of the factors taken into account by the buyers was ABB's experience with asynchronous three-phase traction in tunnels in Switzerland. Brush was in favour with British Rail, having just supplied 100 powerful Class 60 Co-Co diesels. The first order, for 20 Class 92 locos, was placed as

Class 92

Technical details

Built: 1993–1996 by Brush Traction, Loughborough.
Length: 21.34 metres.
Width: 2.67 metres.
Weight: 126 tonnes.
Wheel diameter (new): 1070 mm.
Design speed: 140 km/h.
Maximum speed: 145 km/h (90 mph)
Electrical supply system: 25 kV AC 50 Hz overhead and 750 V DC third rail.
Traction motors: Six ABB Type 6FRA 7059B asynchronous three-phase.
Maximum tractive effort: 400 kN.
Continuous tractive effort: 360 kN.
Continuous power rating: 5040 kW under 25 kV AC; 4000 kW from 750 V DC.
Wheel arrangement: Co-Co

early as 22 July 1990, then was followed by further orders for ten, seven (for EPS) then nine (for SNCF). The 46 locomotives cost a total of £138 million or exactly £3 million each. This would be almost £6 million in today's money, or €6.5 million. Modern multi-voltage locomotives such as Siemens' *Vectron* or Bombardier's *TRAXX*, both produced in large numbers, cost between €3 and €5 million each, depending on how complex their equipment is.

The locomotives were assembled by Brush Traction in Loughborough, north of Leicester. The welded steel loco bodies were first built by Procor (later Bombardier Prorail) at Horbury, south of Leeds, and supplied by road already painted to Loughborough.

Below: The bodyshell of 92006 is being fitted out at Brush Traction on 13 December 1993. *Colin J Marsden*

A good side view of 92031 at Tonbridge on 12 October 1997 showing clearly the third rail shoes of which there were three on each side of each bogie. *Chris Wilson*

Horbury had already supplied bodies for Class 60, but the bodies for the new "European" locomotives had greater crash resistance (70 tonnes – to SNCF standards) and additional lifting points (at the ends) in case of derailment in the Tunnel. Most electrical components came from ABB in Zürich, Switzerland.

The bogies were derived from those under Class 60 although they needed to be lengthened, partly to allow the addition of third rail shoes, of which there are one on each side per axle. These could be retracted when a loco is operating under 25 kV – they are raised by springs and held down by compressed air. The automatic sanders are automatically shut off in the Tunnel. The Class 92 has the usual (Westinghouse) air brakes but also rheostatic brakes, which operate by turning braking energy into dissipated heat, and regenerative brakes which work by "reversing" traction motors so braking energy is fed back as electricity into the overhead system.

Traction motors are nose-suspended, which was possible due to the relatively low maximum speed of 140 km/h. The whole ABB traction chain is very similar to that used for the Eurotunnel Shuttle locomotives which were also built by Brush Traction. This was in turn derived from equipment installed in Austrian Railways (ÖBB) Class 1822, built for work on the mountainous Brenner route. The main transformer supplies one motor block for each bogie. The cooling system is oil-based, like that in Swiss Railways (SBB) Class Re 460. Most of the electrical systems are duplicated to avoid the risk of failure in the Tunnel which has become one of the busiest stretches of railway in the world.

It was specified that a single Class 92 would be able to haul 1600 tonnes on 750 V DC between the Tunnel and Redhill (and under 25 kV AC over Beattock summit – 1 in 75 – in Scotland), but only 1100 tonnes in the Tunnel itself under 25 kV AC. All trains would be double-headed however, allowing up to 2200 tonnes; one Class 92 needed to be able to haul the whole 2200 tonnes out of the Tunnel if the other failed.

On the roof are two pantographs, specified by Eurotunnel, although only one would have sufficed in other circumstances. The system for multiple operation uses time division multiplex (tdm). In addition to the conventional operation of two locos in multiple at the front of a freight train, it was planned that on Nightstar trains, which were expected to reach 16 coaches, or 800 tonnes, there would be one Class 92 at each end, each with a driver – the Nightstar coaches would be wired for tdm throughout.

As with all the traction and rolling stock used in the Tunnel, fire suppression systems are extensive. The interior of a Class 92 is divided into three compartments separated by bulkheads capable of resisting fire for 30 minutes. Those at the extremities each contain a motor block while the one in the middle houses braking equipment, control systems, TVM 430 cab signalling and the train-to-shore radio. Each compartment has its own extinguishing system.

The locos would be maintained entirely at Crewe International Electric Maintenance Depot (IEMD) in north-west England, around 400 km from the Tunnel; SNCF would monitor its nine locomotives from Hellemmes, near Lille, SNCF's nearest workshops to the Tunnel. However, SNCF

Opposite: Trials with 92003 took place on the Verberie–Ormoy-Villers freight-only line in early June 1994 as a section of the line was equipped with TVM 430 cab signalling. 92003 hauled a test coach and SNCF electric locomotive BB 16771 brought up the rear. This combination is seen at Ormoy-Villers (above) and on the freight line from Verberie (below). *David Haydock (2)*

would not be involved in maintenance at any level – if a Class 92 broke down in France it would be repatriated to Crewe for attention. It was originally intended that Eurostar's depot at North Pole could carry out minor exams but this never took place.

Despite being owned by three companies and intended for different types of services, all Class 92 were originally outshopped in RfD's livery of two-tone grey with "British" yellow front ends and a red line at roof level to warn of overhead electrification. The locos also carried three "Tunnel" circles in relief on the sides and the BR double arrows (RfD and EPS) or SNCF symbol at one end and a diamond-shaped plate with an eagle, a symbol of Crewe depot, at the other. All of the locos were named, most of them after authors and composers.

The first loco, 92001, was completed in August 1993. After undergoing static tests at Loughborough 92001 and 92002 were moved by rail and sea in February 1994 to Velim test circuit in the Czech Republic. 92002 then continued its journey to the famous Wien Arsenal centre where the loco underwent climatic tests. Both returned from Velim in August 1995. 92003

Operations further into France?

Class 92 were initially intended to operate no further east than Calais Fréthun with freight trains and as far as Calais Ville with Nightstar trains, thanks to installation of the British AWS system in France as far as Calais Ville. Installation never took place after plans for Nightstar services were dropped completely.

However, over the years there were several proposals to use surplus Class 92s operating further into France. In early 1998 EWS chief Ed Burkhardt told SNCF he would like to see Class 92 operating from Wembley through to the Lille area in order to improve loco and driver productivity, with a single "freight corridor" between London and Lille. However, the French unions were always reluctant to accept Class 92 as the design still did not meet SNCF crashworthiness standards. Nothing came of this plan, and as wagonload traffic was rationalised by SNCF, and intermodal traffic becoming the "future" for the Channel Tunnel, the new container terminal which opened at Dourges, south of Lille, in 2003, was the target destination. It would have been out of the question to install the GB system over the 120 km or so to Lille or Dourges, so the engineers looked into the installation of the French KVB system on board Class 92. Unfortunately, after several attempts to find the space necessary (Europorte had another try in 2011), the idea was dropped – fitting a great deal of traction and signalling equipment into Class 92 had left no space for KVB.

Europorte even considered fitting its surplus locos with a large diesel engine for use by GB Railfreight in Britain. Certainly a GM-EMD engine for John Smith!

Right: 92030 "Ashford" was the first Class 92 to be used to haul an enthusiast's special train and is seen here on the Otford loop on 12 July 1997 with the "Dungeness Pebbledasher" which would continue onto non-electrified lines with 37688 in EWS livery. *Chris Wilson*

Centre right: An unidentified Class 92 is seen with SNCF loco BB 22295 at Calais Fréthun stabling point in 1995. *David Haydock*

Below right: All line drawings in this book are the work of *Thierry Leleu.*

"Beethoven" was handed over to RfD on 15 March 1994 then was moved to France on 1 June 1994 for tests at Calais Rivière Neuve yard (now Calais Fréthun). On 2 June the loco moved on to the old station at Orrouy-Glaignes on the Ormoy-Villers–Verberie line, a freight-only route between the Paris–Creil–Compiègne line and the Paris–Laon lines. A 10 km section of the northbound track on this line, electrified at 25 kV AC, had been equipped to test TVM 430 cab signalling. Later in June 1994 the loco was joined by SNCF-owned 92006 for trials in multiple. After successful tests they returned to the UK on 9 September.

Soon after delivery 92004 was used to test operation on the third rail supply on the Shepperton branch near London then was tested under 25 kV AC on the London–Glasgow West Coast Main Line (WCML) in early September 1994.

Optimistic traffic forecasts

The construction of the Channel Tunnel was based on forecasts of traffic which turned out to be very optimistic. It was expected that within ten years Eurostar would be carrying 15 million passengers (in 2019 the figure reached 11 million), that there would be five daily (or nightly) sleeper trains and that through freight traffic would rapidly reach 5 million tonnes. The latter figure looked achievable when traffic reached 3 million tonnes by 1999, only five years after the Tunnel opened. However, that was the best year and from then on a combination of two migrant crises, the abandonment of wagonload traffic in the UK and poor service quality on the continent meant that traffic is only about 1.3 million tonnes at present – the same as carried on the Nord-Pas-de-Calais ferry just before the Tunnel opened. The Nightstar trains were abandoned before they started. It is therefore the case that no more than half a dozen Class 92s are needed for Channel Tunnel traffic, and these only during the night.

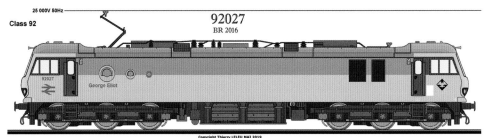

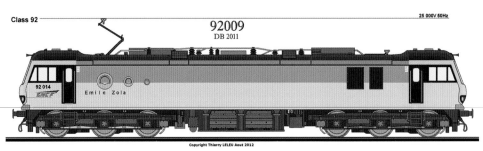

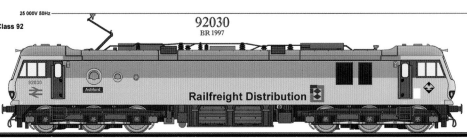

N°.	Original Name	Owner Original	From 1997	From 2007	From 2011	From 2014	Moved Abroad	Livery	New EVN number	New Name
92001	(Victor Hugo)	RfD	EWS	DB		DB	RO 2013		91 53 0 472 002-1	Mircea Eliade
92002	(H. G. Wells)	RfD	EWS	DB		DB	RO 2015		91 53 0 472 003-9	Lucian Blaga
92003	Beethoven	RfD	EWS	DB		DB	RO 2017		91 53 0 472 007-	
92004	Jane Austen	RfD	EWS	DB		DB (S)		EG		
92005	(Mozart)	RfD	EWS	DB		DB	RO 2015		91 53 0 472 005-4	Emil Cioran
92006	(Louis Armand)	SNCF			Europorte	GBRf d		CA		
92007	Schubert	RfD	EWS	DB		DB (S)		EG		
92008	Jules Verne	RfD	EWS	DB		DB (S)		EG		
92009	(Elgar)	RfD	EWS	DB		DB h (S)		DB		Marco Polo
92010	(Molière)	SNCF			Europorte	GBRf d h		CA		
92011	Handel	RfD	EWS	DB		DB h		EG		
92012	(Thomas Hardy)	RfD	EWS	DB		DB	RO 2013		91 53 0 472 001-3	Mihai Eminescu
92013	Puccini	RfD	EWS	DB		DB (S)		EG		
92014	(Emile Zola)	SNCF			Europorte	GBRf d		CA		
92015	(D. H. Lawrence)	RfD	EWS	DB		DB h		DB		
92016	(Brahms)	RfD	EWS	DB		DB h (S)		DB		
92017	(Shakespeare)	RfD	EWS	DB		DB (S)		AL		Bart the Engine
92018	Stendhal	SNCF			Europorte	GBRf d h		CA		
92019	(Wagner)	RfD	EWS	DB		DB h		EG		
92020	(Milton)	Eurostar		Europorte		GBRf (d)		GB		
92021	Purcell	Eurostar		Europorte		GBRf (S)		EP		
92022	Charles Dickens	RfD	EWS	DB		DB	BG 2017			
92023	(Ravel)	SNCF			Europorte	GBRf d h		CA		
92024	(J. S. Bach)	RfD	EWS	DB		DB	RO 2015		91 53 0 472 004-7	Marin Preda
92025	Oscar Wilde	RfD	EWS	DB		DB	BG 2012		91 52 1 688 025-1	
92026	Britten	RfD	EWS	DB		DB	RO 2017		91 53 0 472 008-8	
92027	George Eliot	RfD	EWS	DB		DB	BG 2012		91 52 1 688 027-7	
92028	(Saint Saens)	SNCF	SNCF		Europorte	GBRf d		GB		
92029	Dante	RfD	EWS	DB		DB (S)		EG		
92030	(De Falla)	RfD	EWS	DB		DB	BG 2015		91 52 1 688 030-1	Ashford
92031	(Schiller)	RfD	EWS	DB		DB h (S)		DB		*
92032	(César Franck)	Eurostar		Europorte		GBRf d h		GB		§
92033	(Berlioz)	SNCF			Europorte	GBRf d		CA		
92034	Kipling	RfD	EWS	DB		DB	BG 2012		91 52 1 688 034-3	
92035	Mendelssohn	RfD	EWS	DB		DB (S)		EG		
92036	Bertolt Brecht	RfD	EWS	DB		DB h		EG		
92037	Sullivan	RfD	EWS	DB		DB (S)		EG		
92038	(Voltaire)	SNCF			Europorte	GBRF d h		CA		
92039	(Johann Strauss)	RfD	EWS	DB		DB	RO 2015		91 53 0 472 006-2	Eugen Ionescu
92040	Goethe	Eurostar		Europorte		GBRf (S)		EP		
92041	Vaughan Williams	RfD	EWS	DB		DB h (S)		EG		
92042	(Honegger)	RfD	EWS	DB		DB h		DB		
92043	(Debussy)	SNCF			Europorte	GBRf d h		GB		
92044	Couperin	Eurostar		Europorte		GBRf h		EP		
92045	Chaucer	Eurostar		Europorte		GBRf (S)		EP		
92046	Sweelinck	Eurostar		Europorte		GBRf (S)		EP		

Names in brackets are removed or replaced.
* (The Institute of Logistics and Transport)
§ IMechE Railway Division
d: Equipped with Dellner couplers for Caledonian Sleeper.
h: Equipped with software for TVM 430 used on HS1.
(s): Stored DB: DB Schenker, later DB Cargo
BG: Bulgaria.
EWS: English Welsh & Scottish Railway
GBRf: GB Railfreight
RfD: Railfreight Distribution (British Rail)
RO: Romania.
SNCF: French National Railways

Livery codes:
AL: Advertising livery.
CA: Caledonian Sleeper "Midnight Teal" dark blue with yellow ends.
DB: DB Cargo red with grey roof and solebar.
EG: EWS grey: two-tone grey with black cab doors and window surrounds plus EWS logos.
EP: European Passenger Services: two-tone grey with dark blue roof.
GB: GB Railfreight blue with orange cantrail and solebar, stripes and cabs.

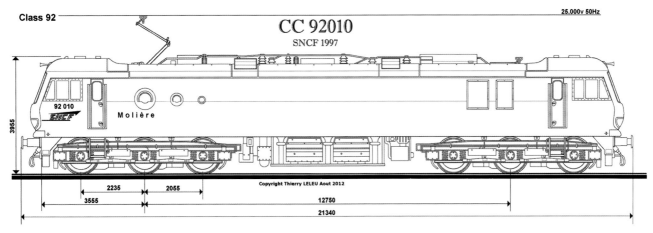

Class 92

CC 92010

SNCF 1997

25.000v 50Hz

92 010 SNCF Molière

3955

2235 | 2055
3555
12750
21340

Copyright Thierry LELEU Aout 2012

A **DIFFICULT** START

A first year without Class 92

Class 92 were intended to be introduced in 1995 but the Channel Tunnel opened to traffic in June 1994. The first revenue freight would be a train of Rover cars from Washwood Heath (Birmingham) to Arluno, near Milano in Italy. In order to cope with through freight traffic from the very first day, it was decided to use SNCF's Class BB 22200. These operated until 13 October 1995. Class 92 were also not able to start work in the UK, due to signalling interference problems, so Railfreight Distribution was forced to create a pool of 14 Class 47 Co-Co diesels which would work freights in multiple.

Tests continued with Class 92, with full traction trials on the WCML in November/ December 1994 and the first tests in the Tunnel with a loco at each end of the train from 12 December. Although regular freights would have both Class 92s in multiple on the front end, Channel Tunnel safety rules for passenger trains were that there would be one locomotive at each end so that, in the event of a problem (particularly a fire) a Nightstar train could be driven out of the Tunnel, away from the incident, with just one loco if necessary. Early tests involved an 1150 tonne intermodal train with a single loco, then the weight was raised to 1300 tonnes. All tracks including crossovers were tested for clearances.

The first loco to be received by European Passenger Services (EPS) was 92020, on 1 February 1995. The first locos to be used in revenue service were 92018 to 92023, approval having been obtained on 9 February 1995. After tests with light engines through the Tunnel, the first revenue operation was with 92021 and 92022 from Dollands Moor to Fréthun on 17 February. The first diagrams, for four locos, were for them operating top-and-tail rather than in multiple. From 17 July 1995, operation with a single Class 92 at the head of a train was authorised.

Operation from the Tunnel to London and beyond

Class 92 was designed to operate not only through the Channel Tunnel itself, but also over 750 V DC third rail lines through Kent from Dollands Moor yard to Kensington Olympia, then over the 25 kV AC network north of London, in particular to Birmingham, Manchester, Glasgow and Edinburgh on Nightstar services and freight. The main problem with this – as with Eurostar sets – was operation on third rail lines. Both Class 92 and Eurostar sets drew very high currents – in order to reach their 5000 kW rating, Class 92 needed to draw 6800 Amps! Power supplies on the route therefore had to be reinforced.

Above: 92022 and a second member of the class emerge from the Channel Tunnel into the Beussingues cutting in France with a mixed freight on 4 October 1996.

However, problems could arise where there are (frequent) gaps in the third rail, such as at level crossings, points, junctions and where the third rail changes sides. When a collector shoe dropped off the third rail or if arcing occurred, electrical "spikes" were generated, giving a wide range of frequencies and harmonics which could interfere with track circuits, leading to false signal aspects, possibly over a wide area.

A solution to these problems was needed not only by immunising track circuits from stray currents, but also work on the locomotives themselves. Class 92 were equipped with an Interference Current Monitoring Unit (ICMU) designed to stop the loco's electrical equipment from being damaged by erratic currents at dangerous frequencies, and even shutting the loco down if necessary. The ICMU therefore needed a great number of adjustments following multiple test runs. If the loco encountered too many gaps in quick succession, the software could shut it down. It was reported at the time that there were around 50 locations in the Wandsworth area of south London where this was the case.

The late delivery of Class 92 and the time taken for tests and modification to the classic line meant that Railfreight Distribution had to start services with pairs of Class 47 diesels and it was only on the night of 20 March 1995 that Class 92 was allowed into revenue service, initially only between 20.30 and 07.00. The first train was hauled by 92013, with 47258 and 47293 as back-up. Regular operations started in July 1995 with two daily return workings between Dollands Moor and Willesden. Software initially limited current draw to 4000 Amps, lifted to 6800 Amps in January 1997. Initially only 92001, 92011 to 92013, 92015 and 92039 were cleared for DC operation. The class entered "squadron service" between Dollands Moor and Wembley in December 1997 after receiving their safety certificate for Dollands Moor–London via Maidstone on 24 November.

Clearly, the decision not to build a new high speed line from London at the same time as construction of the Tunnel itself, or re-electrification of the classic line at 25 kV AC overhead, meant a great deal of investment in the classic line had to be made anyway for a rather sub-standard result.

Above: 92003 "Beethoven" is seen at Dollands Moor on 21 November 1997 carrying a frontal plate showing the British Rail symbol and 1948–1997, commemorating the end of BR following privatisation.

Below: 92010 is more than ample power for a single covered van, seen operating off the third rail at Westwell in Kent on 24 October 1996. *Chris Wilson (3)*

REPLACEMENTS FOR **LATECOMERS**

The Channel Tunnel opened to freight traffic in mid 1994 but it was clear that the first of the 46 Class 92 Co-Cos being built for the Tunnel would not be ready in time. In September 1992 Brits were able to marvel at the sight of SNCF electric loco BB 22317 on show in Birmingham at an exhibition about the potential for international rail freight traffic. Few could have imagined that the class would be running into Kent two years later, as a stopgap until Class 92s arrived! The locos chosen were 22379 and 22380 plus the last seven of the class – 22399 to 22405. All were equipped specially by SNCF's Oullins (Lyon) works for use through the tunnel – with TVM 430 cab signalling, cable sockets for use in multiple, anti fire barriers, improved wheelslip prevention, the ATESS safety recording system, cab air conditioning and UK-specified yellow ends! These earned them the nickname *"yellow submachines"*. They also had to be operated with sandboxes and wheel greasers out of action to avoid polluting the Tunnel and had their mini snowploughs removed.

In order to avoid equipping all locos with TVM 430 equipment and cab air conditioning, leading locos would be identified as TTU (*Transmanche TVM 430 Unité Multiple*: 22379, 22380, 22399, 22401, 22403, 22405) and trailing locos TU (22400, 22402 and 22404). This meant leading locos needed to run round at each end of the Tunnel. In order to check that they could cope with the gradients in the Tunnel, 22399 and 22400 were tested with a 1545 tonne freight over a line with 1.5% gradients in the Alps. Tests were also carried out on the LGV Nord in February 1994 then revenue services began on 1 June 1994.

Left: SNCF BB 22400 TU and 22399 TTU are seen at La Délivrance (Lille) stabling point on 28 September 1993 during driver training.

Right: An unmodified SNCF BB 22242 is seen in the Eurotunnel Coquelles terminal in December 1993 during tests with Passenger Shuttle stock. SNCF locos were used due to the late arrival of Eurotunnel's Bo-Bo-Bo locos. *David Haydock (2)*

The locos only remained in service through the Tunnel for just over a year but SNCF took advantage of those equipped with cab signalling. Once back at Dijon depot all of the TTU locos were equipped with 200 km/h bogies from the BB 22351–22356 batch and the locos were allocated to inspection duties on high speed lines. Then from October 1997 the locos were used to launch a new 200 km/h overnight freight service carrying parcels from Paris Chevaleret to Orange and to Toulouse via Bordeaux. Both of these trains ran over high speed lines. They still power

Below left: A pair of SNCF BB 22200s are seen at Cheriton, about to enter the Tunnel. On the left is the M20 motorway while Eurotunnel's Cheriton depot is visible and the Shuttle terminal is mostly off camera on the right.

Below: BB 22405 (withdrawn in 2019) and another BB 22200 leave the Channel Tunnel at Beussingue cutting with the Dagenham–Silla Ford train in late 1994. *Chris Wilson (2)*

inspection trains, having been allocated to SNCF Infra and all are now in that activity's yellow livery, 22401 and 22405 having been withdrawn in 2019. As for 22400, 22402 and 22404, they were all equipped for push-pull operation and now operate TER services around Lyon and Marseille.

A less well-known episode in the life of this class was the hire of unmodified locos 22242, 22286, 22396, 22397 and 22398

to Eurotunnel, which used them for work around the terminal at Coquelles before the first Shuttle locos were delivered. At one point, in early 1993, it was expected that between nine and 12 BB 22200 would be modified to stand in for Eurotunnel's Shuttle locos which were late. 22297, 22383, 22384, 22386, 22389 and 22394 were modified but in the end Eurotunnel put back the opening date instead.

EWS TAKES OVER

Above: 92001, the first in EWS livery, heads a train of cars at Cow Roast, near Tring, on 8 September 2006. *Chris Wilson*

No sooner had Class 92 entered service in 1997 than privatisation of British Rail's freight operations saw English Welsh and Scottish Railway (EWS) take over Railfreight Distribution, and with it 30 Class 92 locos. 92003 actually hauled the very last British Rail train, a Dollands Moor–Wembley on 21 November (see photo).

Run by no-nonsense American railroader Ed Burkhardt, EWS was sceptical of the need for Class 92, having ordered ultra-reliable Class 66 diesels to replace most of the inherited diesel fleet which the Americans considered highly inferior. There were even jokes at the time about turning Class 92 bodies into henhouses!

EWS became frustrated with delays to approval for Class 92 over the West Coast Main Line (WCML) but test running was eventually permitted from Crewe to Mossend, near Glasgow, in April 1998, after modifications to their AC power equipment. Revenue-earning services started on 11 May 1998, with 92037 hauling

a Mossend–Bescot (Birmingham) non-Channel Tunnel service.

In June 1999 Class 92 were authorised to work over the East Coast Main Line (ECML) from Edinburgh and Glasgow south to Doncaster, while on the WCML, authorisation to operate between Crewe and London came as late as August 1999. Class 92 then quickly started to take over services between Wembley and Scotland and were able to show off their power over the steep gradients at Shap and Beattock. Seeing the superior performance over the WCML EWS was now less sceptical and used Class 92 to replace older electric classes, including the relatively recent Class 90.

Nightstar abandoned

The success of Class 92 over the WCML was good news as abandonment of Nightstar had made the nine Class 92s owned by EPS surplus to requirements and freight traffic through the Channel Tunnel was still

not building up at a rate which would see Class 92 anything like fully employed.

Nightstar (see separate chapter) was the project to operate luxury overnight trains of up to 16 coaches from Glasgow, Edinburgh, Manchester, Bristol and Cardiff to Brussels and Paris plus from London to destinations beyond Paris in France and beyond Brussels in Germany. Trains would need to be topped-and-tailed by Class 92 through the Channel Tunnel as far as Calais Ville. Nightstar would be operated by the same company as Eurostar: European Passenger Services (EPS), later to become Eurostar (UK).

However, after several studies it was decided that Nightstar would never make a profit and on 9 July 1997 London & Continental Railways announced abandonment of the project. Eurostar UK initially advertised its seven locos for hire, then tried to sell them in summer 2000, but with a surplus of Class 92s in service, no-one was interested. They were therefore stored at their Crewe base depot.

Below: 92001, the first in EWS livery, stands beside 92036 and 92028 at Dollands Moor on 1 June 1999, with a plaque celebrating five years of freight trains through the Tunnel. 92001's train was carrying Rover cars from Washwood Heath to Brescia in Italy. *David Haydock*

Above: 92012, carrying an EWS "Beastie" sticker, passes through Kensington Olympia on 17 October 2009 with 4E32 Scunthorpe–Dollands Moor carrying steel slabs to Hayange in France. *Chris Wilson*

25 000V 50Hz

Class 92

92012
EWS 2009

92012
Thomas Hardy
EWS

Copyright Thierry LELEU MAI 2019

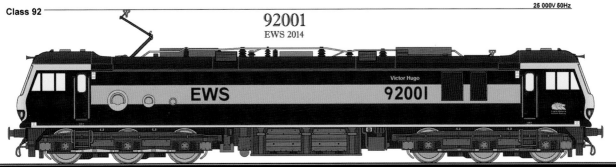

Class 92

25 000V 50Hz

92001
EWS 2014

Victor Hugo
EWS 92001

Copyright Thierry LELEU Mai 2019

EUROTUNNEL BRANCHES OUT

Above: Europorte 92028 is seen under overhaul, lifted off its bogies, at Eurotunnel's Coquelles depot near Calais on 27 February 2014. By this time GB Railfreight had officially taken over management of the fleet.

After almost a decade operating its Shuttle services, Eurotunnel started to expand its activities, partly due to dissatisfaction with the level of freight traffic passing through the Tunnel. After initially rising to over 3 million tonnes a year in 1999, and looking well on the way to the forecast 5 million tonnes a year, traffic had fallen back to 1.46 million tonnes by 2002. Apart from the first migrant crisis, which brought about a fall in traffic of 40%, reliability of freight trains in France was poor, EWS did not seem very interested in Channel Tunnel freight and wagonload services were gradually disappearing. In both the UK and France, open access freight operation was becoming a reality, and in 2003 Eurotunnel founded the subsidiary Europorte 2 and applied to the French Transport Ministry for an operating licence with a view to open access operation. After talking to customers the aim was to introduce a direct service from "northern France to northern England".

Europorte 2 then became the first company to receive a licence to operate open access freights in France – in February 2004. In announcing this Eurotunnel said

it would launch a five-days-a-week service between Britain and Basel, Switzerland, via Metz in France from early 2005, with connections from Metz to Mannheim and München, and Basel to Milano and that it could be operating 30 trains a week by 2008. The company also announced its intention of building an intermodal terminal at Folkestone, known as FIRST (Folkestone International Rail Services Terminal), to be in service by 2005 and with a capacity of four trains a day. However, none of this came to pass immediately and it was not until November 2007 that Europorte 2 started operations.

Europorte takes over Class 92s

Meanwhile, as cooperation between nationalised railways BR and SNCF evaporated with privatisation, EWS and SNCF had separate Class 92 operations through the Channel Tunnel. In early 2006 SNCF decided that it would no longer operate its own locos through the Tunnel and in February and April of that year sent all of its nine locos to Crewe depot for storage. With the seven Eurostar locos that made 16 Class 92s in store – 35% of the class.

A year later, in February 2007, Eurotunnel purchased five of the stored Eurostar locos. 92020, 92021, 92032, 92040 and 92044 were chosen and were dispatched for overhaul by Brush Traction. The company then purchased the other two Eurostar locos, 92045 and 92046, in October 2007.

In June 2007 Eurotunnel announced the launch of a direct freight service between the container port in Dunkerque and the UK but this never started. A more concrete plan emerged in late 2007 when Eurotunnel proposed to manage operation of four of SNCF's Class 92s with Eurotunnel drivers to streamline Tunnel operations. This would allow the cost of a freight train passing through the Tunnel to be cut from €8000 to €5000. In January 2009 this deal was sealed with the transfer of 92010, 92028, 92038 and 92043 from SNCF to Eurotunnel.

Eurotunnel was clearly manoeuvring to move into the rail freight industry – in 2009 the company also purchased the French operations (SNCF took over those outside France) of Veolia Cargo and the company was renamed Europorte France. But by this time Eurotunnel was no longer talking of operating between the UK and

Left: 92023 "Ravel" was one of the few Class 92s which receive a nameplate instead of the usual transfers on the bodyside. It is seen on the same date, still with SNCF markings but having passed to Europorte 2 then to GB Railfreight. *David Haydock (2)*

Below: The Europorte 2 logo on a Class 92.

the continent. The operations with Class 92 through the Tunnel remained, and were managed by subsidiary Europorte Channel.

Europorte Channel then bought the remaining five SNCF Class 92 locos – 92006, 92014, 92018, 92023 and 92033 – in July 2011, taking its fleet to 16 locos. By this time the Eurotunnel group had also bought GB Railfreight (see below) and 92032 was turned out in GBRf orange and blue livery in March 2011. Under Eurotunnel ownership GBRf

expanded quickly and constantly needed additional locomotives. Europorte Channel had a considerable surplus of Class 92s for Tunnel services so where possible, GBRf freed up Class 66 diesels by replacing them "under the wires" with Class 92.

Eventually GBRf took over the whole Europorte Class 92 fleet and then officially purchased them in 2014 (see below).

Below: On 23 October 2010, a year after being transferred from SNCF to Europorte 2, 92010 is seen outside Coquelles depot. This view shows the third rail pick-up shoes on the bogies well. *Keith Fender*

DB SCHENKER BUYS EWS

DB Cargo 92 017 in Stobart Rail livery is caught at Wandel (between Carstairs and Abington) with 4M48 'Tescoliner' from Mossend to Daventry on 29 June 2010.
Robin Ralston

Left: 92 016 is seen at Craigenhill (between Carstairs and Carluke) on the 6S51 infrastructure service from Carlisle to Mossend on 11 October 2011. *Robin Ralston*

Right: DB Schenker 92015 passes through Kensington Olympia on 10 March 2012 with the Scunthorpe–Ebange steel slabs. *Chris Wilson*

In December 2003 EWS and SNCF put all of their 37 Class 92s into a common pool which meant that all of them were cleared to work from Calais Fréthun to Glasgow. Previously 14 locos in the WTWE pool (92001, 2, 3, 10, 12, 23, 28, 29, 31, 33, 37, 38, 39 and 43) could only run between Dollands Moor and Calais Fréthun and had had their 750 V DC collector shoes removed. At the time 92011 and 92036 had been out of service for several months.

By 2005 EWS was using Class 92 on a variety of services, in addition to those between London and the Tunnel, including intermodal trains from Dollands Moor, Wembley and Daventry to Trafford Park and Mossend, Enterprise services from Wembley and Daventry to Bescot and Mossend, Carlisle to Warrington and Bescot and trains of timber from Mossend to Warrington (for Chirk). In addition to these trains over the West Coast Main Line, Class 92 was used over the East Coast Main Line from Dollands Moor to Tyne Yard and Doncaster, plus Doncaster to Mossend.

In 2007 it was announced that German Railways (Deutsche Bahn or DB) had bought English Welsh & Scottish Railway. EWS had already started to operate open access freight services in France, with rumours of trains of stone from quarries in the Calais area to greater London. These never materialised. However, DB subsidiary Euro Cargo Rail (ECR) moved aggressively into the French rail freight market and within a few years had ousted Fret SNCF from the Calais area. One by one ECR and DB Schenker took over all of the cross-Channel freight services from Fret SNCF and therefore took control of the whole transit – within the UK and France plus through the Tunnel.

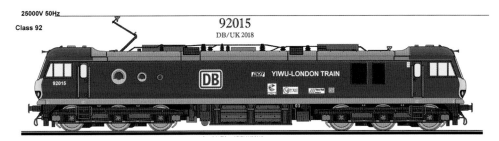

EUROTUNNEL BUYS
GB RAILFREIGHT

On 1 June 2010 Eurotunnel purchased UK freight operator GB Railfreight (GBRf) from First Group. It seemed at the time that this was the final piece of the jigsaw that would turn Eurotunnel into an international rail freight operator, as the company now had the potential – like DB Schenker – to operate freight trains from anywhere in the UK (GBRf) via the Channel Tunnel (Europorte Channel) to anywhere in France (Europorte France). Eurotunnel said its main aim would be to develop freight services between Britain and the continent where rail had a 1% market share.

In February 2014 GBRf announced that it had purchased the 16 Class 92s previously owned by Europorte Channel in order to expand services, including on international routes, and with future electrification of UK freight routes in mind. Of the 16 locos only six were operational and it was expected that up to six more would be reactivated. Through this takeover, GBRf took over haulage of trains through the Channel Tunnel on behalf of Europorte Channel, plus over HS1 as far as the London area.

The first train operated by GBRf for Europorte Channel was on 3 November 2014 when Europorte France/GBRf launched a new intermodal service moving containers from Dourges in northern France to Barking for UK haulage firm John G Russell. After initial optimism that this might be the first of

many new cross-Channel flows this service was withdrawn after only a year, due to a new migrant crisis in Calais. A revived service from Dourges to Daventry was still under discussion in early 2020. In July 2016 GBRf/Europorte ran a trial weekly service carrying new Honda cars from Portbury (Bristol) to Gent in Belgium, but this was not followed up by a regular service.

The potential for international operation was never fulfilled. GB Railfreight expanded aggressively into all

sorts of other lucrative traffics, but not international services, while Europorte France expanded into French domestic traffic such as cereals and chemicals. Eurotunnel has a full-time manager promoting through rail freight but the job is to "encourage and aid" other operators to launch new services rather than for the Eurotunnel group to run services itself. Indeed the author has heard from highly-placed managers at both GB Railfreight and Eurotunnel that the Tunnel usage

Left: The only Class 92 freight working in the UK, excluding the Channel Tunnel and HS1, in early 2019 was a Garston–Dagenham train for Ford. 92020 leads 6L48 14.08 Garston Car Terminal to Wembley (truncated on this date), with 66760 out of shot on the rear of the consist, at Salop Goods Junction (Crewe) on Saturday 6 April 2019. *John Illingworth*

Right: 92032 is seen at the inauguration of Barking Freight Terminal (east London) on 22 May 2012. *Keith Fender*

charges for through freight are "too high". Eurotunnel has a scheme known as ETICA to help operators start up new freight traffic, with lower Tunnel charges in the initial stages. But the fact that the Eurotunnel group has not gone flat out to operate its own international services is telling.

In October 2016, Eurotunnel sold GB Railfreight to EQT Partners, a Swedish group which already owned Swedish company Hector Rail, which now also operates extensively in Germany. In 2019 GB Railfreight was sold by EQT to Infracapital.

Below: 92043 approaches Leggatfoot summit (near Carstairs) on the previous evening's train 1S26 23.50 London Euston to Glasgow Central and Edinburgh on 28 June 2019 in the early days of the new Mk 5 sleeper operation. *Robin Ralston*

CLASS 92 ON HSI

The High Speed 1 high speed line opened between London St Pancras and the Tunnel in two stages in 2003 and on 14 November 2007. Although HS1 had been built with the aim of allowing freight trains to operate, and has passing loops to allow passenger trains to overtake them, it was not until April 2009 that a project emerged to equip DB Schenker Class 92 locos to operate over the new line. Although Class 92 were fitted from the start with French TVM 430 cab signalling for operation through the Tunnel, the version on HS1 was slightly different and locos needed their on-board equipment to be modified. Some of the funds for this would be financed by the EU's Marco Polo fund.

The first test with a DB Schenker Class 92 over HS1 did not take place until 25 March 2011 and the first revenue service was on 27 May 2011 when a Hams Hall–Novara (Italy) train was hauled by 92009 in DB red livery, newly renamed "Marco Polo" (formerly "Elgar").

However, this first train needed diesel assistance over a non-electrified section at Ripple Lane and the use of HS1 has never become the "norm" for Channel Tunnel services, except for those originating near Ripple Lane. In July 2011 there was a trial run from Dollands Moor to Barking with European-gauge swap bodies and on 11 November 2011 a weekly service was introduced from Barking to Poland. Such trains could reach Barking in 70 minutes from Dollands Moor compared with four hours over classic lines. However the train no longer runs.

On 1 December 2011 Eurotunnel announced that all of Europorte Channel's 11 functioning Class 92s had been approved for use on HS1. The aim was to start operating a new Dourges–Barking service from Calais to Barking over HS1 (see above).

In early 2012 the chance of Class 92 finding more work in the Channel Tunnel diminished further when Eurotunnel started to seek approval for other types of loco to be used in the Channel Tunnel, meaning that a TRAXX electric, say, would be able to reach Dollands Moor from anywhere in Europe. In September 2012 Alstom tested its 6400 kW Prima II Bo-Bo prototype loco and in January 2013 Siemens tested its Vectron but these trials have so far come to nothing.

Other services which used HS1 but which no longer operate include a thrice-weekly DFDS service from Novara to Daventry, and a weekly chilled "fruit and veg" service from Valencia in Spain to Barking, for Stobart Rail. The celebrations of a first train arriving from China via HS1 in 2017 were short-lived as the resulting weekly service was curtailed in early 2018 following yet another strike in France.

The only service to use HS1 in early 2020 is the Ford "blue train" between Dagenham and Valencia which runs four times a week operated by DB Cargo. Container services which were running previously were withdrawn after the migrant crisis from 2016 and the SNCF three-month strike in 2018.

All other trains currently operating, such as the almost daily Ditton–Neuss and Scunthorpe–Ebange services are diesel hauled throughout in the UK.

....

Right: 92001 is seen on HS1 with the famous Ford "Blue Train" from Silla, near Valencia in Spain to Dagenham. It is seen crossing the Medway viaduct on 26 May 2017. This train was the only freight using HS1 in early 2020. *Jamie Squibbs*
....

DB Cargo's 92015 was the locomotive chosen to ceremonially head the first container train from Yiwu in China to Barking (London) on 18 January 2017 and carries markings to advertise the fact. However the train no longer runs. *Keith Fender (2)*

GB Railfreight sometimes carries out work for Eurotunnel on High Speed 1. This is super power (12 000 kW) on 30 June 2019 for two wagons with 92044 at the front and 92032 on the rear at Medway. *Jamie Squibbs*

92s FOR THE CALEDONIAN SLEEPER

In February 2015 GB Railfreight won the 15-year contract to supply drivers and locomotives to operate the Caledonian Sleeper trains between London Euston and Scotland on behalf of the franchise winner Serco. GBRf would employ its Class 92 locos for this as trains can load to 16 coaches, the longest passenger trains in Britain, so decided to form a pool of 11 locomotives (seven plus four in reserve) for these trains. The main fleet is 92006, 92010, 92014, 92018, 92023, 92033 and 92038. Several of these were put back into service after a heavy overhaul, having been stored for many years. The back-up fleet of locos in GBRf livery is formed of 92020, 92028, 92032 and 92043.

The locos work the trains on the Lowland Sleeper route between London and Edinburgh/Glasgow and on the Highland Sleeper route between the same cities, although the latter trains divide/combine at Edinburgh so as to serve Fort William, Aberdeen and Inverness.

The seven locos in the main fleet have received a "Midnight Teal" blue livery which is similar to the old British Rail blue. This was applied after the "Tunnel Rings" and cabside depot plaques had been removed.

Class 92 started to haul Caledonian Sleeper services on 31 March 2015, but there were several failures despite the overhauls. Problems were traced to the locos' electrical equipment to which Brush carried out further modifications. It was not until 17 January 2017 that Class 92 haulage resumed on the Caledonian Sleepers.

In 2018 the locos started to be modified with Dellner couplers in order to be used with the new CAF-built sleeper coaches. These are used to reduce shocks in the middle of the night when coupling and uncoupling.

Class 92   92018   CS 2015   25 000V 50Hz
92018
Copyright Thierry LELEU Mai 2019

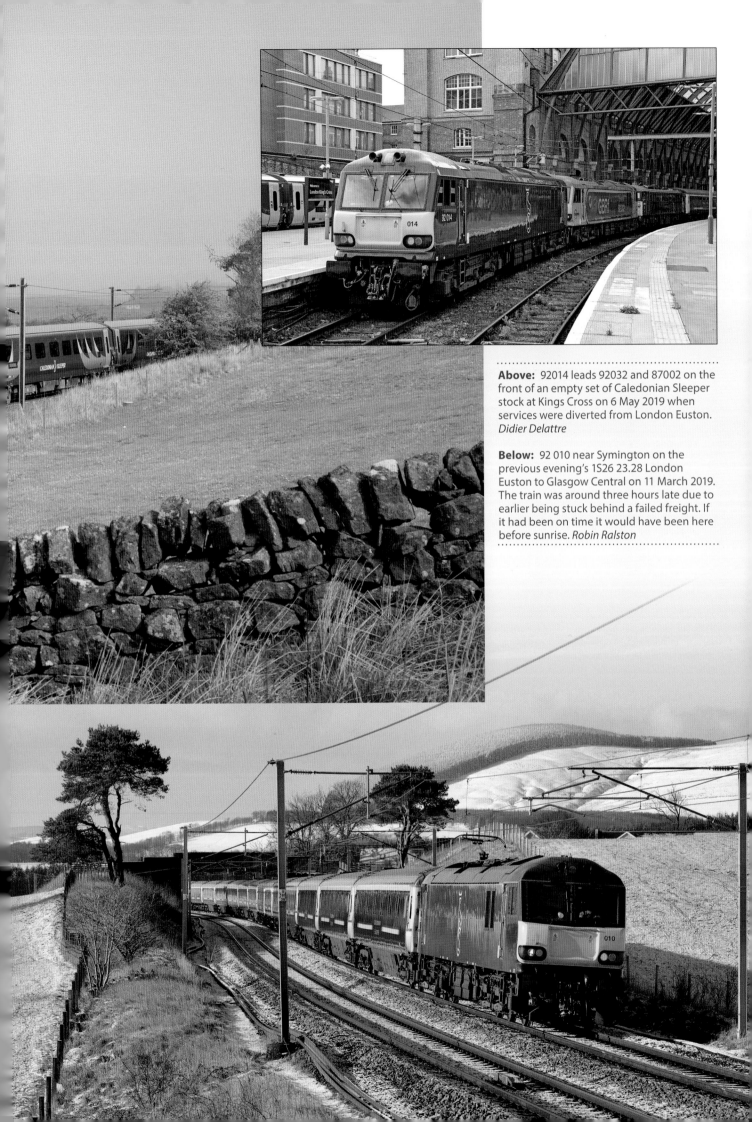

Above: 92014 leads 92032 and 87002 on the front of an empty set of Caledonian Sleeper stock at Kings Cross on 6 May 2019 when services were diverted from London Euston. *Didier Delattre*

Below: 92 010 near Symington on the previous evening's 1S26 23.28 London Euston to Glasgow Central on 11 March 2019. The train was around three hours late due to earlier being stuck behind a failed freight. If it had been on time it would have been here before sunrise. *Robin Ralston*

DB EXPORTS

The largest batch of Class 92s were the 30 locos ordered for British Rail's Railfreight Distribution, which then became part of the EWS fleet in 1997, then moved to DB Schenker when the latter took over EWS in 2007. DB Schenker is now known as DB Cargo, part of Deutsche Bahn, Germany's incumbent operator. Although DB Cargo uses a small number of Class 92s in the Tunnel and within the UK, the Class 92 fleet was obviously far too big for its needs. DB Cargo has subsidiaries in almost every European country and in early 2012, confirmed it was preparing 92034 "Kipling" for use in Bulgaria at Crewe depot. The loco left the UK via the Tunnel on 7 May and arrived in Sofia on 4 June. It then moved to Pirdop copper refinery where the class was used regularly until DB lost the contract to move copper ore from the port of Burgas in January 2017. The loco had started tests on these trains in August 2012, double-heading with a former Danish Railways Class EA loco. Once approval was received for the class, DB Schenker then sent 92025 and 92027 to Bulgaria in December 2012.

92012 was dispatched from the UK in May 2013, but went to the Softronic works in Craiova, Romania, to be prepared to operate

in that country. This time it was reliveried in DB red (but retaining the Channel Tunnel "rings" and BR symbol), renumbered 91 53 0**472 001**-3 and renamed "Mihai Eminescu". 92001 "Victor Hugo", in EWS maroon and gold livery, left the UK in July 2013 for Romania but was rapidly turned out in DB red.

In May 2015 92002 and 92024 were moved to Romania, becoming 91 53 0**472 004** "Marin Preda" and **472 003** "Lucian Blaga" respectively) while 92005 joined its sisters in August 2015, becoming **472 005**. "Emil Cioran". 92030 then moved to Bulgaria in mid 2016, making four locos there.

In April/May 2017 92003 "Beethoven" and 92026 "Britten" were moved to Romania, the latter becoming 472 008. Meanwhile DB had put 472 001 (ex 92012) up for sale. In spring 2019 though 92003 was numbered 472 007 and started operations. Despite an uncertain future, 472 007 and 008 were still in operation in Romania in late 2019 and 472 002 under repair.

Above: DB Cargo Romania 472 004 "Marin Preda", ex 92024 "J. S. Bach", with a container train on 17 July 2016, in Cernavoda Pod adjacent to the bridge over the Danube. *Mircea Dorobantu*

Bulgarian Railways then decided to renumber the Class 92s there as "Class 88". In August 2017, 92022 "Charles Dickens" arrived in Romania, but then moved on to Bulgaria to supply spares.

Following the loss of the Pirdop contract in early 2018, the four Bulgarian locos 92025, 92027, 92030 and 92034 are still operating in Bulgaria sporadically, often on Pernik–Ruse freights, while 92022 supplies spares.

A fifth, sixth and seventh country for Class 92

There was a major surprise in November 2017 when former 92005 (472 005) moved from Romania to Croatia, having been sold

Right: Preserved 1955-vintage DB "Crocodile" 194 580 hauls 92025 and 92027 through Germany on 13 December 2012 on their way to Bulgaria. The photo was taken at Groenhart on the Nürnberg–Treuchtlingen line. *Andreas Dollinger*

Right: TransAgent Rail 472 005 is seen on 24 August 2018 near Zagreb Klara in the unusual checked livery.

Below right: TransAgent Rail 472 004 and 003 are seen on 3 November 2018 on the freight-only Zagreb Klara–Remetinec connecting line.

to Russian company LocoTech. After minor modifications the loco started driver training on 13 December with Croatian freight operator Transagent špedicija based in the port of Rijeka. Following full approval in Croatia, DB Cargo Romania sold four of its locos (472 001, 003, 004 and 005) to LocoTech which then leased them all to TransAgent špedicija.

By August 2018 472 005 had been turned out in a black and blue chequered livery (but still with the Channel Tunnel "rings") and was hauling trains of iron ore (destined for a steel works near Budapest) from the Croatian port of Bakar via Zagreb to Gyékényes, just inside Hungary – a sixth country for the class. 472 003, still in DB livery, then entered service and was used to double-head freight trains with 472 005. 472 003 was being used for spares in autumn 2019. 472 004 has received a different livery with sweeping black/white curves at each end. Class 92 is expected to remain active on the Bakar–Škrljevo, Škrljevo–Rijeka and Rijeka–Šapjane lines.

TransAgent originally said it would take all eight Class 92s in Romania. However, the locos proved to be problematic because of overheating on the Rijeka line, and the company decided not to lease the remaining four locos. As TransAgent also plans to operate open access freights in Serbia, a seventh country, 472 005 was on test from Šid to Sremska Mitrovica in July 2019.

13 DB Cargo Class 92s have now been "exported" to continental Europe – 92001–92003, 92005, 92012, 92022,

Below: The first test run with a Class 92 in Croatia was on 12 January 2018, with very cold but sunny weather in Bakar bay. The locomotive hauled a heavy freight to Lokve; two HŽ Cargo electrics of Class 1141 assisted with the haulage. *Toma Bačić (3)*

92024–92027, 92030, 92034 and 92039. Those in Romania all have 12-figure EVNs, are in DB red livery and are based at Turceni, just north of Filiaşi from where they work over much of Romania, including trains of Ford cars from Craiova to Curtici.

Locos in Bulgaria are all in the original BR livery, have had their electric train heating removed and have wing mirrors. Some have gained striped yellow/black snowploughs. They all have 12-figure EVNs and are numbered as Bulgarian "Class 88".

Liveries

All Class 92 locos were originally delivered in a "triple grey" paint scheme with three large circles on the sides and the "owning" company's logo on the cabsides. RfD later introduced a "European" variation with blue roof and "Railfreight Distribution" on the lower bodysides.

EWS repainted 92001 in its bordeaux red and gold livery in August 1998 and 92031 was the only other one in that livery. Most of the other EWS locos received "Beastie" stickers on the mid-bodysides.

Following the takeover by DB Schenker, 92017 received a special blue and white livery to advertise a new Stobart Rail service but the first loco in DB Schenker red was 92009, which also had its "Elgar" name replaced by "Marco Polo". Other locos in DB red are 92015, 92016, 92031 and 92042.

92032 was the first recipient of the GB Railfreight orange and blue livery, on 19 May 2017, This was followed by 92043 in September 2017. Other GBRf locos are still in EPS livery of two-tone grey with a dark blue roof and Europorte vinyls. All but 92044 are stored.

The first loco to receive Caledonian Sleeper dark blue livery was 92010, followed by 92006, 92014, 92018, 92023, 92033 and 92038.

Names

The original names given to Class 92 honoured well-known European composers and writers; with a few exceptions, those on SNCF locos were French, the others British and other nationalities. An exception to this rule was 92006 "Louis Armand", a French railway engineer and former SNCF chief.

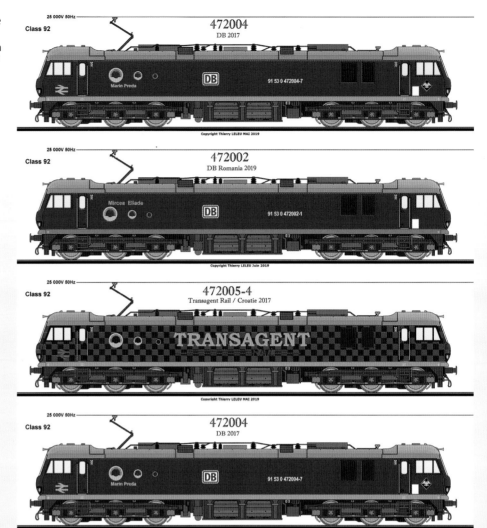

92030 "Da Falla" was renamed "Ashford" in 1996 and 92031 never carried its allocated name "Schiller" but was named the much more prosaic "The Institute of Logistics and Transport". in 2001. 92009 "Elgar" became "Marco Polo" in 2011.

Most of the other locos have lost their names over the years, the ones in Romania receiving names of Romanian poets, playwrights and so on.

Ex-British 92025 "Oscar Wilde", now DB Bulgaria's 88 025 in the company of a former Danish Railways (DSB) Class 86, near Burgas with a copper ore train in November 2017. The Channel Tunnel rings and UK depot identity (Crewe) are still visible. *Konstantin Planinski*

The situation 25 years on

Of the 46 Class 92 locos built, none has been officially withdrawn, but a good number are stored. 13 have been "exported" (see above).

There are therefore just 33 Class 92 still in the UK. Of these, DB has 17 and GB Railfreight has 16, although the latter uses far more in service. Of the GB Railfreight locos, there are now eight locos in the main Caledonian Sleeper fleet and four in reserve while the other four locos are at the Brush plant in Loughborough. These supply spares and are unlikely to return to service. GBRf now rarely uses its locos for freight services: 92006, 92010, 92014, 92018, 92020, 92021 (S), 92023, 92028, 92032, 92033, 92038, 92040 (S), 92043, 92044, 92045 (S), 92046 (S).

The DB Cargo fleet (in the UK) consists of 17 locos, but only six are serviceable and these are based at Dollands Moor, working only freights through the Channel Tunnel, singly or in multiple, plus the Ford train four times a week between Dollands Moor and Barking. All the 11 other locos are stored at Crewe Electric depot: 92004, 92007, 92008, 92009, 92011, 92013, 92015, 92016, 92017, 92019, 92029, 92031, 92035, 92036, 92037, 92041, 92042.

So, out of the 46 Class 92s, only six of them (13%) are being used for the purpose for which they were designed, and a total of 15 locos (almost a third) are in store.

In principle all GBRf locos could operate over third rail lines in spring 2020 but DB Cargo locos could not. Some DB Cargo locos have had their third rail shoes removed, whilst all have had them isolated.

Above: Former DB Cargo Romania 472 003 is being used to supply spares to the TransAgent locos and is seen in the depot at Buzin (Zagreb) on 8 August 2019. *Thierry Leleu*

Below: The only freight train currently using HS1 is the Dagenham–Silla (Spain) car parts service for Ford. Here DB Cargo loco 92015 heads the northbound train as 6L23 Dollands Moor–Ripple Lane, seen coming off the Medway viaduct on 14 June 2017. *Jamie Squibbs*

CHANNEL TUNNEL FREIGHT:
GREAT EXPECTATIONS... DASHED

Before the Channel Tunnel opened rail wagons were only able to cross the Channel by ferry via Dover and Dunkerque. Most traffic was moved in mixed wagonload trains by Railfreight Distribution in the UK and SNCF in France. The ferry was able to carry wagons loaded with hazardous goods but these were banned through the Tunnel. Immediately before the Tunnel opened the ferry being used was the "Nord-Pas-de-Calais", launched in 1987, which carried only rail wagons and lorries. In the distant past freight wagons had even been carried on passenger ferries.

In Dunkerque, wagons were shunted on and off the ferry at the Port Ouest, then moved to Grande Synthe marshalling yard which was linked to other yards across France and in other countries. However, in May 1993 SNCF rationalised its wagonload services – Grande Synthe would no longer sort wagons for the whole of France but instead forwarded complete trains for sorting at Lille La Délivrance (87 km) or Somain (120 km) which had overnight services to most parts of France plus Belgium and Germany. Ironically La Délivrance has since been closed, Somain yard near Douai cut back and Dunkerque is the main yard for the region.

The only "block" trains in 1993 were those bringing mineral water to the UK from Evian, Volvic and Perrier and beer from Strasbourg. A flow of pet food from Orléans to Cricklewood (north London) had been

lost in 1992. In the years leading up to the Tunnel opening the ferry was carrying about 1.5 million tonnes a year.

Wagons for the Tunnel

With the prospect of massive amounts of new freight traffic passing through the Tunnel, and operating over very long routes, large numbers of new wagons were built. British Rail's Railfreight Distribution subsidiary ordered 450 low platform "Multifret" double

Above: On 7 October 1995 92029 exits the French portal of the Channel Tunnel with a Wembley–Valencia intermodal service formed mainly of Bell containers.

Below: SNCB Class 12 dual-voltage locos were early performers on Tunnel freights to and through Belgium. Here 1212 is seen at Ruminghem, approaching Calais on 24 March 1999. *Chris Wilson (2)*

intermodal wagons from Arbel Fauvet Rail in Douai, northern France. SNCF and Intercontainer ordered no less than 750 more. The company also manufactured 300 fully enclosed car carrying wagons built to the UK loading gauge for RfD. Other wagons used by SNCF and Intercontainer complemented this fleet – around 1000 wagons were made available for the start of services. Container wagons had a low floor at 945 mm above rail level but despite this some £50 million had to be spent on clearing loading gauges in the UK to allow containers 2.77 metres high.

Service start up

The first revenue-earning through freight trains were on 1 June 1994, the first service carrying Rover cars from Washwood Heath (Birmingham) to Arluno near Milano in Italy. This service had been running since March using the "*Nord-Pas-de-Calais*" ferry. The train was hauled through the Tunnel by specially-adapted SNCF electric locos BB 22379 and 22403 (see section on Class 92). The following day a container train ran from Muizen in Belgium to Wembley then a Wembley to Milano intermodal service was launched on 13 June. On 27 June Wembley–Lyon–Avignon–Perpignan (France) and Wembley–Muizen–Duisburg container trains started up. Also in June 1994, a service moving Peugeot cars from Montbéliard in France to Bathgate, Scotland began.

Due to the late delivery of Class 92 electric locos, it was necessary for operator Railfreight Distribution to constitute a special fleet of Class 47 diesels for use in multiple in the UK. In France, traction from Calais Fréthun yard was mainly in the hands of Class BB 26000 5600 kW "*Sybic*" electric locomotives. Trains from Fréthun to Belgium were hauled by SNCB's Class 12 3310 kW electrics.

By 20 December 1994 1000 freight trains had passed through the Tunnel and the timetable totalled 80 trains a week. After only a year of operation this had risen to 15 train pairs a day – about four times the current number. A full list is contained in Table 1 on page 114. The list of trains is quite remarkable in that Wembley container terminal, north of London, was dispatching 11 container trains a day, of which one to Belgium/Germany, one to Luxembourg, three to France, one to Spain and no less than five to Italy! Three services carried finished cars, including one which was often loaded in both directions, taking Rover cars from Longbridge (Birmingham) to Arluno, near Milano, then returning from Torino with Fiats for Avonmouth near Bristol. There are no intermodal services through the Tunnel now, except the Dagenham–Silla Ford car parts which ran almost from day one, no finished cars and no wagonload traffic.

From 29 September 1996 the UK was plugged into the important "Qualitynet" network of intermodal services operated by Intercontainer-Interfrigo (ICF) from a hub at Metz, north-eastern France. Daily container trains ran between Wembley

Above: SNCF 1947-vintage "Baldwin" diesel loco A1AA1A 62011 is seen shunting the train ferry at Dunkerque Port Ouest on 8 August 1989. The train in the foreground is formed of weighted "reach wagons" and was pushed by 62005. *David Haydock (2)*

and Metz, connecting into a dozen daily services to Spain (3), Switzerland (2), other parts of France (2), Italy (4) and Austria (1). The Metz hub was ICF's solution for having less-than-trainloads of containers – sections of trains would be shunted between trains at Metz, and if traffic built up on an origin–destination pair, a direct train would be introduced.

However, the network depended entirely on trains being roughly on time and each year ICF would complain that this was not the case, and regular strikes, particularly in France and Italy, made it difficult to maintain.

It should be noted that the forecasts were for traffic to reach 35 freight trains par day per direction by 1997, so in the first year almost half of this was reached. Optimism was *de rigueur*. Intermodal operator ACI was talking of up to five further services, including to Germany and Austria while CTL was talking of extra services to Spain, Germany, eastern Europe and more to Italy.

EWS takes over

At the time of the launch of Channel Tunnel freight services France had a monopoly service provider (SNCF) as did nearby Belgium (SNCB) but in the UK the government was in the throes of privatising the railways. In the case of freight, domestic conventional services were divided into three and each of the companies was put up for sale. In the end all three were bought by US railroad Wisconsin Central which re-merged them as English Welsh and Scottish Railway (EWS). Freight services between Britain and the continent initially remained within the nationalised Railfreight Distribution (RfD) but this was also eventually sold off, and bought by EWS.

In the end the very last British Rail train, was an RfD service which ran on Friday 20 November 1997 from Dollands Moor to Wembley – an intermodal service from Milano Rogoredo hauled through from Calais

Fréthun to Wembley by 92003 "Beethoven". At the time new Tunnel services included steel from Fos-sur-Mer in France to Brierley Hill (Birmingham) and Peugeot cars from Mulhouse in France to Corby. In December 1997 RfD became EWS International.

All time high reached

In 1998 freight through the Channel Tunnel reached an all-time high of 3 141 000 tonnes, already half of the 6 million tonnes predicted for the route. Then in the first quarter of 1999, traffic slipped back by no less than 17%, which was put down to excess capacity in the trucking sector which was reducing prices and taking intermodal traffic in particular from the railways.

A three-week SNCF strike in 1995 had sown doubts in the minds of some logistics operators, and frequent strikes on both French and Italian railways were given as the main reason for operators to withdraw services or hold off from launching them. The 1996 Tunnel fire had less of an effect. Some hesitation could be expected from Railfreight Distribution, as it was to be sold off, but the takeover by EWS did not bring a new surge in traffic. Ed Burkhardt, the hard-nosed American then in charge was initially optimistic about doubling cross-Channel traffic, but saw more potential in wagonload and block trains than intermodal. However, he was not impressed by his "partner" Fret SNCF. Both EWS and Fret SNCF proceeded to hack back loss-making wagonload services around the turn of the Century. In the meantime DB showed little interest in using the Tunnel, German companies preferring to export via the North Sea ports.

Train routeing

In the UK the majority of trains ran to the Tunnel between Wembley/Willesden in north London skirting the west and south of the capital via Kensington Olympia, then over the Kent main line via Ashford to Dollands Moor yard near Folkestone. A small number of trains reached London via the West Coast Main Line from Garston (Liverpool), Bescot and Longbridge (Birmingham), whilst just one train, carrying china clay to Italy started from Exeter.

All of the Tunnel trains had to travel through France where a wide variety

Above: Due to the late delivery of the Class 92 electric locos, Railfreight Distribution had to form a temporary fleet of Class 47 diesels which hauled Tunnel freights through Kent in multiple. A smoky 47237 leads 47241 through Redhill on 17 August 1995 with 4M36 Perpignan–Wembley. *Chris Wilson*

of routes have been used. The majority of trains operated via SNCF's "north-east corridor" via Hazebrouck, then Lille or Douai, Valenciennes, Mohon (near Charleville-Mézières) then to Metz or turning south to Dijon. Most trains

Above: BB 22379 and 22403 leave the Tunnel in Calais with the Longbridge–Arluno Rover car train on 1 June 1994. *David Haydock*

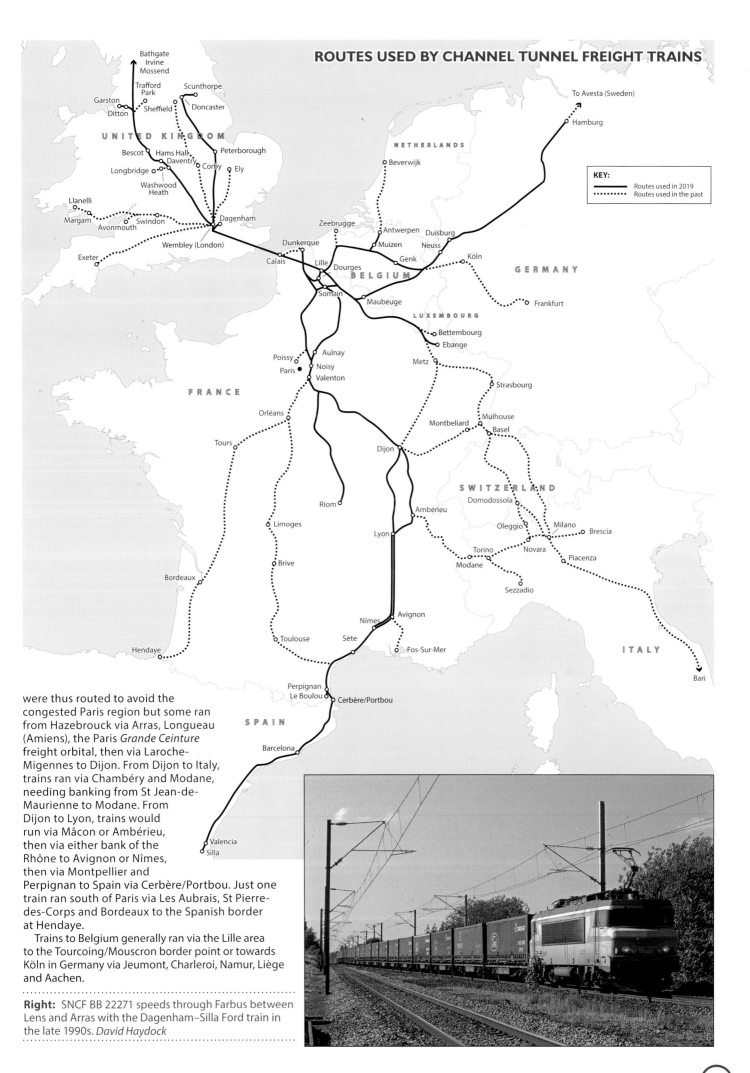

KEY:
Routes used in 2019
Routes used in the past

were thus routed to avoid the congested Paris region but some ran from Hazebrouck via Arras, Longueau (Amiens), the Paris *Grande Ceinture* freight orbital, then via Laroche-Migennes to Dijon. From Dijon to Italy, trains ran via Chambéry and Modane, needing banking from St Jean-de-Maurienne to Modane. From Dijon to Lyon, trains would run via Mâcon or Ambérieu, then via either bank of the Rhône to Avignon or Nîmes, then via Montpellier and Perpignan to Spain via Cerbère/Portbou. Just one train ran south of Paris via Les Aubrais, St Pierre-des-Corps and Bordeaux to the Spanish border at Hendaye.

Trains to Belgium generally ran via the Lille area to the Tourcoing/Mouscron border point or towards Köln in Germany via Jeumont, Charleroi, Namur, Liège and Aachen.

Right: SNCF BB 22271 speeds through Farbus between Lens and Arras with the Dagenham–Silla Ford train in the late 1990s. *David Haydock*

FIVE YEARS ON

On 1 June 1999 EWS International, Eurotunnel and SNCF celebrated five years of freight through the Tunnel. The celebratory train was a Washwood Heath–Brescia (Italy) carrying Rover cars, hauled by 92001 in EWS livery. On the French side SNCF was preparing to introduce tri-voltage Class BB 36000 "universal" locomotives which were built to operate all the way from Calais via France to Italy.

Unfortunately by mid 1999 traffic was falling – tonnage being down 17% – blamed on a strong Pound hitting UK exports and spare capacity in the road haulage industry depressing rates. The Trafford Park–Muizen (Belgium) intermodal and Genk–Garston

Ford train were withdrawn while other services were reduced in frequency. On the other hand wagonload freight was increasing slightly, with a new direct service from Wembley to Gremberg (Köln) in Germany. However this train initially covered the 400 km journey in 18 hours, an average of just over 20 km/h, with four traction changes. In 1999 Belgian Railways (SNCB) started to use its Class 12 dual-voltage locos through to Calais, thus cutting out some loco changes.

Other services operating at the time included a Mossend (Glasgow)–Valenton (Paris) intermodal with a stop at Daventry. The Ford "Blue Train" was diverted via the

Above: A few Channel Tunnel services were worked by SNCF's "flat iron" Class BB 12000 electrics before they disappeared. BB 12091 is seen at Ecaillon on 21 February 1996 having just left Somain with the 14.30 mixed freight to Wembley which it will take as far as Calais Fréthun.

hilly route via Limoges and Toulouse but has since reverted to its original route via Lyon and Nîmes.

A marathon run

The turn of the century looked like bringing improved fortunes, with three new flows starting, the first being a twice-weekly intermodal service run by GTS, mainly carrying furniture, from the Italian city of Bari, to Manchester, one of the longest through freight services in Europe, at about 2600 km. This took about 50 hours southbound and 58 hours northbound, with "only" four loco changes – SNCF's Class BB 36000 never did run through from Calais to Italy, only running Calais–Modane.

The second service was a daily train of paper and pulp for Swedish company Stora which sent its products by sea to Zeebrugge, with a train from Zeebrugge to Barking (London). Another flow of paper was from Brive in central France to Ely or Cricklewood, north London. Finally, Ford reintroduced its service carrying finished cars from Genk (Belgium), but to Corby, rather than Garston (Liverpool).

Left: A variety of traction at Calais Fréthun stabling point on 1 October 1997: SNCF electric BB 22295 and diesel CC 72086, with Class 92 92031 plus a Class BB 16500 electric and a pair of BB 66000 diesels in the background. *David Haydock (2)*

Right: 92011 is seen at Sevington on 1 May 1997 with a short Wembley–Lille La Délivrance wagonload service. Behind 92011 is GM EMD diesel loco 59003 en route to Germany for tests with Deutsche Bahn. The loco was later operated by Heavy Haul Power International before returning to the UK.

The migrant disaster

In late 2000 and early 2001 there was a flood of migrants trying to reach the UK, causing problems to transport operators in the Calais area. As well as many people trying to climb onto lorries, a group of people in poor health were found in a train of Evian mineral water when it reached Calais. The British government put the blame on transporters and brought in regulations under which they would be fined £200 for every migrant brought into the country. EWS was fined £186 000 in just 23 days and pointed out that it could not carry out inspections itself in Calais; this had to be done by SNCF at the time. By mid 2001 EWS had been fined £500 000.

Through rail freight services were very badly hit because other modes tightened their security first and migrants reduced their attempts to climb on lorries and moved to trains. A local newspaper at the time said that Eurotunnel was employing 370 staff to prevent intrusion by migrants but that SNCF employed just eight security staff. EWS, a private company with no government to bail it out, threatened to pull out of Channel Tunnel traffic completely if the government did not relent.

Eurotunnel took early action to protect its terminal and the Tunnel entrance but even with some increased security there were "invasions" in August 2001 when asylum seekers broke through fences. The situation became so bad that EWS/SNCF freight services through the Tunnel were suspended from 6 November 2001 and after this freight trains passing through Calais slowed to a trickle. Some customers and train operators reacted by diverting trains to Zeebrugge. It was only at this point, after almost a year, that SNCF decided to invest in considerably increased security.

By January 2002 the problems were starting to ease and the British government had stopped fining EWS and Eurotunnel. However on 12 March SNCF suspended all rail freight through the Tunnel until the number of *gendarmes* was raised to 80 and the number of security staff to 30. Traffic was supposed to return to "normal" but until 28 March trains would only run between 19.00 and 03.00 each night. Severe problems continued into May. Only then did SNCF start installing razor wire barriers, something Eurotunnel had done a year before. The situation then improved slowly, being "much better" by the end of 2002.

However it was said that Britain's international freight services were "near collapse". With hindsight, traffic never recovered and operators now still hesitate to use the Tunnel. Through freight was halved from 2.95 million tonnes in 2000 to 1.46 million in 2002 – basically the same as the ferry had been carrying in 1993, and representing a market share of about 5% in cross-Channel traffic. This compared with SNCF's market share of 21% in France and rail

Below: SNCF "Sybic" BB 26089 passes Pont d'Ain station with an intermodal service from Wembley to Italy on 16 July 1998. *Chris Wilson (2)*

freight's 9.5% share in the UK at the time. The 5% was the lowest share of cross-border traffic with France – even worse than the 5.5% share on the Spanish border, where there is a track gauge change to surmount.

At a post-crisis conference in February 2002 on Tunnel rail freight SNCF said it expected traffic to rebound and reach 4–5 million tonnes by 2010 – a very ambitious target, although less than the increase expected in lorry traffic. Other participants were less optimistic and cited other difficulties such as aligning paths over three different railways and, a regular complaint over the past 25 years, the high level of Eurotunnel access charges (see below), which, it was claimed, were 70% of total charges for services such as Wembley–Paris.

Right: SNCF BB 26026 is seen at Douai on 2 April 1996 with the Longbridge–Arluno train of Rover cars. *David Haydock*

Table 1
Channel Tunnel freight trains summer 1995/1999

Route	Traffic	Train pairs/week 1995	1999
Intermodal			
Wembley–Muizen–Duisburg	CTL	5	
Wembley–Muizen			6
Wembley–Bettembourg	ACI	4	
Wembley–Metz			6
Wembley–Nolsy	CTL	5	
Wembley–Valenton	ACI	5	
Mossend/Wembley–Noisy/Valenton			8
Wembley–Perpignan		5	
Wembley–Lyon/Avignon/Perpignan			3
Wembley–Melzo	CTL	5	3
Wembley–Rogoredo	ACI	5	
Wembley–Rogoredo	CTL	6	
Hams Hall/Wembley–Rogoredo			9
Wembley–Pioltello	ICF	5	
Wembley–Novara	CTL	5	5
Wembley–Ollegio			5
Wembley–Valencia	ACI	5	
Dagenham–Silla	Car parts (Ford)	5	6

Route	Traffic	Train pairs/week 1995	1999
Block trains			
Genk–Garston	Ford cars	5	
Longbridge–Arluno	Rover cars	5	
Washwood Heath–Brescia	Rover cars		6
Torino–Avonmouth	Fiat cars	5	1
Sheffield Avesta	Steel slabs	1	
Exeter–Sezzadio (Italy)	China clay		1
Brookgate–Frankfurt	Paper		1
Evian–Daventry	Mineral water		C
Various	Peugeot cars		C
Wagonload			
Wembley–Lille Délivrance		5	
Bescot/Wembley–Lille/Somain			12
Wembley–Köln Gremberg			5
TOTAL TRAINS A WEEK		**81**	**77**

ACI: Associated Containers Inc   ICF: Intercontainer-Interfrigo
CTL: Combined Transport Ltd   C: conditional

92016 "Brahms" passes Wandsworth Road with an Intermodal train for Dollands Moor on 25 February 1998. *Chris Booth*

TEN YEARS ON:
GREAT DISAPPOINTMENT

In 2004, after ten years of through freight operations via the Tunnel, it was clear that things were not going well at all, but by no means all of the problems had come from the illegal immigration. The hoped-for "seamless" rail journeys across Europe were anything but. And just as services returned to normal after the migrant crisis SNCF workers went on strike for almost two months, followed by Belgian and Italian rail staff. However, strikes were not the only problem. In spring 2004 SNCF was "holding" freights at Calais Fréthun due to "drivers being on holiday" while there were also cases of no locomotive being available for the Dagenham–Silla train at either Calais or Cerbère. This is a train with four drivers lined up to take the train from one side of France to the other. Usually lack of a loco causes a full day's delay.

Intermodal services were the most important sources of through Tunnel freight traffic over the first five years but after ten years, the number of routes to Italy had dropped from five to three. The usual problems of unreliability were compounded from mid-2003 when the French infrastructure manager announced that it would have to restrict traffic through the Fréjus tunnel between France and Italy during its rebuilding. This meant that most Tunnel services had to be diverted via Switzerland. This cannot have helped their survival.

Apart from the Dagenham–Silla Ford train, there were no more intermodal services to Spain, traffic to Barcelona having stopped due to unreliability, mainly on the border with France. As for intermodal traffic to France, every train had been stopped by mid 2003.

The service from Wembley to Metz, which was designed to plug into ICF's Qualitynet network (see above) did not survive for the strange reason that it was too difficult to supply enough wagons then to trace them to the many countries served by the company!

Above: SNCF BB 22277 passes Glanges on 26 January 2007 with the Ford train from Dagenham to Silla in Spain. *Fabrice Lanoue*

And after ten years there were no intermodal services at all between the UK and its biggest trading partner, Germany, DB showing no apparent interest.

Long distance steel slabs

As far as block trains are concerned, the service carrying newsprint from Aylesford in Kent to Frankfurt in Germany was unsuccessful but in mid 2003 a service was tested, carrying slabs of steel (blooms) from Scunthorpe in north-east England to Ebange in France, for transformation at Hayange into long rails, in particular for French high speed lines. For once, this became a major success and continues today, 16 years later, to run daily. The train carrying steel both ways between Sheffield and Avesta (Sweden) was torpedoed by rotten reliability.

Automotive traffic was almost completely eliminated due to the illegal immigration problem, but also by industry restructuring and poor reliability. One of the reasons that trains carrying finished cars to the UK have not come back to the Tunnel can be found in Zeebrugge. The Belgian port has gradually grown into a centre of excellence for handling cars, especially those being exported from continental Europe to the UK.

Hope from the new operators?

Just before the Tunnel's tenth anniversary Fret SNCF passed through one of its regular crises and asked for a large cash injection from the French government. Under EU rules this is not normally possible; in this case the EU allowed the rescue package with the proviso that France opened up its rail freight market to competition earlier than the EU deadline.

The first company to take advantage of the new rules was Eurotunnel which applied for an operating licence to run in France so as to launch its own container shuttles to the UK. Eurotunnel received a flat rate "minimum usage charge" from through freight until then, but this arrangement was due to lapse in 2016. The Tunnel owner was disappointed by the efforts of the incumbent operators

Below: SNCF "Sybic" BB 26093 approaches Douai on 2 April 1996 with the Wembley–Melzo (Milano) intermodal service. The loco headed the train all the way from Calais Fréthun to Modane on the Italian border. *David Haydock*

Right: On 26 September 2003 92015 heads the Manchester–Bari container train at Sevington, where the conventional line runs next to the HS1 high speed line. *Chris Wilson*

and thus wanted to run its own services. For this purpose the company founded a subsidiary known as Freight Solutions, which later became Europorte 2. Eurotunnel said it wanted to triple the number of freights using the Tunnel by the end of 2007 from 100 to 300 per week. The first service was to run between Daventry and Dourges near Lille from 2005.

On 16 March 2004 it was announced that Europorte 2 was going to purchase, via a leasing company, five Alstom Prima tri-voltage locomotives of the same design as Fret SNCF's BB 37000 (which can operate in France, Germany and Switzerland) to be delivered from the end of that year. The plan was to launch a daily UK–Basel (Switzerland) intermodal service via Dourges and Metz. There would be connecting services at each of the latter points. The plan was to reach 30 weekly trains by 2008. Europorte 2 asked Alstom to investigate the cost of equipping its new locos to operate through the Tunnel but it was thought it would have to contract EWS or SNCF to operate through the Tunnel or buy one or more Class 92 locos.

Intercontainer pulls out of Metz

Possibly, with hindsight, the most significant development (or more precisely contraction) in Channel Tunnel freight services occurred on 12 December 2004 when Intercontainer-Interfrigo (ICF) pulled out of its long-standing hub at Metz in north-eastern France. The company blamed an increase in rates from traction

suppliers, principally SNCF and SNCB, and persistent poor service. At the same time ICF withdrew its two direct services between the UK and Milano: Hams Hall (Birmingham) Segrate and Trafford Park (Manchester)–Milano Smistamento, due to "prohibitive costs". These were replaced by increased capacity on ICF's Zeebrugge–Italy services.

ICF replaced its dozen or so services passing via Metz with direct services avoiding France and Belgium completely, hauled by SBB Cargo which was expanding into Germany. 15 years later there is still no rail freight traffic whatsoever routed from the Channel Tunnel or the Benelux ports via France to Italy.

Another, more insidious cause of the decline in traffic was the gradual running

down of wagonload services in both the UK and France. At the turn of the century wagonload services were an important part of SNCF's traffic. However, the company implemented a series of restructuring exercises which saw the number of points and lines reduced drastically and the number of wagons hauled falling by around 80%. In the UK the takeover of EWS by DB Schenker had a negative effect on wagonload services. The company tried to carry traffic in less frequent trainload services but the traffic gradually shrunk to nothing.

Below: RENFE 269 519 is seen on 17 January 2010 at Sant Sadurní with the Silla–Dagenham Ford train. *Juanjo Rodriguez*

TUNNEL CHARGING
– A CONSTANT GRIPE

In early 2005 EWS announced that it was planning to expand operations into continental Europe starting with France. The move was possibly motivated by the company steadily losing traffic to competitors in the UK and therefore putting locos into store, including Class 92 electric locos for the Tunnel.

However, the very next year, EWS was threatening to withdraw all of its Channel Tunnel services on 30 November 2006 if a solution was not found for charging for freight trains under the "Minimum Usage Charge". EWS took Eurotunnel to court to require the company to conform with EU open access rules, and impose charging which the market could bear. EWS was supported by the UK lobby organisation Rail Freight Group which said Tunnel freight traffic could be five to ten times greater with "reasonable" charges.

At the last minute a temporary agreement was reached with the UK Department for Transport, although EWS still found charges too high.

Meanwhile Tunnel traffic continued to fall in early 2007 when Belgian company Unilog withdrew its Manchester–Daventry–Muizen service due to a 24% rise in traction charges, mainly passing on a rise for the Tunnel. It was reported at the same time that GTS was to suspend its Manchester–Bari service and on 4 April 2007 Norfolk Line was told that the cost of running its Hams Hall to Novara service would rise by 15%, mainly due to a rise

Above: A relatively rare event – a Class BB 16500 with a Channel Tunnel service. BB 16665 passes Lens station with an unidentified Wembley–Italy intermodal service. *David Haydock*

in Tunnel usage charges. The only other remaining services (40 train pairs a week) at the time were:

- Dagenham–Silla, Ford car parts
- Scunthorpe–Ebange, steel slabs
- Wembley–Gremberg, wagonload
- Wembley–Somain, wagonload
- Evian/Riom–Coventry/Knowsley, mineral water
- Swindon–Gent, Honda cars
- Aulnay/Poissy–Corby, Peugeot/Citroën cars
- Zeebrugge–Wembley, paper

Then, on 23 October 2007 Eurotunnel announced that it would cut track charges to an average of £3000 per freight train and that the company would offer traction to all comers for a further £400 per journey, having bought its own Class 92 locomotives. The company must have hoped that traffic would then recover; only 1.21 million tonnes were carried in 2007 and 1.24 million in 2008.

However, the criticism has never gone away. In early 2010, former head of EWS then DB Schenker in the UK, Keith Heller, said that complex rules for using the Tunnel and high usage charges were "hampering the development of rail freight between the UK and mainland Europe".

Eurotunnel has consistently denied that its charges are too high, but in the face of through freight traffic stagnating at a low level, the company launched ETICA (Eurotunnel Incentive for Capacity Additions) in 2013 to provide financial aid to railway undertakings setting up new services between the UK and France via the Tunnel. Eurotunnel claimed at the time that its access charges were about €100 per 40 foot container for a 750 metre train loaded to 1800 tonnes (a very rare beast in France) but that ETICA would help pay for marketing, traffic build up and customs checks in France. The aid would be limited to the first year.

ETICA has certainly had a positive effect on Channel Tunnel traffic but it is highly marginal. Despite its unassailable knowledge of the cross-Channel market. Eurotunnel has been unable to generate through freight traffic.

The number of lorries crossing the Channel each day is still enough to fill 100 container trains. But an average of only one container train operates each way, each day through the Tunnel. The stated aim of ETICA was to double the number of freights passing through the Tunnel to 5000 by 2018. In 2013 there were 2547, up from 2325. The number did start to rise but the second migrant crisis stopped growth in its tracks.

EWS TAKES OVER IN FRANCE

Having received approval to operate its Class 66 Co-Co diesels in France, EWS subsidiary Euro Cargo Rail (ECR) started to take over Channel Tunnel freight trains from Fret SNCF. From October 2007, ECR took over traction of the Dagenham–Silla Ford train within France – a 1300 km run from Calais to Cerbère. At the same time ECR took over the Hams Hall–Novara Norfolk Line intermodal service between Calais and Basel. This train was later cut back to Domodossola and was still running four times a week in 2014.

EWS then announced that it would launch more European intermodal services in 2008:
• Daventry–Brussels
• Manchester–Duisburg
• Manchester–Milano

The positive trend continued with news that the Manchester–Bari GTS service restarted in December 2007, although cut back to Piacenza. However, by 2011 this had stopped again.

In March 2008, the Manchester–Duisburg (Rheinhausen) train started, although initially conveyed by the Wembley–Gremberg wagonload service. In the same month French intermodal operator Novatrans announced new services from France to the UK.

Then, in autumn 2008, Europorte 2 started driver training between Calais Fréthun and Dourges, near Lille, with Class E 37500 Alstom Prima tri-voltage locomotives with a view to launching a Daventry–Dourges intermodal service. This was followed by tests with a rake of empty wagons through to January 2009.

However, no sooner had these plans been progressed than an economic crisis set in and most plans were put on the

back burner or dropped. It was not until 3 November 2014 that GB Railfreight and Europorte France finally launched a Barking–Dourges service, with the train running direct from Barking to Calais Fréthun behind a pair of GBRf Class 92s then running to Dourges (two hours from Calais) and back behind a Class E 37500 electric, in the daytime. The train ran at suitable times to allow containers to be transferred to or from services linking Dourges overnight with the south of France.

The new service was run on behalf of John G Russell, a Scottish logistics provider. It can be considered a success, running daily

Above: Above: Euro Cargo Rail 186 306 with DB-liveried 186 327 dead-in-train are seen at Gerzat on 31 January 2014 with a train of empty mineral water vans heading for the Volvic bottling plant.

Below: Below: Euro Cargo Rail 66195 heads a similar train at Gerzat on 11 April 2014. *Lionel Suty (2)*

Monday–Friday. However, it fell victim to the second migrant crisis. At the time of writing a relaunch, with the service running Daventry–Dourges, was planned.

Fret SNCF fights back

On 28 June 2007 Deutsche Bahn announced that it had acquired the whole of EWS, including Euro Cargo Rail, thus allowing German Railways to own the biggest rail freight operator in the UK and the biggest competitor to Fret SNCF in France. From 1 January 2009, EWS became DB Schenker UK, but Euro Cargo Rail retained its name, possibly to avoid frightening the French too much.

Having lost considerable amounts of Tunnel freight traffic to EWS/ECR, SNCF set up a subsidiary in the UK, known as Freight Europe (UK) and on 10 March 2009 launched a weekly service carrying steel coil from Dunkerque to Burton-on-Trent. SNCF had no operating unit in the UK and subcontracted traction between Dollands Moor and Burton-on-Trent to Colas Rail.

Later in 2009 Fret SNCF plus Colas Rail in the UK, Europorte 2 in the Tunnel, and Crossrail in Switzerland and Italy, launched a new Hams Hall–Novara service in addition to the DB Schenker service on the same route. At the time Fret SNCF said it would obtain its own traction and staff in the UK over the long term but this never happened. Then in January 2011 GB Railfreight and Europorte Channel took over the section from the UK to Calais, also moving from Hams Hall to Daventry, with the aim of using a Class 92 throughout. At the same time SNCF subsidiary Captrain took over operation in Switzerland and Italy. This service had been on the point of being withdrawn but GB Railfreight had been able to offer a price to

Above: Euro Cargo Rail 186 313 is seen on 18 January 2012 near Cerbère with the Silla–Dagenham Ford train. The loco will stay with the train to Calais, about 15 hours later. *Juanjo Rodriguez*

restore the train's profitability. By 2014 the train was operating three times a week, but SNCB had taken over from Fret SNCF from Calais Fréthun to Uckange and Sibelit (an SNCB, CFL, SNCF and SBB joint venture) from Uckange to Basel. SBB Cargo took over from Captrain from Basel to Novara.

Below: Euro Cargo Rail 186 302 is seen at Aouste near Liart on the French "north-east corridor" on 5 August 2004 with the Hams Hall–Novara "Unit 45" intermodal. *Pascal Dumont*

FREIGHT USES **HIGH SPEED 1**

In 2007 the high speed line from the Channel Tunnel to London, by then known as High Speed 1, or HS1, was completed. Although the line has some steep gradients, it was designed to allow freight trains to use it, having several loops to allow overtaking.

However, it was not until 16 April 2009 that HS1 managers and DB Schenker Rail signed an agreement to cooperate on developing modifications to Class 92 locomotives (see chapter on these locos) to allow them to operate over the new line. The idea was to start operations over HS1 in early 2010.

On 23 July 2011 DB Schenker transported the first "European sized" (UIC loading gauge) wagons over HS1 – two wagons with Mega Combi containers for Transfesa and four European-sized swap bodies were moved from Dollands Moor to a rail terminal in east London. DB Schenker followed this up with its first UIC loading gauge freight service over HS1 in November 2011 – a weekly train from Barking, east London, to Wrocław in Poland, a distance of about 1400 km. This service was twice-weekly by 2014.

Another step forward was taken in May 2012 when Europorte operated the first "piggyback" service – carrying complete lorry trailers in special "pocket wagons" – between mainland Europe and the UK, using HS1. The train carried road trailers loaded with Vauxhall car parts from Antwerpen to Barking. Journey time was around seven hours for 400 km. Europorte said it would launch a regular service of three trains a week with Ewals Cargo Care from Antwerpen, Genk (both in

Belgium) or Duisburg in Germany, another plan which never came to fruition.

Eurotunnel takes over Veolia Cargo

In 2009 France's first open access freight operator, Veolia Cargo, was put up for sale. SNCF was prevented from taking over its French operations but bought its activities in the rest of Europe. Eurotunnel acquired the French activities and eventually merged it with Europorte 2 which, in the end, had not launched any Channel Tunnel freight services. Veolia Cargo was merged with Europorte 2 as Europorte France, Class 92 operations through the Tunnel becoming Europorte Channel. Eurotunnel told its shareholders at the time that it would use this acquisition to develop services linked to the French ports and the Tunnel. Europorte Channel would also support other operators aiming to launch new freight services.

Fruit and veg train

On 27 October 2009 DB Schenker and UK company Stobart Rail launched a new service carrying fruit and vegetables in temperature-controlled containers from Spain to the UK. Like the well-established Ford train this train ran from Silla, near Valencia in Spain, to Dagenham,

east of London. Much of the produce arrived at Silla by road from the Alacant and Murcia areas further south. The service began running once a week, with DB Schenker expecting it to run three times a week by late 2010 and Stobart Rail predicting five times a week.

In mid June 2010 DB Schenker then ran a trial intermodal service for Stobart from Bönen in the Dortmund area of Germany to Ditton, near Liverpool. Unfortunately this was not followed up by a regular service.

By mid 2011 the Stobart Rail train from Spain had been suspended due to a lack of traffic, having never run more than weekly. Although the traffic was somewhat seasonal, sources said that the train was sabotaged by Spanish road hauliers who did not want to lose traffic.

In November 2011 the weekly service was revived, the driving force behind the project being Europorte, which was expected to take over operation, after a start using Fret SNCF in France and COMSA in Spain.

However, in January 2013, the Stobart train again disappeared. Instead, shorter rakes of wagons carrying Stobart containers were added to the Silla–Dagenham Ford train which runs almost daily. However, this arrangement, which seemed to provide a perfect solution to providing a better frequency, did not continue for very long.

Above: An unidentified (because of the dirt covering the number panel) Euro Cargo Rail Class 77 passes Dourges station with the Stobart "fruit and veg" train from Valencia to London on 4 March 2010. *David Haydock*

Below: The Dagenham–Silla train is seen on 20 February 2011 at Castelbisbal near Barcelona behind RENFE TRAXX 253 002. *Juanjo Rodriguez*

STEEL TRAFFIC BOOSTS TONNAGES

Above: During a short period when Fret SNCF worked the train in France, the Scunthorpe–Ebange is seen on 9 March 2014 at Pont Maugis behind BB 27078 and 27061. *Pascal Dumont*

Early in 2011 fire damaged the galvanising line at the Tata Steel works at Beverwijk in the Netherlands. In order to maintain production, DB Schenker and SNCB Logistics in Belgium set up a four-times weekly shuttle from March between Beverwijk and Trostre, near Llanelli in South Wales. Trains were backloaded from Llanwern steel works, near Newport, to Beverwijk. The trains ran for much of the year.

The following April SNCF and subsidiary Captrain started hauling steel coils from Port Talbot, South Wales, to Botlek in the port of Rotterdam. Trains were hauled by Colas Rail in the UK. This service ran on and off through to 2016.

In 2011 steel traffic was very important for the Tunnel. In addition to the above flows, the near daily Scunthorpe–Ebange train of steel slabs continued, while a regular service – about three times a week – carrying steel coil was by then running from Margam and Llanwern in South Wales to Sous-le-Bois, near Maubeuge, in northern France. Both these flows were for Tata Steel.

Aluminium in both directions

On 24 February 2014 DB Schenker Rail announced that it had won a contract with Novelis Deutschland (formerly Alcan) – trains actually started running on 31 December 2013 – to carry aluminium slabs and coils, previously moved by ship, between Germany and England. The trains carry ten-tonne aluminium coils from the Alunorf plant in Norf, near Neuss (north of Köln in Germany) to Ditton, near Liverpool, on trains formed of covered bogie *Cargowaggons*, the coils being taken by lorry to Widnes. The same trains are then backloaded with 27-tonne slabs of recycled aluminium from nearby Latchford.

The train was initially operated by a DB Class 92 throughout between Ditton and Dollands Moor but a Class 66 diesel is now in charge in the UK. Initially SNCB Logistics operated the train between Calais and Germany, but DB Cargo/Euro Cargo Rail took over in June 2016 and now uses Class 186 locomotives throughout.

The train initially operated three days a week but rapidly increased to five days a week. The initial traffic was added to in early 2016 by the addition/removal at Daventry of flat wagons carrying swap bodies which carry aluminium for Jaguar-Land Rover and the service increased to daily. This is the reason why the train now also serves the container terminal in Neuss. The train also connects with another Novelis service in Neuss, with some wagons going forward to eastern Germany.

Traffic avoiding the Tunnel

There is an enormous amount of suitable traffic avoiding the Tunnel at present for a variety of reasons. In addition to freight which travels entirely by lorry, there are significant flows to ports just across the Channel from England which travel long distances across continental Europe but are then transferred to ships for the last part of the journey.

In the early 2010s the PSA group (Peugeot-Citroën) was dispatching about one train a day of finished cars from its plants at Montbéliard and Mulhouse in eastern France, plus Poissy near Paris and Rennes, to Calais. Traction was by Euro

Cargo Rail for PSA's logistics subsidiary GEFCO. In Calais the cars were transferred to a ship which took them the short distance to Sheerness in Kent. This seemed a perfect flow for Eurotunnel to capture via its Europorte subsidiary. However, in 2016 GEFCO dropped ECR in favour of Fret SNCF and diverted the trains via Belgium to Zeebrugge. In January 2020 this traffic was taken over by Europorte.

"Rolling motorways"

With its massive experience in running the Freight Shuttle service between Cheriton (UK) and Coquelles (France), Eurotunnel portrays itself as Europe's biggest operator of "piggyback" services – complete lorries on trains. In the past five years, a terminal has been built in Calais using the Lohr piggyback technique and services now carry lorry semi-trailers from Calais to Le Boulou, on the France/Spain border and to Torino in Italy. Both these services are operated by SNCF's VIIA subsidiary. From December 2019 a service started running from Sète, a port in southern France, to Calais for Turkish company Ekol, which runs a ferry shuttle between Sète and Turkey. Finally, at least for now, the German company Cargobeamer is to build a "competing" piggyback terminal at Marcq, near Calais, and is to operate services to Italy via Germany. All of these are designed to carry lorries which cross the Channel, either through the Tunnel or on ferries.

Eurotunnel has watched these developments with interest – in 2014 the company was seeking a site for a transfer terminal south-east of London with the idea of launching such "rolling motorway" services one day.

The second migrant crisis

A combination of wars and oppression in the Middle East and North Africa led to a massive migrant crisis across Europe during 2015/16. One of the results of this, from spring 2015, was an increasing number of migrants trying to reach the UK via Calais. The nightmare of 2000 was repeated, with attempts to reach England in the back of lorries, on trains or by walking through the Tunnel. The fences, some electrified, erected after the first crisis were found to be inadequate. There were cases of 2000 people trying to storm them. By July 2015 a dozen people had died trying to cross the Channel. The British government reacted by paying Eurotunnel to build more and higher fences, and asking the French government to stop the build up of migrant numbers in the Calais area.

As in 2000 Eurotunnel was the quickest to defend its business and increase security. This included clearing 56 hectares of woodland, adding more personnel, plus 29 km of higher fences and more CCTV cameras. The migrants therefore turned their attention to SNCF Réseau lines which were less difficult to penetrate causing disruption to Eurostar services and reaching freight trains standing at Calais Fréthun, waiting to depart for the UK. As Eurotunnel is responsible for security and safety in the Tunnel, the company stopped accepting trains which were not "migrant-free", thus severely delaying freight trains. Freights were halted completely on some days in August and September 2015.

Above: Euro Cargo Rail 77027 is seen at Lesquin, near Lille on 6 June 2013 with the Calais Fréthun–Maubeuge loaded steel train from Port Talbot for Tata Steel. The loco has now been "exported" to DB Cargo in Germany and this traffic has now stopped. *Didier Delattre*

Already at this point operators were forced to suspend or abandon their rail services.

Through freight traffic had started to recover before this crisis and was creeping towards 2 million tonnes a year. Traffic in the first quarter of 2015 was up 13%. But in October 2015 it was reported that the number of through freights was down 33% and tonnage by 27% in the third quarter of the year. Both of the services run by Europorte had been stopped completely – the Barking–Dourges was "suspended" (still not reintroduced in early 2020) but the Daventry–Novara was withdrawn permanently. The Margam–Maubeuge

steel train was another casualty of the crisis, stopping in the last quarter of 2015.

Unfortunately the chaos in the Calais area continued into 2016, one of the problems being a massive "village" of up to 9000 migrants known as the "Jungle" being gradually established to the east of the port of Calais. This was finally dismantled in late 2016. By the end of this period, traffic had fallen to only 1 million tonnes a year while lorry numbers carried by Eurotunnel were up 14% in late 2016. The final figures for 2016 were 1 041 294 tonnes, down 27% on 2015 to an all-time low, carried in just 1797 trains, down 26%.

ECR 66202 is seen at Lesquin with the return Maubeuge–Calais steel empties on 15 June 2013. *Didier Delattre*

CHINA TO LONDON

On 18 January 2017 a train loaded with 34 40-foot containers arrived at Barking from Yiwu in China, having taken 17 days for the 12 451 km journey. The train ran via Kazakhstan, Russia, Belarus, Poland, Germany, Belgium and France, the Channel Tunnel and HS1 to reach London. In fact, the containers had been transferred between wagons at the gauge changes on the China/Kazakhstan and Belarus/Poland borders then ran to Duisburg where 34 of the 44 containers were transferred to Channel Tunnel-approved wagons. Even then the route was not direct as the train then passed via Antwerpen in Belgium.

The first return service from London to China ran on 10 April 2017 with InterRail Group as the manager and DB Cargo operating from London (DP World London Gateway) to Calais, B-Logistics (ex SNCB) to Duisburg via Antwerpen, and PKP Cargo from there to Małaszewice on the border with Belarus. Arrival in Yiwu was on 29 April. The consignment included whisky, soft drinks, baby food and pharmaceuticals.

However, despite all the publicity, a regular service has never operated.

Future security

On 29 June 2017 Eurotunnel started work on building a new installation at Calais Fréthun which is able to scan freight trains headed for the UK as they arrive in the yard. Inspections are currently carried out in such a way that two Eurotunnel staff have to open the wagons or containers when requested by the French customs staff who carry out the inspections – an expensive deployment of three or four staff. This can take two hours for a complete train and involves a walk of up to 1.5 km in all weathers for staff.

New x-ray equipment will scan the train, passing at up to 20 km/h, and customs staff will be able to inspect the contents of a train on a screen. A wagon will only be opened is something suspicious is spotted. It is hoped that dwell time at Fréthun can be cut by half from 3–4 hours at present, although a loco

Above: The China to UK freight makes a symbolic entry to DB's Eurohub freight terminal at Barking, near London, on 18 January 2017. The train was pushed from the rear by a diesel loco. *Keith Fender*

change will still be needed. The scanner cost €7.4 million, of which €6.4 million came from Eurotunnel.

New traffic hit by SNCF strikes

In early 2018 things started to look up, with a new intermodal service running once a week from Padova in Italy to Tilbury carrying Birra Peroni beer for Japanese brewing company Asahi. Traction in France was provided by Fret SNCF.

A second new less-than-daily service carried continuous welded rail from Scunthorpe to Duisburg and Hamburg in Germany. The third service to be launched carried containers for shipping company CMA CGM between London Gateway and Duisburg in Germany, with connections there to Chinese "Silk Road" trains and to Poland. The initial service – a very long train – ran once a week, but was expected to build up to six train pairs a week.

However, 2018 was a year when a new French government decided to reform the railway system. SNCF staff responded by calling a "rolling strike" with three days of stoppages followed by two days of "normal" work from March through to June. Freight is particularly badly hit by such strikes – whereas a passenger may put off a non-

Below: A computer-generated image of the new train scanner at Calais Fréthun. This was not yet in service in early 2020. *Courtesy Eurotunnel*

DB Cargo 66108 is seen near Eastriggs with 6S94 02.03 Dollands Moor to Irvine on 14 September 2016. The train carries china clay slurry from the port of Antwerpen, Belgium, for the Caledonian Paper Mill. China clay formerly arrived from Burngullow in Cornwall. The train is now operated by GB Railfreight. *Robin Ralston*

essential journey or find another way of travelling to work, a freight train has to wait (at least) until the next day. If no spare staff are available to take the train on, it may be necessary to wait for a weekend to "clear" traffic. In many cases companies have to find a road transport alternative and may need to sign a long-term contract which means the traffic does not return to rail after the strike.

The first month saw a large number of trains of all types cancelled, although in May and June the situation was somewhat better. But SNCF found it impossible to run the Padova–Tilbury train and it was rapidly "suspended indefinitely".

One new traffic which was tested in late summer 2019 was 108 metre lengths of continuous welded rails from the Voestalpin Schienen plant at Leoben Donawitz in Austria, which operates via Germany and Belgium, then via the Tunnel to Eastleigh, near Southampton.

Eurotunnel is still hopeful that traffic will bounce back and hopes that traffic will double to 5000 trains a year by 2023.

An analysis of the traffic which remains today shows that most traffic consists of heavy bulk goods which can be stockpiled quite easily. From 2018 British Steel dispatched extra loads of steel slabs from Scunthorpe to Hayange with the aim of building up stocks in case of a "hard Brexit". This boosted Tunnel freight traffic temporarily.

Ford's "blue train" carrying components in swap bodies is an exception to this rule, although components can also be stockpiled. However, most customers of intermodal services are not willing to accept regular disruption and are sticking with road transport.

RegioRail BB 27137 heads a train of empty mineral water vans which originated in Daventry from Ambérieu to Publier (the Evian bottling plant) on 3 January 2019. There is a second loco at the tail end of the train. *Pierre Julien*

CHANNEL TUNNEL FREIGHT
25 YEARS ON

Above: 92017 "Shakespeare" is seen at Grassthorpe Crossing near Tuxford working 4E32 11.55 Dollands Moor to Scunthorpe on 20 April 2009. The train of empty steel flats originated at Ebange. *Chris Booth*

After peaking at over 3 million tonnes in 1999, the amount of freight has fallen and for 20 years has been stuck around the 1.5 million tonne mark. The most worrying point is that these volumes are concentrated in just four flows – others are inconsequential; they include the delivery of new trains from continental train builders such as Siemens in Germany, Hitachi in Italy and Stadler in Poland. At least one of these flows is threatened by Brexit.

The four flows which make up the base traffic are:

- Ford containers, three or four times a week, between the Dagenham plant, east of London, and the Silla plant, south of Valencia in Spain. The trains are hauled by a DB Class 92 over HS1 between Dagenham and Fréthun via Dollands Moor, by Euro Cargo Rail in France, then by RENFE in Spain. The route through France changes regularly but is currently from Calais Fréthun to Cerbère on the Spanish border via the Paris region, Dijon, Lyon, Nîmes and Perpignan. At Cerbère containers are transferred between standard gauge and broad gauge wagons. Containers are loaded in both directions.
- Mineral water, daily for most of the year, for Danone Waters from the Evian and Volvic sources to Daventry for distribution. Operations in France have changed over time. At present RegioRail shuttles the Evian trains between Publier and Ambérieu then Euro Cargo Rail takes trains forward from there direct via Dijon to Calais or Lille Délivrance, where some trains may be split for Calais and Zeebrugge. Euro Cargo Rail carries out the complete run from Volvic via Paris to Calais direct or via Lille Délivrance. Wagons return empty.
- High quality steel slabs from the British Steel (formerly Tata Steel) plant at Scunthorpe to Ebange, for the company's Hayange plant in north-east France which produces rails, used in particular on France's high speed lines. Wagons return empty. In France the train is routed via Lille, Valenciennes and Mohon. Ebange is near Uckange, south of Thionville and trains are moved between there and Hayange over an industrial branch. There were worries in 2019 that this lucrative traffic might disappear from the Tunnel. The UK part of company which owned the Scunthorpe plant went into liquidation. At the same time the still-solvent French part of British Steel moved to buy an ailing steel plant at Saint Saulve near Valenciennes in France. One of the options for saving the plant was to transfer the production of steel slabs from Scunthorpe to Saint Saulve. This would mean the end of the Scunthorpe flow.
- Aluminium for Novalis from Ditton, near Liverpool, to Neuss in Germany. Trains are loaded in both directions, with mainly scrap aluminium (empty cans) for recycling from Ditton, and mainly new aluminium slabs from Neuss. Neuss is a hub from which most wagons go to a massive plant at Norf, between Köln and Neuss, but some go forward to Göttingen and others too Nachterstedt-Hoym, near Halberstadt. Around a year after this service started, a stop at Daventry was introduced to attach a set of wagons carrying swap bodies owned by Jaguar Land Rover. These return loaded with aluminium for car building. The train is routed via Lille and Valenciennes to Jeumont in France then Charleroi and Liège in Belgium and Aachen in Germany.

All of the above trains are hauled by Euro Cargo Rail Class 186 electric locomotives, about half of which are in ECR white livery and the other half in DB red livery.

Euro Cargo Rail DB-liveried 186 322 heads the Calais Fréthun–Lille Délivrance mineral water vans on 3 September 2019. This is part of the journey taking the empties back from Daventry to either Publier (Evian) or Riom (Volvic). *David Haydock*

One of the only types of traffic which has remained for the whole 25 years of the Tunnel's existence is mineral water from Evian in the French Alps. This was already travelling by the Dover–Dunkerque train ferry before the Tunnel was built – in 1989 50 000 tonnes travelled to Neasden in the UK this way and the production company hoped to double this. Trains were formed of ten "twin-set" Type IVA covered vans and these had priority on the train ferry on two days a week. Traction was by SNCF in France and British Rail in England.

Today the flow is much heavier – between 150 000 and 200 000 tonnes a year – and organised differently. Danone Waters, which now owns the business, is committed to using rail as much as possible and reorganised its rail logistics in December 2015. All wagons of mineral water are moved out of the bottling plant at Publier, near Evian-les-Bains, by private operator RegioRail using a Class BB 27000 electric loco at each end as gradients on the line are steep. Trains operate to Ambérieu (160 km) then are re-marshalled. Trains to Calais are hauled by Euro Cargo Rail using Class 186 TRAXX electrics, then in the UK are taken over by DB Cargo. Three or four trains run per week for most of the year, but a train a day can operate in periods of hot weather and when stocks are being built up.

In addition to this Danone Waters also owns Volvic which also dispatches mineral water to the UK, also hauled by Euro Cargo Rail. ECR works all of the trains from Ambérieu and Volvic to Lille (La Délivrance yard) then works them forward to Calais or to Zeebrugge. Much of the water heading to Zeebrugge then goes forward to the UK too. Danone Waters stated in 2015 that the equivalent of 12 trains a week was destined for the UK.

Channel Tunnel freight timings winter 2019/2020

Northbound

48430	TO	02.57	Antwerpen Rhodesie –Fréthun	07.31	China clay	Lineas 13
6S94	WO	04.28	Wembley–Irvine	17.51	China clay	GBRf 66
46461	Daily	01.50	Neuss–Fréthun	11.15	Aluminium	ECR 186
6M13‡	Daily	01.04	Dollands Moor–Ditton	(13.00)	Aluminium	DB 66
48470	MWX	05.30	Cerbère-Fréthun	02.49	Ford empties	ECR 186
6L21	Tu-Sat	21.03	Dollands Moor–Dagenham	(22.10)	Ford empties	DB 92
47420	Daily	00.43	Ebange–Fréthun	06.57	Steel empties	ECR 186
4E26	Daily	08.09	Dollands Moor–Scunthorpe	(16.00)	Steel empties	DB 66
49411	Daily	06.16	Lille Délivrance–Fréthun	07.57	Mineral water	ECR 66
6M45	Daily	09.27	Dollands Moor–Daventry	(14.30)	Mineral water	DB 66

‡ stops to leave/pick up traffic at Daventry 05.53/09.13
In addition to the daily La Délivrance–Fréthun, there are irregular trains from Valenton, either from Ambérieu or Riom.

Southbound

6O16	Daily	11.42†	Ditton–Dollands Moor		Aluminium	DB 66
46470	Daily	14.00	Fréthun–Neuss	00.30	Aluminium	ECR 186
6071	Daily	15.06*	Daventry–Dollands Moor	(21.00)	Mineral water empties	DB 66
49420	Daily	14.11	Fréthun–Lille Délivrance	15.32	Mineral water empties	ECR 66
4028	Daily	22.40§	Scunthorpe–Dollands Moor	(06.20)	Steel slabs	DB 66
47411	Daily	16.10	Fréthun–Ebange	23.03	Steel slabs	ECR 186
7O81	MWX	18.25	Dagenham–Dollands Moor	(22.05)	Ford intermodal	DB 66
48460	Tu-Sat	01.44	Fréthun–Cerbère	22.17	Ford intermodal	ECR 186
6M74	ThO	20.50	Irvine–Wembley		China clay empties	GBRf 66
6B63	FO		Wembley–Dollands Moor	19.16	China clay empties	GBRf 66
48421	SO	05.12	Fréthun–Antwerpen Rhodesie	10.43	China clay empties	Lineas 13

† Recessed at Warrington Arpley (13.50–21.07)
* (14.47) Mon, Tue
§ (20.15) Sunday 6O07
Some timings simplified for clarity.
Other traffic (timings vary): new train delivery from various builders to various depots
Timings in brackets are approximate.

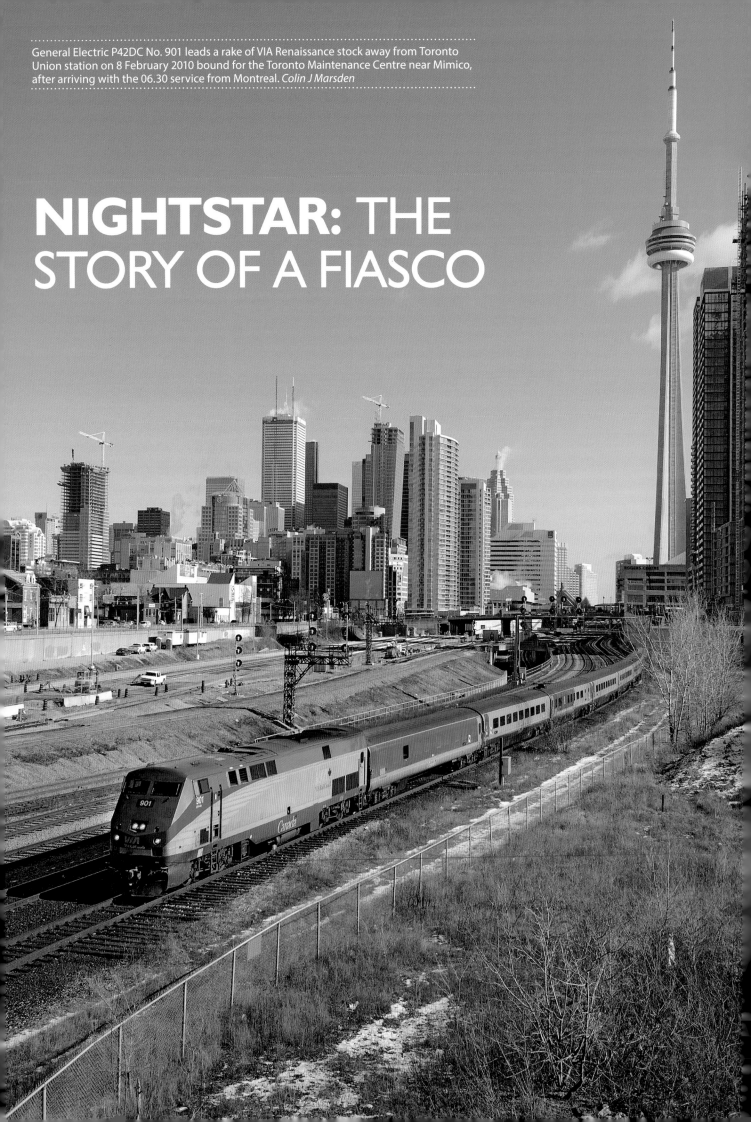

NIGHTSTAR: THE
STORY OF A FIASCO

Although all of the elements of the Channel Tunnel story involved over-optimistic traffic forecasts and, in several cases, over-engineered and therefore over-expensive trains, the story of Nightstar was by far the worst – a disaster from start to finish, although the curtain has not yet fallen on the final conclusion.

It seemed like a good idea. For the many people in the UK who would not be able to take advantage of direct Eurostar services, the idea of overnight trains – falling asleep in Cardiff or Edinburgh and waking up in Paris or Brussels – seemed like a good idea. At the time, the late 1980s, nobody had thought of budget airlines, air travel was still quite expensive, high speed trains were only just starting to spread across Europe and night trains were still common and well used.

A consortium known as European Night Services (ENS) was formed by European Passenger Services (Eurostar) in the UK, SNCF in France, NS in the Netherlands and DB in Germany. Trains would run through Belgium but SNCB was not a partner. The consortium called for bids to build around 200 200 km/h coaches in late 1990 with delivery from December 1992. The expiry date was extended several times and the preferred bidder – GEC-Alsthom (formerly Metropolitan-Cammell in Birmingham) – was not announced until 4 February 1992. By then the order had been reduced to 139 coaches costing £110 million (another source says £153 million), to be delivered from July 1994 to June 1995. However signing of the order was blocked by the Conservative government on the grounds that the deal between consortium members was anti-competitive. In order for work to start, funds were allocated to GEC-Alsthom but these soon ran out and

work stopped. Eventually the contract was signed on 7 July 1992, and delivery of the first set put back to late 1994/early 1995. In the end construction did not begin until autumn 1994.

Stock and services

The steel-bodied rolling stock was to be based on the Mark 4 daytime stock built by Metro-Cammell from the late 1980s for the East Coast Main Line electrification. The stock would be air conditioned and have power operated doors. Trains would have to meet the stringent safety rules of the Channel Tunnel and countries where it would run – the UK, France, Belgium and the Netherlands, but also Germany. The routes originally planned in 1992, most trains consisting of two portions which would divide and combine, were:
- London to Amsterdam and Köln via Brussels
- London to Dortmund and Frankfurt via Brussels
- Plymouth and Bristol to Brussels
- Swansea and Cardiff to Paris
- Glasgow to Paris and Brussels

By the time European Night Services produced a brochure in May 1995 the routes had already been revised as:
- Glasgow/Manchester–Paris
- Swansea/Plymouth–Paris
- London–Dortmund/Frankfurt
- London–Amsterdam

The Plymouth and Swansea routes were not electrified and would therefore have to be diesel-hauled as far as Kensington Olympia west of London from where they would go forward to Calais hauled by Class 92 electric locomotives. The other services would be Class 92 hauled throughout in the UK. All

trains would have a second Class 92 attached at the rear of the train to operate through the Tunnel.

For the Swansea and Plymouth services six pairs of specially modified Class 37/6 diesels would be used with a generator car between them to provide electricity for heating and air conditioning – the auxiliaries in the Nightstar coaches would be very greedy for energy. The Class 37 top speed was raised to 90 mph (144.8 km/h).

The 139 coaches were as follows:
- 47 cars with 50 reclining seats arranged 2+1 for budget travellers. Each seat had a table, footrest and reading light. Baggage was to be stored under seats and in overhead lockers. There were three toilets with washing facilities per car. A trolley service would serve refreshments in the evening, then snacks and drinks could be bought from a counter in the lounge car.
- 72 sleeper cars, each with 20 bunk beds in ten cabins. Six cabins had a compact en-suite shower room with washbasin, toilet and hairdryer. Four cabins had only an en-suite toilet and washing facilities. Each cabin had two armchairs with fold-out tables, which converted into the bunk beds at night. Other facilities included a fitted wardrobe and cupboard and facilities for making hot drinks. The cabins had intercoms for room service. The ticket price would include complimentary drinks on departure and breakfast and exclusive access to the lounge bar. Cabin doors would have punch card locks which would be handed over on boarding.

Below: Plans of the sleeper, seated and lounge cars from a May 1995 brochure produced by European Night Services.

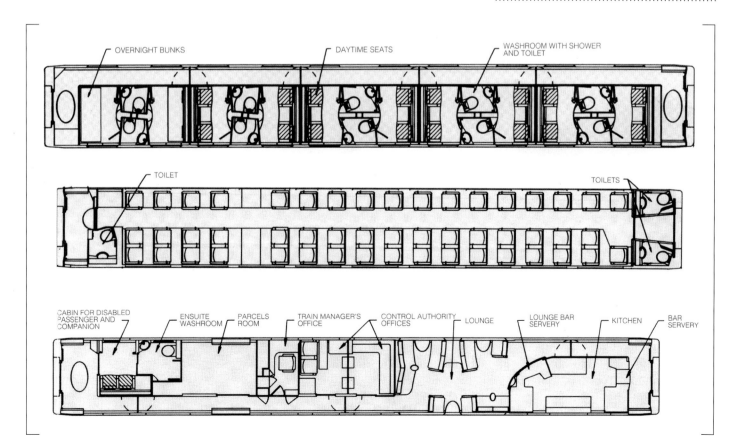

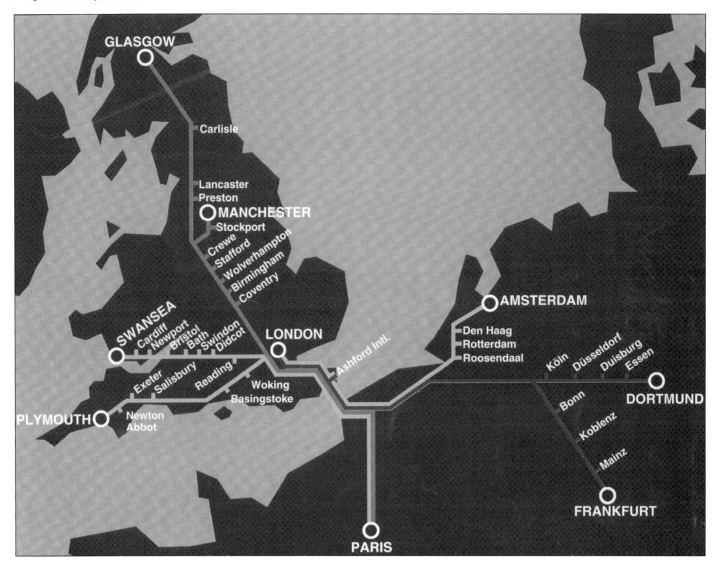

The coaches would be formed into nine 7-car subsets with three seated, one lounge and three sleeper cars and nine 8-car subsets, formed of two seated, one lounge and five sleeper cars. There would be two seated cars and two service cars spare. Trains from London, from where more business traffic was expected, would be formed of two 8-car sets, with more sleeper than seated accommodation, while trains from the "provinces" would be formed of two 7-car sets. All stock would be based at North Pole depot which would be shared with Eurostar.

Couplings between the coach sets and a locomotive would be very complicated as British practice is very different from that in the other four countries which apply standard European UIC couplings. This meant there were no less than 17 flexible connections at the coach ends.

Braking was standard for all countries although Germany insisted on magnetic track brakes for emergencies.

All coaches had to be designed to meet the stringent Channel Tunnel fire standards with barriers capable of holding back a fire for 30 minutes at up to 840° C. A full smoke and fire detection system was also fitted.

Problems, problems

Following the delays to tendering and contract signing, delivery slipped again to early 1996 due to problems with a subcontractor. In autumn 1995 European Night Services announced that the first services would begin in July 1996, following delivery of the first trains in January 1996. The idea would be to build services up gradually, starting with the West of England to Paris service in July 1996 with portions from Swansea, calling at Cardiff, Newport, Bristol, Bath Spa, Swindon, Didcot Parkway and Reading and from Plymouth, calling at Newton Abbott, Exeter, Salisbury, Basingstoke and Woking. In September 1996 this would be followed by Glasgow and Manchester via Birmingham to Paris, London to Amsterdam in November 1996 and London–Dortmund/Frankfurt in January 1997.

But delivery then slipped to late 1996 due to "the incredible complexity of the stock". Infrastructure work on the West Coast Main Line was running late and it was by then thought that Class 92 locomotives running on the third rail would not be able to supply enough power for a complete train's heating and air conditioning. It was later found that Class 92 could manage a full train.

• 20 lounge cars with 15 seats in a lounge area and one large two-bed cabin and washroom suitable for wheelchair users. This was also the service car with a parcels room, train manager's office and control authority offices.

Above: The map from European Night Services' brochure produced in May 1995 which publicised the rolling stock and services to be introduced in "mid 1996".

A similar problem was later found in France where the locomotives to be used (expected to be SNCF Class BB 36000) could not heat and haul a 16-coach train without multiple operation for which they were not equipped. Each coach would weigh as much as 60 tonnes fully loaded which meant a 16-coach train could weigh as much as 960 tonnes. The heavy weight was put down to the large amount of water carried for showers and toilets plus materials needed for fire regulations in the Tunnel while massive amounts of energy would be needed to heat or air condition the trains as well as heating water for showers, for example. At one moment an option considered was to couple a DB Class 234 diesel to trains to produced electricity in the Tunnel!

In April 1996 three coaches were sent to the Wien Arsenal climatic test centre. The first subset was outshopped in early July 1996 and initially tested with 37609 and 37610 plus a generator set. A second subset was completed in September 1996, coupled to the first and tested in the Channel Tunnel first with 37609 and 37610 then with 92032 and 92039. This was followed by tests in northern France.

The coaches were tested in France, then Belgium and even made it to Germany by February 1997 where they were tested on the steep Geislinger Steige gradient between Stuttgart and Ulm. Tests were carried out with two 8-car half sets in the Channel Tunnel starting in October 1997.

Cancellation

In October 1996, as a result of the privatisation of British Rail, Eurostar (UK) was taken over by a new company London and Continental Railways (LCR) which started a review of the project. By now the project was two years behind schedule, Ryanair was established and Easyjet had just been founded. Travellers were starting to get a taste for "low-cost" air travel and the market for high cost overnight services was shrinking. LCR started to review proposed services, with trains from the UK provinces looking doubtful and new destinations from London such as Zürich and Berlin under consideration.

With no imminent launch, completed trains started to be stored at Kineton and Long Marston army bases from June 1997. Some of the unfinished body shells were stored at Washwood Heath (Birmingham). In July 1997 LCR finally announced the complete cancellation of "regional" Nightstar services – those serving points north and west of London – although services from London to Amsterdam and Frankfurt were still being re-assessed. LCR therefore placed a moratorium on building the coaches given a lower level of service. LCR blamed the deregulation of air services and the poor performance of new hotel trains in the rest of Europe. A month later, services to Germany were dropped as DB had baulked at the cost of security measures necessary in Frankfurt.

Final cancellation of trains from points north and west of London was confirmed on 9 July 1999 and services from London soon after. Most of the other completed coaches plus many incomplete vehicles were moved to Kineton.

Above: A set of Nightstar stock is seen stabled on 14 October 1996 at Tourcoing, near Lille, alongside SNCF Class BB 16500 locos plus local push-pull trains and, just in shot, Regional Eurostar 3301/2.

Below: On 24 October 1996 26135 heads the Nightstar test rake through Douai with a run to the Paris region. *David Haydock (2)*

Eurostar (UK) decided to sell half of its Class 37/6 locos (37607–37612) to Direct Rail Services in 1997 but initially retained the generator vans and its seven Class 92 locos. Eurostar then put the generator vans and Class 92s up for sale in July 2000. Scotrail considered the generator vans for use north of Glasgow but rejected the idea. The Class 92s found no takers as there was already a big surplus of the class.

Left: Nightstar stock was tested in Belgium, initially hauled by a Class 18 C-C, the only Belgian loco type capable of supplying enough electricity. After tests on 21/22 December 1996, the train was moved to Minden test centre in Germany. Here 1802 heads the train near Ath, with a regular Eurostar service passing on 21 December 1996. *Michel van Ussel*

Export to Canada

By the time the project was finally abandoned only 64 coaches had actually been completed. The UK government tried to find a buyer in order to recoup some of the wasted money. In 1999 Scotrail considered buying some of the stock to update the Caledonian Sleeper services but found them too heavy and plumped for refurbishing existing Mark 3 trains.

In June 2000 Canadian operator VIA Rail took three vehicles for trial running – one coach with reclining seats, one sleeping car and a service/lounge car which also housed the operating systems. VIA Rail announced six months later that it had struck a deal to obtain all 139 vehicles, of which the incomplete 75 vehicles were in "kit" form. The "bargain basement" price was CAD 125 million, just €83 million at today's exchange rate. However, a year later the cost had risen to CAD 160 million due to safety modifications, cold-weather retrofits and a lawsuit over access for disabled persons which led to 14 modifications.

Bombardier carried out all the modifications to the coaches at its Thunder Bay plant in Ontario – winterisation, addition of luggage space, creation of three dining cars from empty body shells, removal of magnetic track brakes and conversion of the electrical system. Other work was done by VIA itself in the light of experience in service – a heating element was added to stop the piston which extends and retracts the steps from freezing and the addition of insulation around piping. VIA de-activated the emergency handles and intercoms in each compartment, installed brake handles in the coach ends and replaced woollen carpets. One point which caused problems was the permanent couplings between coaches – VIA was forced to introduce a completely new maintenance regime to deal with a full rake at a time.

In mid 2002 three six-car sets were formed then used on the overnight Montreal–Toronto "Enterprise" service. From early 2003 25 vehicles entered service from Montreal to Quebec and Ottawa. Then from mid 2003 a set started operation on the "Ocean" service between Montreal and Halifax. Within two years three 17-car sets were formed.

By the end of 2005 VIA had the following coaches in service: 47 vehicles with reclining seats of which 14 were classified as "Club" cars, 51 sleeper cars, 12 sleeper car body shells rebuilt as baggage cars and three more as dining cars (three of the baggage cars were later further converted to baggage/transition cars) and 20 service cars. VIA branded the coaches "Renaissance" stock.

However, there were many complaints about the stock – a lack of panoramic "dome cars" to see the scenery, cramped, uncomfortable service car lounges, warmed up rather than fresh meals, and the absence of open sections, roomettes and triple bedrooms.

Many changes have been made since then and in 2019 the stock was restricted to the "Ocean" between Montreal and Halifax and on the Montreal–Quebec/Ottawa route. However, VIA Rail has said that the Renaissance stock is "not in the company's plan for the long term because they are challenged in cold weather" and as they must work in permanently coupled sets, any failure sidelines the whole train.

In mid 2019 78% of the former Nightstar stock was out of action, leaving two sets working the "Ocean". With new VIA stock on order the cascade of LRC stock is likely to end the Nightstar use, although in 2019 VIA was still overhauling Renaissance stock.

A second stab at night services?

For over a decade the London Sleeper Company has been developing a new hotel train service to run between London St Pancras and a number of major European cities. These would be multiple units with sleeper accommodation, able to run over high speed lines at the beginning and end of their journeys – most high speed lines are closed for maintenance during the night. However, the Brexit process and higher access charges on HS1 in the UK are putting the future of this project in doubt.

I am grateful to Bob Johnston and Colin Marsden for some of the information in this chapter.

Right: VIA loco 901 with Nightstar stock, passes Toronto Sunneyside, running empty stock to Toronto Union from Mimico car shops to form train 66, the 17.00 departure to Montreal on 8 February 2010. *Colin J. Marsden (3)*

Left: EPS 37604 and 37608 are seen at Putney on 21 April 1996 hauling Eurostar set 3105/6 empty from Kensington Olympia to Waterloo, with barrier wagons at each end of the locos. *Chris Wilson*

Right: Former Nightstar Coach Class vehicle 7216 (61 19 20-90 003-6) in the consist of the 06.30 Montreal–Toronto on 8 February 2010.

Below: Another view of the empty stock working below.

WHAT NEXT FOR THE CHANNEL TUNNEL?

Crystal ball gazing was particularly difficult at the beginning of 2020, especially as the UK had just left the European Union, but before negotiating new rules with EU countries, and also because of the global climate crisis which was starting to change consumer behaviour.

Let us look first at Brexit. Although the UK officially left the EU at midnight on 31 January 2020, there were no immediate effects as this date was the start of a period of 11 months for negotiation during which the UK would still apply all EU rules. At the end of this period, the accords negotiated may mean that travel and trade will continue more or less as before, but a more likely result is that there will be more checks on goods and passengers than now.

In case of the latter Eurotunnel and Eurostar have already made preparations for a "hard Brexit" under which there would be increased checks. For Eurostar passengers this may mean slightly longer check-ins and this may start to cause serious congestion at St Pancras International where there are already problems when there are more than two departures per hour, in the early morning.

However the most trouble is expected on the approaches to the Channel ports and Eurotunnel terminals. The authorities in the UK and France already have special arrangements in force in case of disruption in the Tunnel or the ports, the best-known being "Operation Stack" which allows lorries to queue or even park on the hard shoulder of motorways approaching the coast. The UK government has been so concerned by the likely effects of a "hard Brexit" that measures under "Operation Brock" such as parking lorries on the closed Manston airport and the temporary hire of ferries has been planned.

The question for the author is whether such problems will permanently affect the Channel Tunnel and how. In the short term transport companies could well divert lorries via other, less congested ports. However, in the longer term this could not continue for cost reasons.

The Tunnel is currently an important link in many logistics chains which demand just-in-time performance in order to reduce stocks. The most crucial are the 100-or-so lorries which take the Shuttle each day carrying valuable stocks of automotive parts. These not only have to arrive on time, but also in the right order! The many car builders in the

Above: Eurostar e320 sets started to operate to Bourg St Maurice on 27 December 2019. This is set 4031/32 with train 9094 to London at Cluses-Les Hôpitaux on the Culoz–Ambérieu line on 11 January 2020.

UK have repeatedly warned the government that they will not be able to support prolonged disruption or higher costs, and that they could decamp to other countries in the EU. Honda has already decided to do so. The UK is already a peripheral (although very important) country in the EU and additional costs or inconveniencies in logistics chains could weigh heavy in keeping car plants open, or in decisions on future investment.

Eurotunnel has invested in extra Freight Shuttles in recent years based on the assumption that traffic in lorries will continue to rise, the target being to carry 2 million trucks a year. After gradual growth to around 1.7 million lorries, the number fell in 2019, above all due to doubts over Brexit. To a lesser extent, the number of passengers using the Shuttle fell too and passengers could be put off in the longer term by increased controls. A significant number of passengers travelling across the Channel are those from other EU Member States who have chosen to live and work in the UK. One of the main aims of those supporting Brexit has been to reduce immigration and this is likely to reduce the number of passengers toing and froing between the UK and countries such as Poland.

Amsterdam at last

There have been a number of very important recent developments for Eurostar, which at last passed the threshold of 11 million passengers in 2019. The first of these was the